The future is in your hands Ann

GOLDA MEIR ~
TRUE GRIT

Ann Atkins

FLASH HISTORY PRESS

GOLDA MEIR ~ TRUE GRIT
By Ann Atkins

Published by: Flash History Press LLC
Address: Paoli, Pennsylvania
Website: www.AnnAtkins.com

ISBN: 978-0-9834784-5-4
Library of Congress Control Number: 2014913224
First Edition. Printed in the United States of America
10 9 8 7 6 5 4 3 2 1

Photos from the Golda Meir Collection, University of Michigan, Wisconsin

Page Design by One on One Book Productions, West Hills, California

Cover Design by Lindsey Mottola Riches–Argus Printing and Invitation Studio, Wayne, Pennsylvania

Author photo by Dave Campli–Campli Photography, Malvern, Pennsylvania

DEDICATION

In an obscure village in Pakistan, 9 October 2012, a girl, Malala Yousafzai, makes a decision to go to school.

Malala Yousafzai

Education is taken for granted every day by millions of families across the world, but for some children pursuing an education endangers their lives. In Malala's town, the Taliban was determined to intimidate those who would defy their decree–girls were not to be educated. The Talibs boarded Malala's school bus and shot her in the face. Malala survived.

This brutal retaliation put Malala on the world stage before government leaders. Addressing the United Nations on July 12, 2013, Malala's speech is a message of peace and understanding. She is the next generation carrying in her the spirit of Nelson Mandela, and she is the youngest person to ever be nominated for the Nobel Peace Prize. Here is an excerpt from her UN speech:

I speak–not for myself, but for all girls and boys.
I raise up my voice–not so that I can shout,
but so that those without a voice can be heard.
Those who have fought for their rights:
Their right to live in peace, Their right to be treated with dignity,
Their right to equality of opportunity, Their right to be educated.

Golda Meir would have been the first to applaud Malala's speech. Golda, forever pragmatic, would have found ways to help Malala bring to life these ideals because these were Golda's ideals too. Malala, a Muslim, would have accepted this kindness from Golda, a Jew, because Malala also says in her speech:

This is what my soul is telling me, be peaceful and love everyone.

Malala Yousafzai, this book, *Golda Meir ~ True Grit*, is dedicated to you. May your spirit of peace and understanding continue to stir in us the courage to stand for justice.

ACKNOWLEDGMENTS

I would like to thank the wonderful people who took the time to read and give input to the Golda book. Your insights and comments helped shape my writing. Future readers won't be able to express their thanks, but I do.

Ed Atkins
Dr. C. Riley Augé
Dorothy Ernst
John Haynes
Ray Kelso
Dr. Mary Powell Lewis
Ken Woodward

I would also like to thank the University of Wisconsin and their staff that graciously accommodates authors. Their foresight to have the Golda Meir Photo Collection continues to ensure history will be recorded.

Flash History Biograhy Series

Eleanor Roosevelt's Life of Soul Searching and Self Discovery
Golda Meir ~ True Grit
Marie Curie ~ A Nobel Life (available 2016)

In Memory of
Edward J. Atkins, Colonel, USAF (retired)
July 10, 1948 – June 9, 2014

The dash between Ed's date of arrival and departure is both literally and figuratively a very small way to represent his magnificent life. The full measure of his character is not in the public arena of the 26 years he dedicated to serving his country as an aviator in the USAF or the 17 years of leadership to Chester County, Pennsylvania as the Director of Emergency Services. The full measure of Edward J. Atkins is in the private arena. His love to us, his family, is where this magnificent life is measured.

Ed, you are the love of my life. I am forever grateful for the 19 years we had together and the thousands of happy moments we shared.

PROLOGUE

From the Writer to the Reader

Readers of the first Flash History biography, *Eleanor Roosevelt's Life of Soul Searching and Self Discovery*, acknowledged the three core intentions I aimed to achieve as an author. Eleanor's story inspired their own life choices and, as busy people, they appreciated a book to be read in a couple days, not a couple months. The more elusive point was also accomplished. The book stirred the reader's interest to further their understanding of the other events and people connected with Eleanor's story. This multi-dimensional impact continues to be the signature mark of "Flash History." I am grateful to everyone who contacted me to give their insights. Your comments and encouragement are fuel for my writing fire. Thank you.

This biography, *Golda Meir ~ True Grit*, presents another unique story of a person's audacity and determination to insure a just society. Golda's success is not a "one man show" but involves a cast of characters each worthy of several books. It is my hope that you, the reader, will respond as you did with Eleanor's story by expanding your understanding of the people and events with a Google search, a library visit or a bookstore purchase.

As I continue to explore cultures, one theme holds true. When everyday people stand by an internal pledge of allegiance to guarantee "liberty and justice for all," their attitude can abrogate the power of extremists who market fear, hysteria and hate as facts. People of any nationality or religion can create a world of dignity and respect rather than discrimination and derision. For some, the decision to live each day with a noble purpose may put them on the world stage as it did for Malala Yousafzai, a Muslim girl standing up to the Taliban. For others, the decision to live this pledge will mean their life is cut short. The glory of their noble efforts are enshrouded at the bottom of a Mississippi swamp or enshrined at the Lincoln Memorial.

It just works like that.

Ann Atkins

TABLE OF CONTENTS

PART THREE

PART FOUR

PART ONE

CONTEXT AND COMMENTS

Social Media ~ 1903

A decision is made. And we say, "The rest is history." Truly. Just ask Pontius Pilate. Poor Pilate had no idea that his decision to crucify one man would send shock waves two thousand years into the future.

His decision brought him to his destiny.

Ask George Washington–a stand for representation leads to a revolution, the birth of a nation, a new form of government and tourists visit the Washington Monument today.

Harriet Beecher Stowe decides to write a novel. The impact of *Uncle Tom's Cabin* inspires the north to action and angers the south into secession. Lincoln says to her, "So you are the little woman who wrote the book that started this great war?"

Robert E. Lee decides to turn down Lincoln's request to lead the Union troops and instead he becomes the south's greatest general in a war that causes the death of 625,000 people. What if Lee had decided differently and said "Yes," to Lincoln?

Our decisions make our destiny. The impact of those decisions makes history. Ralph Waldo Emerson said: "All history is biography"

Golda's journey is a story of her decisions; decisions that made her destiny and made history.

For the context of Golda's beginnings we go to Russia. It is the spring of 1903, a few days before Easter. Decisions by politicians and peasants are being made. The fallout of these decisions will descend on the Russian Jews.

Posters were the social media of the day. Someone decided to write and distribute one entitled:

"A Proclamation Inciting a Pogrom of the Jews, Easter, 1903"

Fellow Christians:

Our great festival of the Resurrection of Christ draws near. It is many years since, put to death by the Jews, Our Lord expiated by his blood our sins and those of all the world, ...

But the vile Jews are not content with having shed the blood of our Savior, whom they crucified, and who suffered for them. Every year they shed the innocent blood of Christians. They shed it and use it in their religious rites.

... they bled to death an innocent child and afterwards threw its body into the street. ....let us join on Easter Day in the cry, "Down with the Jews!" Let us massacre these sanguinary monsters who slake their thirst with Russian blood!![1]

It doesn't matter that the story is false. It doesn't matter that "*the death of an innocent child*" is a girl who committed suicide and died at a Jewish hospital that was trying to save her. What matters is the need of the extremely wealthy to direct the brewing civil unrest away from their corrupt government. The answer is a scapegoat. And who better than a group having no government that will defend them? The rest of the poster shouted:

> *They aspire to seize our beloved Russia. They issue proclamations in order to incite the people against the authorities, even against our Little Father, the Tsar, who know them for a cowardly, vile, rapacious people, and will not give them liberty."*[2]

And if that didn't drum up enough fear to instigate the masses then the post script reads:

> *P.S. Make your visitors read this, or else your establishment will be sacked. We shall be kept informed of this by those of us who go amongst you.*[3]

The P.S. is the real point. The elite want to keep their place. They will intimidate the masses to avert any inclination toward dismantling their power. Fueling fear to a class of struggling people in order to create a feeding frenzy and to find someone else to blame—works well.

> This is a familiar tool of intimidation in the entrenched echelons of any culture. In the United States, the violence of the Ku Klux Klan is allowed to continue, diverting the attention of the exploited lower white class from the advantages allowed to the upper white class.

The intended long-term effect of the poster is successful. The rumblings of civil unrest are averted. The Russian Revolution, the fall of Tsarist autocracy, is delayed another decade.

The short-term effect of the poster is felt in the village of Kishinev. It is a *pogrom*. Gangs fill the streets. Their fires and sledge hammers leave two thousand Jews without homes. Forty-nine Jews are dead. Bodies of babies are found torn apart. Hundreds are crippled, beaten, maimed and humiliated.

It is not the first pogrom and it won't be the last. Undeterred by officials, gangs of violent peasants can instigate *pogroms* any time. They will ransack and burn homes, shops and synagogues, while murdering, raping and torturing the residents.

The author of the 1903 Russian poster doesn't know his announcement will have a far reaching effect on a little girl in Russia, a Jew. She will become a founder of the State of Israel.

The author, Harriet Beecher Stowe, doesn't know the effect of her writing on this same young girl who, upon seeing the play, *Uncle Tom's Cabin*, jumps up from her seat, shouting at the injustice. She will become Prime Minister to the State of Israel and stand before the United Nations petitioning that audience for justice.

In the stories of people's decisions, Golda Meir's decisions are an automatic, integral reflex making her leap in a single bound from the audience into the arena of life and fight for people to live in peace and with dignity. In an era of history, when Super Man fights to protect only gentile women and children, Golda flies to any fight to defend Jews. She doesn't take time to look for a phone booth and don a red cape. She shows up in sturdy shoes and a plain ironed dress.

Unlike a comic book hero whose faults are fictional, Golda's missteps will cause death. Unlike comic book coloring of bold reds and blues that never fade, Golda's bold idealism is muted with the glare of war. Unlike a comic book, where adoring crowds give thanks with the turn of a page, Golda contends with the frustrations of her people, the growing pains of a nation.

Against empires shrouding their advantages with an air of superiority, Golda's radar vision unnerves the upper echelons throughout the world. She can see that the "P.S." on the poster is always the real problem–in any language, in any media. She will demand of these extremists to stop using the fears of un-protected people as a means of exploiting an economic upper hand. And for rulers who are sellouts, Golda will not rant, al-though her quiet, cold stare cuts them no slack.

She lives her resolve to bring forth a place in the world where her family and fellow Jews will be free and safe. Golda Meir will be a signer of the Declaration of Inde-pendence for the State of Israel.

From the Archives Department,
University of Wisconsin-Milwaukee Libraries

1

RUSSIAN ROULETTE

For the story of Golda Meir, the curtain rises on May 3, 1898. The stage is Russia against a backdrop of civil unrest. Politics, a twisted character in any play, has a leading role to thwart the intentions of Justice. As in Greek mythology, where a mortal human is used to reveal the glory of a noble life, Golda is born with defiance in her DNA. Her script is written by the incorruptible North Star. Let the drama begin...

However, Golda's story is not a myth. It is an epic legend.

Poverty and filth permeate the masses infecting their kindness like a Black Plague of the heart. Diverting any attention from the true source of this misery, the Russian government aligns with the church to place the blame on liberalism where the principal proponents of this sin can be found in the community of Jews. Therefore, if Holy Russia is to be saved, then, the progress of Jews must be stopped. This policy can be seen from the top: Catherine the Great referring to the "evil influence" of the Jews down through the courts enacting more laws against the Jews (dating from late 1800s over six hundred laws are passed restricting Jewish life), down to the village *pogroms* often led by priests.

From 1881-1884, over 200 Jewish communities were attacked. Much like lynchings in America, the *pogroms* were free entertainment, public affairs which thousands would attend. "The Christians did not raise a finger to put a stop to the plunder and assaults… Many of them even rode through the streets in their carriages in holiday attire in order to witness the cruelties that were being perpetrated."[1]

As a prerequisite to survival, Jews were obliged to obey laws written only for them. Jews lived in Siberia or within a given geographic area of Russia called "Pale of Settlement." The term "pale" is specifically picked because it means more than just an area fenced off. "Pale" is a word used to describe an area where one race of people live under the control of another race. The Russian Government was sending the message–Russian Jews are subordinate to Russian Christians. Life within the Pale of Settlement was **not** a sanctuary from the anti-Semitic violence nor was there justice.

The laws included: No Jews can own property outside of their town. No Jews can become judges, sit on a jury, run their own school (schools must be run by Christians), be employed at the post office or the Stock Exchange or the Department of Railways. No Jews can buy land outside of town to use as a cemetery, or exceed the quota of 5% Jewish surgeons (unless there is a war). Jews moving from town to town within the Pale or wanting to move outside the Pale must have special permission (Jewish prostitutes are exempt from this rule).

Restrictions on Jewish merchants include: If a Jewish shop is for watch repair, it is against the law to sell a watch chain; a baker can't sell coffee; and kosher butchers can't sell to non-Jews. To paralyze the possibilities of the next generation, it is against the law to teach young Jews the Russian language in Hebrew schools. Other laws, with no purpose other than being punitive, stipulate **if** a Jewish couple can marry, **when** a Jewish couple can marry, and **how many** Jewish marriages can take place each year.[2]

Uncertainty was the daily bread of the Jewish citizens under the control of police lining their pockets with bribes. Any person caught standing up for himself would incur his house being raided, his arrest on trumped up charges and then being dragged through the streets (a message to everyone else) and thrown into a jail cell for several days. Worse still, families or whole villages could be given only a three-day notice to pack up and leave.

The legal suffering and persecution listed here is only a wisp of the evidence of Jews being used as a religious deflection by those hiding behind walls of economic advantage. In the years to come, Golda will not forget the lesson that tyranny, not religion, within any group gives rise to corruption and extortion. Future British officials and US officials will insinuate to Golda that she appease Arab extremists, but Golda never forgets that no amount of subservience or bribery will avert despotism.

For now, Golda is a little girl, and her birth name is Goldie Mabovitch. Born to Blume and Moshe, the importance of her parent's background is this—they are unimportant. They are not the wealthy, not the noble class, and not the intelligentsia. Given these circumstances, it is most unlikely Golda will ever go far unless one notices she is stubborn like her great-grandmother, Buba Goldie. Buba Goldie, dubbed "the man in the family" would have laughed hearing this repeated by the future Prime Minister of Israel, David Ben-Gurion, referring to her namesake as, "The only man in my cabinet." As they say, the apple doesn't fall far from the tree

Golda's parents meet in Pinsk (within the Pale of Settlement) where her mother's family lives. Moshe Mabovitch has come to town from the Ukraine to register for mandatory military duty. Jewish quotas within the army must be filled or families are ruined with fines beyond their finances. There is also the fact that children are taken by the Russian soldiers. Moshe knows the stories of his grandfather, who was kidnapped when he was thirteen and conscripted into the Russian army for a twenty-five year commitment. The grandfather was lucky and escaped after thirteen years. Moshe, wondering what dangers might befall him on this trip to Pinsk, need not worry. He falls in love.

Blume announces to her family that she met a "tall handsome young man" and she "instantly fell in love."[3] Golda's grandmother recognizes Moshe's integrity and gives this union her blessing.

Over the next few years Blume and Moshe have a daughter, Sheyna. Blume's next five children, four boys and one girl, will die before their first birthdays due to ill health and disease caused by poverty. When their living conditions improve because Blume is the wet nurse/nanny for a wealthy family, they have their daughter Golda. Golda's innate strong will is evidenced by her early nickname–Kochleffl–a stirring spoon. One more daughter, Zipke, is born (referred to in future text as "Clara" her name after the family immigrates). Although Blume will continue to struggle with pregnancies and miscarriages, the three daughters will be the extent of the immediate Mabovitch family.

Moshe, working as an artisan and woodworker, has limited opportunities living in Pinsk. He is not able to provide for his family by staying inside the Pale. However, in order to live outside the Pale he needs permission. Moshe builds a chess table. Proving his skills grants him the special pass he needs to live in Kiev. His optimism sees the wealth of the city and ignores the fact that in all of Russia, Kiev is the most anti-Semitic.

His hard work and a family loan support Moshe building a wood shop. He steps closer to success when he is awarded a contract. He finishes a furniture request for schools and libraries. The officials don't pay him. Why? They either find out Moshe is a Jew or they knew it and planned the increase in profit from free goods. Regardless, Moshe has no recourse because he has no rights. He is a Jew.

Golda's earliest memories are of Kiev. Not romanticizing she recalls, "I have very few happy or even pleasant memories of this time." We "suffered, with poverty, cold, hunger and fear, and I suppose my recollection of being frightened is the clearest of all memories."[4] Her reference to fear is the night (April 19, 1903) of a pogrom in Kiev. Mobs with knives, crowbars and big sticks screaming "Christ killers" could be heard coming down the street.

Golda recalls, "I remember how scared I was and how angry that all my father could do to protect me was to nail a few planks together…"[5] Her fear as a child and the anger of her inability to protect herself will translate into action in the years to come. Golda will never fall to a victim mentality nor will she engage in polite repartee that diminishes the grim reality of mob violence.

> Another child remembers a night in Russia, "lying on a blanket by the side of a road, watching his house burn to the ground." Immigrating to America, he becomes a great composer. Irving Berlin writes "God Bless America." [6]

Moshe is unable to succeed against the twisted legal discrimi-
nations of Kiev. His family is starving and living with fear, so
they return to Pinsk, moving in with his father-in-law. Moshe's
next plan is to immigrate to America. Aside from the cost, going to live on the other side of the world is an enormous decision. It is the 1903 Kishinev Pogrom connected to the poster
described earlier in the "Context and Commentary" which
pushes him to make the move. Here is an account of what
happened during the pogrom:

> "Some Jews had nails driven into their heads. Some
> had their eyes out. Children were thrown from garret
> windows, dashed to pieces on the street below. Women
> were raped, after which their stomachs were ripped
> open, their breasts cut off. Still the police did nothing.
> Nor did the city officials. Or the so-called intelligentsia.
> Students. Doctors. Lawyers. Priests. They walked lei-
> surely along the streets watching the show."7

Under the gaze of 5,000 Czarist troops, the wrath of the
Kishinev Pogrom lasts three days. Over 2,000 families are homeless because 1,300 homes and stores are looted and destroyed.

**1903—Kishinev
Pogrom**

Figure 40. Five of the 49 victims of the Kishinev Pogroms in
1903. From a memorial album, J.N.U.L., Jerusalem.

Golda will carry these memories of pogroms into her future. With any attempt to understand her life she reminds us, "If there is any logical explanation… for the direction which my life has taken… [it is] the desire and determination to save Jewish children… from similar experience."[8]

How can Jews protest? What are their options? Take to the streets and fight? They have no army and no guns. They will be murdered and their fewer numbers will mean survival of their race even less likely. Many will immigrate and leave Russia behind. But for those who stay, their protest is to announce a day-long fast.

Golda, just turning five, declares that she will fast. Blume attempts to dissuade her daughter explaining the adults are the ones that will fast. Golda dismisses her mother's rationale with her own. Golda will fast for the children.

1904–Childhood photo of Golda in Pinsk, Russia

From the Archives Department, University of Wisconsin-Milwaukee Libraries

Golda is already living up to the words she would speak later in life, "It isn't really important to decide when you are very young just exactly what you want to become when you grow up. It is much more important to decide on the way you want to live. If you are going to be honest with yourself and honest with your friends, if you are going to get involved with causes which are good for others, not only for yourselves, then it seems to me that that is sufficient, and maybe what you will be is only a matter of chance."[9]

Amidst the wave of immigrants that leave after the Kishinev Pogrom, Moshe is one of them. He makes plans to go to America and return in three years with enough money to support his family. Blume and the girls remain in Pinsk.

For Golda, the next few years will provide some warm memories of her grandfather's house full of aunts, uncles and cousins. Blume, baking bread and selling it door to door, earns enough money for a small apartment for her and her daughters. Although, any image of a cozy life is not totally correct, because next door is a police station. Blume and the girls can hear the screams of men and women being interrogated and beaten. Blume has particular reason to worry. Sheyna, at any moment, could be one of those prisoners.

> This is the same time as Bloody Sunday. A protest in St Petersburg to petition the tsar results in soldiers firing into the crowd and at least 1,000 people are killed by bullets or trampled to death as they try to flee.

Sheyna's involvement in revolutionary activities, like handing out pamphlets to protest the tsar, could get the whole family killed, imprisoned or sent to Siberia. Sheyna is also having illegal meetings at the apartment. Bluma, frantically stays out front to watch for police.

The debates within the Jewish community on how to move forward as a people are over these options: 1. stay in the country and advocate for change within the Russian government; 2. immigrate to another country, assimilate there and hope to not be persecuted; 3. return to the land of their origins and work toward the rebirth of Israel.

Option 3 is called Zionism: The belief of Jews having their own nation state in a territory defined as the Land of Israel. Here, Jews and their Jewish culture will be free of anti-Semitism. Assimilating to a foreign culture in order to escape persecution will not be necessary.

> The descriptor, 'Wandering Jew' becomes so common it is a cliché entombed by a 13th century folk story of a Jew who taunted Jesus and is condemned to wander the rest of his life. To date, the term 'Wandering Jew' is the name of a plant that roots easily and thrives with little care.

A debate is not necessary if the rights of your citizenship are upheld in your country. But for centuries, in dominions around the world, Jews live in a status of *Diaspora* in order to survive.

> Diaspora: A population of common origin, from a smaller geographic area, being scattered outside of their country. Due to escaping war, persecution, or sold as slaves–Jews had "dispersed" worldwide since six hundred years before Christ.

As a Diaspora, Jews are the minorities in any country and as such they are convenient scapegoats for social, economic and government ills. This leads to the growing popularity of option 3 in the debate.

Golda, eavesdropping on Sheyna's meetings, is learning the pros and cons of each option.

Sheyna is nine years older than Golda. Golda adores Sheyna and describes her as, "a remarkable intense, intelligent girl who became and remained one of the greatest influences of my life."[10] Sheyna has illegal political meetings at the apartment and Golda, listening from a hiding place, is beginning her education. Golda later explains what she started to learn at such a young age, "I must have begun, when I was about six or seven, to grasp the philosophy that underlay everything that Sheyna did." [11]

What Golda hasn't learned yet is to not overstep her bounds. When Sheyna discovers Golda in her hiding spot, Sheyna threatens that Golda be banished from any future meetings. Golda retorts with her own threat. "Look out, or I'll tell the police what you're saying." Sheyna responds, "If you do, I'll be sent to Siberia and I'll never return."[12]

The drama Sheyna brings to the family continues to escalate. Sheyna is in love with Shamai (referred to in future text by his American name, Sam), a fellow revolutionary. Sheyna also learns that Theodore Herzl is dead. Mourning his death, Sheyna will wear only black for the next two years.

"If you will it, it is no dream."

Theodore Herzl

Theodore Herzl: Like the future Gandhi giving his people hope, Herzl is not only a spokesman for the Jews but a rallying icon of Jews returning to Palestine, the Zionists. In 1902, Herzl publishes a novel *Altneuland* (*Old New Land*). Translated to Hebrew the title is–*Tel Aviv*. He might be surprised to know that someday the title *Tel Aviv* will be used as the name of a city in Israel. Herzl's photo will hang behind the signers of the Declaration of Independence for the State of Israel on the day of their independence. Herzl's quote had come true. "If you will it, it is no dream."[13]

**1948 David Ben-Gurion reads
the Declaration of Israeli Independence**

*From the Archives Department,
University of Wisconsin-Milwaukee Libraries*

Any dream for Blume right now is a nightmare. She lives in constant fear of Sheyna being caught by the Cossacks (groups of military horsemen who delight in the dirty work of enforcing laws and taking bribes). Blume's breaking point comes the day a drunken peasant sees Golda and a friend playing in the street. He grabs their heads and bangs them together yelling, "That's what we'll do to the Jews. We'll knock their heads together and we'll be through with them."[14]

Blume writes to Moshe whom she hasn't seen in three years–"We are coming now."

Golda has always heard her people say in solemn remembrance at the conclusion of the Yom Kippur service–"Next year in Jerusalem." Now Golda hears her mother saying–Next year in Milwaukee.

2
NEXT YEAR IN MILWAUKEE

"It doesn't matter if you've saved enough money or not," Blume writes to Moshe. "Believe me, we must come. Now!"[1]

It's the spring of 1906 and Blume is packing up. They will join the stream of two million Jews who leave Russia during the years 1881-1914. Forced to abandon their wealth, one man says, "I don't want to own anything. I want my family alive."[2]

However, while trying to leave Russia you risk your life. For those applying for a visa, officials can kidnap you and put you in the army, tax you while denying your visa, put you out of business, or beat you. The illegal guides, hired to escort the caravans, are little assurance for safe passage. Jewish girls are kidnapped and sold to brothels as far away as South America or Asia. Soldiers have little incentive to not shoot and kill anyone they find. The Russian policy is not to admit they don't want Jews, so they are loath to let them leave.

If Blume and the girls go, they will face 5,300 miles ahead where a lot can go wrong. But Blume sees the Cossacks out of control and knows they could all be dead if they stay. The odds of surviving, navigating her girls through the impending dangers, seem better.

Moshe is living and working in Milwaukee as a carpenter. He doesn't have enough money to pay for legal exit permits for his family, but he can buy fake permits. Far less than a good match, Blume and the girls must assume different identities. The discrepancies raise the risk of being arrested.

Blume, now forty, has the passport of a twenty-year-old girl. Sheyna, seventeen, must look twelve. Golda is eight but the papers say five. And for the youngest, Clara, she must pose as the daughter of another immigrant and call her "Momma."[3] The four of them practice and rehearse their new names as if their lives depend on it, because they do.

As the journey starts, so do the snags that could trip them. A man paid to purchase train tickets is playing out his scam to keep the money and instead make them ride in a wagon. Blume threatens to return to Pinsk and tell everyone he's a cheat. They get their train tickets.

Arriving at the Russian-Polish border, their luggage is lost or stolen and Blume has no recourse. (Who would dare file a complaint if your travel papers are forged?) The loss is counterbalanced by one fact: they are alive.

At the border, Blume faces questioning by guards who have God-like authority to change any family's escape route to end them up in Siberia. Blume's fierce determination is aided with money to pave the way. Hesitation by border guards is squelched with bribes.

Once in Poland, their next train is delayed. Waiting two days, in an unheated shack, they are not the only family freezing in the wood hut. Children are crying, and the soldier, plied with money to watch over them, threatens to kill the baby and its mother if they don't shut up.[4] The baby is quieted and the small band of refugees makes it to the station.

The train ride to Vienna takes two days. Each clack of the wheels takes them further from their homeland and closer to America. After Vienna, the next stop is the port of Antwerp. The hurdle here is hoping their papers are processed and approved. This success overrides any resentment that they each tolerate a disinfectant bath. Following all this, the émigrés wait. There is another delay.

Blume, Sheyna, Golda and Clara stay two days at the immigration center as the ship owners hold the departure. Waiting to load as many passengers as possible, the owners will increase their profit. Once the human freight boards, they are ordered below deck. The next fourteen days are spent in a dark cabin with four strangers. Golda's memories are blurred, but she does remember, "We were very scared."[5]

Their country, their community, their family, their friends are miles behind them. They might have known they will never see them again. They don't know that in the coming years those left behind in their homeland will all be dead–killed in the impending world wars. For Sheyna, still in mourning for Herzl, she is also grieving the loss of her beloved Sam. Leaving him behind, going so far away and his risk of being arrested are all valid fears that she has seen the last of him. For a poor Russian Jew, this journey to America might as well be a one-way ticket to the moon.

The ship is packed with immigrants. Most are exhausted, many are sick. Blume worries that because of the squalid conditions during their travels someone within her family could become ill, thus prevent them from getting through customs and into the United States. They could arrive at the shores of America only to be turned back. If there is a quote of Blume saying she is "stressed out," it is an understatement.

Passengers are allowed to spend time up on the deck. It is

here, watching the waves, feeling the wind, we find Golda. "I felt well and can remember staring at the sea for hours, wondering what Milwaukee would be like."[6]

Blume and her three girls are on their way to a new country, a new language, a new life. Communication is cut off from their old country, and there is no way to "connect" to their new culture. No Google search, no "app" to answer inquiries and no 3-minute YouTube video on "How To Assimilate to the USA"–all out of the question. And yet, all they have are questions. What does Father look like now? Will I recognize him? Will I ever see my aunts and uncles again? What will be different? And Sheyna wonders, "Will I ever see Sam again?"

US customs grants entry to the Mabovitch family of four. This last leg of the trip is crossing miles of America–next stop Milwaukee. The train is clacking along to their final destination–carrying them closer to answers and more questions.

Arriving in Milwaukee, one piece of life that remains the same is Yiddish. This one thousand-year-old language is a combination of German, Slavonic and Hebrew. It is spoken in the Jewish neighborhoods all over the world, from Siberia of Russian to the Midwest of America. Eleven million Jews have this bond.

Another common bond is the divisions among the Jews. Within the 8,000 Jews of Milwaukee there are forty-nine synagogues.[7] Partitions are by occupation; the laundrymen's synagogue, the carpenter's synagogue, and even a synagogue for politicians. A local newspaper notes there are more opinions than, "there are more political parties in central Europe."[8] This divisiveness amidst Jews, as in any group free to ques-

"True, we are a very small people, but remarkably hard to take."

Golda Meir

tion, isn't going to improve. The success of Golda's future will be due in part to her ability to negotiate with groups, stay sensitive to any slight, and merge them to the common cause of Zionism. This unification will be furthered by Hitler's Holocaust.

Poverty is also a familiar interlocking force. Although, the Hebrew Relief Society reports in 1905 that "only two percent of Jewish immigrants who land on our shores ever asked for aid."[9] This is an amazing statistic considering the immigration laws of most countries were written to enrich the government and force Jews to leave their wealth behind.

Here in Milwaukee, the communities create their own entertainment, enjoy the free steam baths (compliments of the Schlitz Brewery), drink cups of hot tea, gossip, or go to the nickel show at the local movie theater. Living with poverty is easy compared to living with *pogroms*.

Moshe is waiting at the station. His beard is gone and his clothes are the dress not of an immigrant but an American. Moshe has answers for his arriving family and he is expecting to have those answers accepted, especially by daughters. He assumes Sheyna is undermining his authority before she even gets off the train. Moshe believes, if Sheyna had not pursued her political activities, they could have stayed in Russia and waited his return. A father/daughter clash will take less than one day to occur.

Aghast, or maybe even embarrassed at their "Old World" appearance, Moshe insists their first stop will be a clothing store. Golda and Clara are thrilled to get new outfits and transform into modern Americans. Sheyna, still in black mourning for Herzl, refuses. Golda recalls, "Sheyna was already a perfectionist at fifteen, a girl who lived according to the highest principles, whatever the price, a severe taskmaster, and very austere."[10] Arriving in America, Sheyna is now seventeen and nothing has changed. What she wants is to be back in Russia with Sam. Instead her father buys Sheyna a frilly blouse and a straw hat with a broad brim covered in fake flowers. He proceeds to tell her, "Now you look like a human being."[11] Sheyna proceeds to tell him, "Maybe that's how you dress in America. But I am certainly not going to dress like that!"[12]

Assimilation to American ways is the new code of conduct to survive. Moshe can't see any other means. He has joined a labor union; he dresses and acts the part. He doesn't want to see his chances screwed up by an idealistic daughter. Moshe will lose this battle.

Blume, ever resourceful, finds an apartment with an empty store front, and she converts it to a grocery shop. Imagine that–newly arrived, no experience–and Blume starts a business. Moshe refuses to help out in the store, and the same sentiments come from Sheyna. Golda will be stuck with this assignment and resents it tremendously. However, the family is enjoying indoor plumbing, a flush toilet, and ice in the ice box.

At the end of their first few months, the summer of 1906, the Mabovitch ladies are going to their first Labor Day parade. Moshe, as a member of his union, will be marching in the parade and tells his family where to stand along the route. But the shift to a new culture isn't a smooth transition, so Mother and the girls are wondering, "What's a parade?"[13] What might be funny now wasn't then because the parade includes police mounted on horses, and when Clara sees them coming, she is terrified and starts to scream, "Mommy, the Cossacks are coming!"[14] The idea that police are here to protect the crowd not promote terror is an alien idea. Unable to calm the little girl's terror, Blume takes Clara home.

Golda, older and innately able to adapt more readily, remembers, "But for me, the parade, the crowds, the brass bands, the floats, the smell of popcorn and the hotdogs–symbolized American freedom…. To see my father marching on that September day was like coming out of the dark and into the light."[15]

Golda quickly learns English and makes friends. Regina Hamburger, Golda's best friend, will be a part of Golda's group that immigrates to Palestine. For now they go to the movies. It is Regina who witnesses Golda's outburst while watching *Uncle Tom's Cabin*.

However, Golda's reaction will never be staged rhetoric. Golda has realized that in spite of school being free for the children of Milwaukee, there is a nominal charge for textbooks. For many children, their families don't have money to buy the books. Golda recalls, "Obviously, someone had to do something to solve the problem, so I decided to launch a fund raiser."[16]

Using the word "obviously" is an indication of Golda's views not the community's. No one else had seen this problem, let alone, made a plan to resolve it. Golda, an eleven-year-old, takes action and organizes the "American Young Sister's Society." With Golda as chairman, she and her group knock on doors, post signs and gather forms of entertainment to sell tickets, put on a show, and raise money. Golda persuades the owner of a local hall to donate the room for the event. The evening includes children reading poetry, playing piano pieces and reciting memorized bits of literature.

Opening the program, Golda is to give a speech. Blume encourages her to write out the speech. Golda refuses. She explains, "It made more sense to me to say what was in my heart."[17] The power of Golda's persuasion will come from her authentic voice. Speaking from her heart will later raise millions to buy arms for the defense of Israel's new borders. That night they raise enough money to buy books for poor children.

The beginning glimpse of Golda's character includes this story. A girlfriend informs Golda that a boy threw a penny at a girl and said, "Pick it up!" When the girl does pick it up the boy responds, "A dirty Jew will pick up every penny." So what does Golda do? Doing nothing is never an answer. She doesn't wait either. Golda organizes a demonstration in front of the boy's house that same night. A friend recalls, "When it came to anti-Semitism, Golda never lowered her head!"[18]

Conflicts within the family are still brewing. Golda resents that she must tend the store in the morning while her mother is out buying the goods that stock the shelves. Being late for classes causes the truant officer to visit Blume, and only then does Blume comply.

Golda is also busy writing letters to Sheyna who had moved out and was able to get a job in Chicago. However, Sheyna contracted tuberculosis and now is living in a sanatorium in Denver. The good news for Sheyna is she had heard from Sam. He escaped from a Russian prison and made his way to America, and now they are to be married. Blume's reaction to this news, "But he has no prospects at all. He is a pauper, a greenhorn, a young man with no means and without a future."[19]

Blume and Moshe forget their own past of making their own choice. They will repeat this mistake with Golda when they decide that continuing Golda's education to be a teacher is out of the question. Instead, Blume is considering who would be a good marriage match.

Golda remembers, "My mother didn't want me to have an education. She thought it was for men only. [Women were suppose to] marry, marry, marry, while quite young."[20] And Moshe tells his daughter, "It doesn't pay to be too clever. Men don't like smart girls."[21] Hearing Golda's plans to attend a teaching school, Blume and Moshe decide to compromise and let Golda go to secretarial school. Golda refuses. The tensions rise and then snap.

Golda discovers Blume has a prospective husband in mind. He's a good man. He owns a shop. OK, so he's twice Golda's age.

Golda is furious.

Parent/child conflict is not uncommon. The turmoil of an immigrant family integrating into a new society is not noteworthy. What is remarkable is Golda's ability to see beyond the safe social expectations and to believe there can be more in her life. She doesn't know yet what that "more" will be, but she knows it's not marrying a shop keeper or being a secretary.

Moshe and Blume's good intentions are not playing out the way they expected for their daughters. Sheyna is not speaking to them, and she is living in Denver. Golda's plan is not at all what her parents are expecting either. Golda's spark has always surprised them, but when Moshe and Blume read the note left by Golda in her room they are shocked.

Golda has breached the walls of her parent's jurisdiction.

3

RUNAWAY

Golda as a girl
From the Archives Department,
University of Wisconsin-Milwaukee
Libraries

"I can honestly say that I was never affected by the question of the success of an undertaking. If I felt it was the right thing to do, I was for it regardless of the possible outcome."

Golda Meir

Golda lives by this quote. Fasting to protest *pogroms* or launching fund raisers for books, now she is fourteen and refusing to quit her education to become a wife. Sheyna and Sam, offering the chance to continue school, write to Golda, "You must come immediately."[1]

Sheyna has given her sister a lifeline. Golda will never forget it. It is one more factor in Golda's concrete admiration for her older sister–the generous offer to share their home and their food which now is more limited with the arrival of their baby.

Golda recalls, "That letter, written from Denver in November 1912, was a turning point in my life because it was in Denver that my real education began and that I started to grow up."[2]

The getaway plot includes her best friend Regina, who has been relaying letters between the sisters over the last couple years. Sheyna has advised in one of the letters, "The main thing is never to be excited. Always be calm and act coolly. This way of action will always bring you good results. Be brave."[3] Golda follows this advice for her escape as well as for the rest of her life.

The money needed gradually comes together and the train ticket is purchased. The run-away note reads:

"I am going to live with Sheyna, so that I can study." [4]

On the train ride Golda sits and thinks. For the next 1,043 miles, Golda is "disconnected." Decades before cell phones, there will be no text message from Regina telling about Moshe and Blume coming to the house. Regina's mother, upset that her daughter was an accomplice, slaps Regina on the face. Nor will Golda hear the rumors that she has run-away with an Italian. Golda only hears the clacking of the train on the tracks. Golda has cut the umbilical cord from a domineering Jewish mother. Not easy at any age, let alone fourteen. There is no record in the coming months of letters between Golda and her parents because there is no correspondence.

The next two years, in Denver, Golda is back in classes every day. After school, Golda helps Sam in the dry cleaning store: pressing clothes, waiting on customers and shutting the shop at seven o'clock.

Evenings at the house, Sheyna and Sam continue being involved with political groups and discourse. The difference now—they don't fear the Cossacks catching them. Golda's education in social politics continues to expand. Still the junior member, she stays quiet, but at least not having to hide. There are many in this group who don't want Golda to hide. She is intense, passionate and full of questions. The young men are interested in her, but one in particular, Morris, has her attention.

Any free time is spent with Morris: the park, outdoor concerts, and book discussions with Morris' latest recommendation. Golda gradually learns his story: family immigrated to America from Lithuania, and his father died when Morris was a boy. Morris works to support his mother and three sisters. He is in Denver because one of his sisters has tuberculosis.

Golda recalls: "I admired Morris enormously—more than I had ever admired anyone except Sheyna—not only for his encyclopedic knowledge, but for his gentleness, his intelligence and his wonderful sense of humor. He was only five or six years my senior, but he seemed much older, much calmer and much steadier. Without at first being aware of what was happening to me, I fell in love with him and couldn't help realizing that he loved me, too, although for a long time we said nothing to each other about the way we felt."[5]

This balance—Morris's quiet patience to Golda's gutsy energy—will prove to be their demise. Golda will always love to be with people, right in the mix where the decisions are being made. Morris, a private person, is content to read books and listen to the classical music on his record player. Sheyna's daughter Judy accurately reflects about Morris, "He didn't like a lot of people around. He liked his family, but everybody else, 'Stay away…'"[6]

Sheyna, now acting as "mother," has an eagle eye over her little sister. There are arguments about curfew and conflicts about which suitors are coming around. Regina remembers, "Sheyna thought that what she said was direct from God. She was always driving people to do things according to her precise standards, constantly criticizing; she could be a very hard person, dogmatic and domineering, often very difficult and very selfish like her mother. She was not a warm person…"[7]

Golda realizes she wants something more than Sheyna's approval; she wants to prove to Sheyna that she is her own person. Golda moves out.

Sheyna, speaking of Golda, remembers, "When she makes up her mind she carries out her decision."[8]

"I marched out of the house in the black skirt and white blouse I had been wearing all day, taking nothing else with me."[9] Golda, sixteen-years-old, is on her own. She moves in with a couple that are tuberculosis patients and lives in a niche at the end of their hall. Still wanting to study, Golda reads in the bathroom during the nights. She can have a light on and not disturb the couple, but their incessant coughing (due to their medical condition), keeps Golda awake most nights. Golda gets a job taking measurements for skirts and earns enough to rent her own small room.

The new job means quitting school–not what Golda wanted. Months go by and the silence between the sisters remains. Golda is lonely, misses Sheyna, and frustrated that she is not continuing her education. After seven months the two make amends, and Golda returns. Sheyna still stands firm in her opinions, but a shift toward self-assurance has occurred within Golda.

During this time a letter arrives from Moshe. Golda remembers what he wrote to her, "If I value my mother's life, I should come home at once."[10] The parents make promises: no interfering and Golda can continue her education. Morris and Golda agree to keep their relationship a secret for now. He will soon follow. Golda is going back to Milwaukee.

· Having defied both her parents and an overbearing sister, Golda's aplomb includes proving she can live on her own and support herself. Golda's self-confidence also includes new ideas. She has learned about Socialist-Zionists. She is intrigued with the concept: having a socialist government within Zionism (having a Jewish nation state) and this is applied to living in a Kibbutz. Golda has never been a religious Jew, so she is taken with the Zionist concept–"religion of labor."

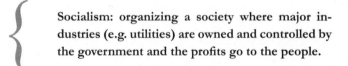

> Socialism: organizing a society where major industries (e.g. utilities) are owned and controlled by the government and the profits go to the people.

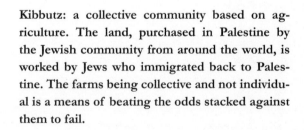

> Kibbutz: a collective community based on agriculture. The land, purchased in Palestine by the Jewish community from around the world, is worked by Jews who immigrated back to Palestine. The farms being collective and not individual is a means of beating the odds stacked against them to fail.

Morris, still in Denver, writes to Golda, "I do not know whether to say that I am glad or sorry that you have joined the Zionist Party … I am altogether passive in the matter, though I give you full credit for your activity, as I do to all others engaged in doing something toward helping a distressed nation, …the idea of Palestine or any other territory for the Jews is, to me, ridiculous."[11] And later he tells Golda, "You get your new Jewish state. So there'll be another country in the world. So what?"[12]

The "So what?" is Morris' articulation in two words of what will become the great divide between him and Golda. For Golda, she is formulating her answer to that rhetorical question with one word–Everything.

Golda will not obligate herself to becoming a Zionist, socialist or otherwise, until she knows she is completely committed to move to Palestine. Before her eighteenth birthday, Golda is slowly coming to that fork in the road.

At home in Milwaukee things have changed. The family has moved to a bigger apartment, there is more food, and Blume is always cooking for guests. With the country entering World War I, Blume has turned the house into a stopover for the young men who volunteer for the Jewish Legion.

Jewish immigrants are not allowed to join US forces. Volunteering for the Jewish Legion, they will fight with the British army to break the four-hundred-year rule of the Ottoman Empire and liberate Palestine. One soldier from the Jewish Legion said, "We Jews didn't want Palestine handed to us on a platter. We wanted to earn it."[13] Another Jewish soldier wrote home and said, "Jews have died for all other countries. It is good to die for our Palestine."[14] Golda wants to join these troops with their cause, but she is turned down. No girls.

A group that will accept her is the Poale Zion (Workers of Zion). Golda is able to join because they wave the age requirement for her. Blending Zionism and Socialism, they believe that Jews can build a nation by the sweat of their brows. Golda, their new recruit, helps raise money to support the mission.

Golda is fulfilling the desire to be a part of something bigger, a purpose that benefits people, a movement not just an individual. In the midst of her outspoken opinions at school, a classmate asks Golda, "Goldie, if everything's wrong, why don't you start your own country?" Golda responds, "I might just do that."[15]

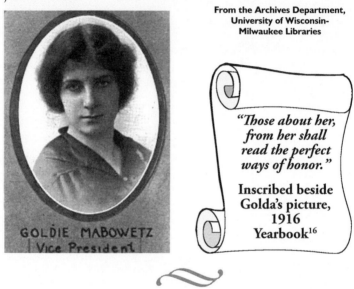

From the Archives Department, University of Wisconsin-Milwaukee Libraries

GOLDIE MABOWETZ
Vice President

"Those about her, from her shall read the perfect ways of honor."

Inscribed beside Golda's picture, 1916 Yearbook[16]

In spite of battles raging in a world war, the battles in the war of wills at home are few. Golda has finished high school and is enrolled in teacher training college. Her relations with her father have improved. The fact that Blume has been reading Golda's mail from Morris causes only a minor skirmish. Overall the Mabovitch family is enjoying their lives and the benefits of their hard work. Golda sees her parents relaxing and reading the newspaper. Sunday afternoons are spent in the park, and Golda watches children playing without fear. Some of these children are her students at the Folkschule where she is giving lessons to Jewish children and passing to the next generation their heritage of Yiddish reading, writing, history and literature.

**1916, Golda (far right) and the
Zionist Jewish Folk School in Milwaukee**
From the Archives Department,
University of Wisconsin-Milwaukee Libraries

Golda is not satisfied. Life challenges have not quenched her spirit but rather the opposite. Golda is thirsting for more. She explains:

> *"Anybody who believes in something without reservation, believes that this thing is right and should be, has the stamina to meet obstacles and overcome them. The best example, of course, is somebody who is very, very religious, who honestly and sincerely believes. He has an enormous source of strength. From my early youth I believed in two things: one, the need for Jewish sovereignty, so that Jews—and this has become a cliché—can be master of their own fate; and two, a society based on justice and equality, without exploitation. But I was never so naïve or foolish as to think that if you merely believe in something it happens. You must struggle for it."[17]*

For Golda, the struggle is just beginning.

4
MARRIED TO ZION
NOT MORRIS

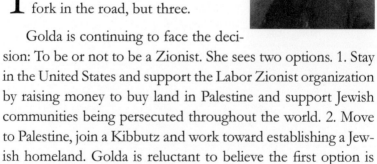

Milwaukee, Wisconsin 1917.
Golda Meir, a school teacher
in Milwaukee
From the Archives Department,
University of Wisconsin-Milwaukee Libraries

The year 1917 will bring not just one
fork in the road, but three.

Golda is continuing to face the deci-
sion: To be or not to be a Zionist. She sees two options. 1. Stay
in the United States and support the Labor Zionist organization
by raising money to buy land in Palestine and support Jewish
communities being persecuted throughout the world. 2. Move
to Palestine, join a Kibbutz and work toward establishing a Jewish homeland. Golda is reluctant to believe the first option is
the answer. Considering the experience of Jews in Russia, her
doubts have credence.

The future of the Jewish people is a constant debate. The
author of an article for the *Jewish Daily Chronicle* writes, "Here in

America lays the destiny of the Jew. ... Every condition is right here for the accommodation of the conditions of modern life to the demands of the old faith."[1] This game plan of American Jews is assimilation while maintaining their Jewish identity. By showing good citizenship, Jews hope their civil rights will not be denied. A rabbi in Milwaukee believes, "A religion can never make a man a foreigner."[2]

Jews cannot imagine that it won't matter how well they assimilate. In the above article's reference to "modern life," the inference is *pogroms* are a thing of the past. If, during this debate, they recall the Dreyfus Affair, the fact that it happened in France, not America, keeps the Jewish trust alive.

Degradation of Alfred Dreyfus 5 January 1895

Picture by Henri Meyer, cover of *Petit Journal*, 13 January 1895, captioned "The Traitor"

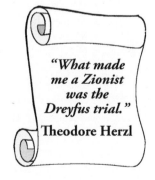

"What made me a Zionist was the Dreyfus trial."
Theodore Herzl

Alfred Dreyfus was of Jewish descent and had assimilated so well to his country of France that he was a French Army officer. At a public trial he was accused and found guilty of treason. Dreyfus was sent to Devil's Island where he spent over four years. With overwhelming contrary evidence and public outcry on an international scale, the truth prevailed that this was a cover up of mistakes by non-Jewish superior officers. The ruling was overturned and eventually Dreyfus was reinstated.

Theodor Herzl, also of Jewish descent, had also lived the policy of assimilation in his country, Austria. He was the Paris correspondent of a Viennese newspaper. In 1894, Herzl was assigned to cover the Dreyfus Affair. It was here, any illusion of society accepting Jews was shattered.

The use of public humiliation, stripping Dreyfus of his rank, witnessing the mass rallies in Paris after the trial and the crowds chanting "Death to the Jews!" was the seal on Herzl's decision that Jews must have a land of their own. He authored the book, *The Jewish State*.

In August 1897 he convened the first Zionist Congress in Basel, Switzerland. This marked the beginning of modern political Zionism. Herzl predicted there would be a Jewish state within fifty years. (Herzl's death was what Sheyna was still mourning when she arrived in Milwaukee.)

Like Herzl, Golda will have her own epiphany that pushes her to Zionism.

For now, Golda and her father are raising money for Jews in war torn areas of Europe. Regina remembers, "Goldie and her hard-working father did a tremendous amount of work raising money for the Jewish Relief Society for clothes and food. I think Goldie felt too that it was the kind of thing Sheyna would have done and she was following in her footsteps."[3]

Some of this money is sent to their hometown in Pinsk. Russian troops have ripped through the streets murdering, raping and pillaging on their way to the front, while the opposing army does the same through Pinsk as they push back. A news report comes out—more than forty men have been taken and lined up to a wall of a church, a wall Golda walked by as a child. Against this wall, the men are shot. Their crime? Receiving and distributing the funds from a relief committee, in America.

Were the funds the very money that Golda had helped raise? Were some of these men Golda's uncles or friends who had visited her grandfather's tavern?

More than one hundred years earlier a quote by Edmond Burke had become famous: "An event has happened, upon which it is difficult to speak, and impossible to be silent." There is no record of Golda knowing Burke's sentiment but she is going to live it. For Golda, it is impossible to be silent. She will not allow this event, the murder of innocent Jews, to go unnoticed.

Golda plans a protest parade. She believed, "they could earn the respect and sympathy of the rest of the city"[4] by showing how they felt about the murder of these Jews. Like the yearly Labor Day parade, they will march through downtown Milwaukee. Everyone—Jew or Christian—will be made aware of the events. Not everyone is pleased with this idea, Jews included.

The Jewish owner at one of Milwaukee's biggest department stores gives Golda the warning, "You'll make a laughing-stock of the Jews. They won't even be able to march straight down the street." Golda is not deterred. She responds, "I don't worry about that." The owner tries again, "You are going to embarrass me so much that I am going to move out of town." Golda responds, "That's your privilege."[5]

In Milwaukee that day, Golda's efforts have an effect. Men, women, and children march four abreast, including a band and a color guard of army veterans. The Stars and Stripes is carried along with a flag bearing the Zionist colors. Many non-Jews join the march of the thousands of Jews, representing fifty organizations in the parade. Golda remembers, "It came as a surprise to me… that so many non-Jews participated in that [parade] and I can remember looking into the eyes of the people who lined the street watching us and feeling how supportive they were."[6] She later writes, "There weren't many protest marches in those days, and we got publicity all over America."[7]

Like the Dreyfus Affair for Herzl, the massacre in Pinsk is the turning point for Golda. She explains, "I think it was while we were marching through town that day that I realized I could no longer postpone a final decision about Palestine. However hard it might be for those who were dearest to me, I could no longer put off making up my mind about where I was going to live. Palestine, I felt, not parades in Milwaukee, was the only real, meaningful answer… The Jews must have a land of their own again and I must help build it, not by making speeches or raising funds, but by living and working there."[8]

{ Aliyah–Jews returning to their Holy Land. Large scale waves of immigrants began in 1882. The Third Aliyah occurs between 1904 and the end of WWI when 40,000 Jews immigrate to Palestine. It is this group that buys land to establish the kibbutz, creates the town of Tel Aviv, builds an electric power plant, a salt plant, a flour mill, and networks of schools (kindergarten through university). This third wave will include Golda. }

Golda explains, "In 1901, the Jewish National Fund had already been formed by the Zionist movement for the exclusive purpose of buying and developing land in Palestine in the name of the entire Jewish people." She remembers, "… the small tin blue collection box that stood next to the Sabbath candles in our living room and into which not only we but our guests dropped coins every week."[9] Golda goes on to clarify, "What was often purchased were deadly black swamps that brought malaria and black water fever. Still, what mattered most was that this pestilential land could be bought, though not cheaply; much of it, incidentally, was sold to the Jewish National Fund by a single well-to-do Arab family that lived in Beirut."[10]

> Blue Box or *Pushke* - Started with a passing of the hat, Theodor Herzl's hat, in 1901, the Blue Box or pushke was born. Millions of these boxes were distributed around the world raising funds to buy and develop the land of Israel. The land was sold by wealthy Turkish and Arab landowners interested in selling off malaria infested swamps, land of no value, at exorbitant prices.

Jewish National Fund, Blue Box

Golda's zeal for the Zionist cause inspires her to address a Jewish congregation. The problem is, she's a woman and not allowed. Undaunted, she picks the High Holidays, gets a soap box, and plans to stand on it outside the synagogue, and people will have to listen to her as they go by. (At that time it is common to make speeches on street corners that provided an immediate audience and no need to hire a meeting room.) When Moshe hears of Golda's plan he threatens to pull Golda away by her braids.

Golda has friends stand guard to watch for and block her father. Moshe arrives but stops to listen to his daughter. Before he can take hold of Golda, her message takes hold of him. He returns home and tells Blume, "I don't know where she gets it from."[11] Golda, for the rest of her life, considers this her most successful speech–having her father change his mind. A growing regard for their daughter is germinating within both Moshe and Blume.

Golda continues giving speeches. Her reputation is expanding but not the number of American Jews willing to follow the Zionist cause to the point of becoming fellow pioneers. Their support for Zionism will be monetary. In the years ahead Golda will be grateful to this group that will provide the millions of dollars needed to buy the arms that protect the new borders of Israel.

Traveling around the country, garnering support for the Zionist cause are two leaders in the movement, David Ben-Gurion and Yitzhak Ben-Zvi. Their overnight stay in Milwaukee includes a speech Saturday night and on Sunday the Mabovitch family will be honored to have them as guests for lunch. Golda knows the future of these guests could be comparable to George Washington and John Adams and she wants to attend the speech. She is torn by the promise to Morris that she will go to a concert that same night with him. She remembers, "That I just didn't have the courage to say that I would not go to the concert."[12]

Golda will forever remember that moment of weakness because the consequence is Ben-Gurion cancels the lunch commitment. His response, "somebody who could not come to listen to him speak is not deserving to have him as a guest."[13] It will be Golda's last time that Zionism does not come first.

Golda is trying to convince Morris to be on board with her Zionist cause. Her case for moving to Palestine is bolstered by the British. The Balfour Agreement is announced to the world.

> **The Balfour Agreement–This proclamation by England, November 2, 1917, declares a portion of the defeated Ottoman Empire (being divided up for Arabs–Syria, Iraq, Iran etc) is to be given to the Jews to reestablish their homeland.**

David Ben-Gurion writes, "England has done a great deal: she has recognized our existence as a political entity and our right to the country." Expecting no assistance from outsiders Ben-Gurion goes on to write, "The Jewish people must now transform this recognition into a living reality, by investing their strength, spirit, energy, and capital in building a National Home and achieving full national salvation."[14]

The Balfour Agreement is the crack in the proverbial door that Golda needs. Armed with this evidence, Golda is convinced that now is the time to go to Palestine, although this won't be possible until WWI ends (in another year), and they must save enough money for the trip.

Morris wants to marry Golda who will only agree to tie the knot if he promises they can emigrate. Morris concedes. Golda writes the wedding vows to include the promise.

Determined to have a simple ceremony, Golda wants to go to the courthouse. Blume won't hear of it and for this argument she wins. Blume is even more thrilled when she finds out the ceremony will be conducted by Rabbi Solomon Scheinfeld, the most important rabbi in Milwaukee.

Golda's work for the Zionist cause, with Rabbi Scheinfeld, has garnered his attention. Could the rabbi have imagined this brazen young woman, who is rewriting wedding vows, will be a prime minister of the new country? Could the rabbi have known that the Hebrew University in Jerusalem will have a wing of the library bearing his name?[15] No—on this day, December 24, 1917, it is simply the wedding of two Jews in Milwaukee.

In the ceremony, the bridegroom is given a glass, which he stomps on and smashes. The sound of broken glass is a reminder of the destruction of the Temple in Jerusalem—the yearning for their lost nationhood. Morris is the one to stomp on the glass but it is Golda who yearns. Raising the funds to travel will take three and one-half years.

**1918 Golda Meir (then Meyerson)
with her husband Morris**

*From the Archives Department,
University of Wisconsin-Milwaukee Libraries*

Life isn't settling down to quiet days of matrimony. If that is what Morris is expecting, he is sorely disappointed. Poale Zion offers Golda a full-time job traveling across the United States and organizing new branches of the group. The job pays fifteen dollars a week plus expenses. Golda is thrilled with the opportunity to earn money for tickets to Palestine plus help the Zionist cause. What a deal! It doesn't matter that these meetings sometimes last until 4:00 am and she is taking medication for migraine headaches. It doesn't matter she is gone from Morris for weeks at a time.

But it does matter to Golda's family. Blume, Moshe and Sheyna are upset.

"My father was furious," Golda recalls.[16] She remembers his rant, "A few minutes after the wedding, you are leaving your husband and going? Who leaves a new husband and goes on the road?" A letter from Sheyna reads, "And as far as personal happiness is concerned, grasp it, Goldie, and hold it tight. There are not many who can speak about happiness. You behold happiness without much effort and don't grasp the real value of it... The only thing I heartily wish you is that you should not try to be what you *ought* to be but what you are. If everybody would only be what they are, we would have a much finer world... find you own self."[17]

Sheyna's dictates, "be what you are" and "find your own self" are good advice if the person being told is free to "be" and "find." Sheyna isn't giving her sister that option and believes Golda should "be" happy as a wife. Golda should stop reaching for a dream and settle for "a much finer world" where everyone fits traditional expectations. Golda will struggle with this conflict fueled by her family and her own dark nights. Golda acknowledges that Morris is patient. She writes, "Morris consoled himself for my being away so much by turning our tiny apartment into a real home that awaited me whenever I was in Milwaukee."[18]

These trips and talks are the next stage of training for Golda's future. Coordinating a unity among the Jewish communities, educating them to the cause–she is clearly being respected because the Milwaukee Poale Zion group elect Golda to be the delegate for the American Jewish Congress in 1918. Golda is nineteen years old. A fellow delegate writes, "She had this natural flair for getting along with people. I tell you her mouth was gold. Every time Goldie opened her mouth, it had impact somewhere. When she appeared among delegates, talking about issues, everybody saw that she was more than the average girl."[19] Another attendee at the conference said, "Few speakers were more moving than Goldie. She could move people to tears. And herself as well. We used to stand offstage with huge man-sized handkerchiefs."[20]

Golda's authentic voice has already been formed by her own short history of experiences. As an up and coming tour de force, she has displayed discernment and action that outweighs an older person's hesitancy. Her keen awareness for the dignity of others resonates within the audience. She is "in her element" at this stage of her life and writes to Morris, "some moments [at the convention] reached such heights that after them one could have died happy."[21]

And Morris is home in Milwaukee–waiting. Even when Golda is back, she is often out four or five nights a week for meetings. Her memory of disappointing Ben-Gurion, disappointing herself, will never be repeated. In fact, another offer comes to Golda. The Zionists need her in Chicago. Her friend Regina writes from there, "I am sure if you came, Chicago would wake from its deep sleep. You are a good motor."[22] Golda goes. Working at the Chicago Public Library in the afternoons is convenient for keeping the schedule of meetings late into the night–mornings Golda can sleep in a little.

Morris still voices his doubts that the Jews will have their own homeland, but he moves to Chicago to be with Golda. Sheyna and Sam with their family of two children are in Chicago, and they express their dismay that the roles in Golda and Morris' marriage are backwards.

When Golda travels to Canada to help raise money for the Poale Zion paper she needs a US passport. The current law states that wives can become US citizens only if their husbands are citizens. Morris is not. Golda then asks her father if she can use his passport. He refuses saying, "Oh, no, if that's what you need in order to go, then you don't go." Golda goes anyway. At the border she is taken by authorities but contacts a Jew on the Canadian side to sort out the legalities. The point being; nothing is going to stop her. Golda will always scoff at excuses and "I can't" is never the right answer.

Golda and Morris move to New York City. They are getting ready for their immigration to Palestine.

PART TWO

CONTEXT AND COMMENTS

Imperial Perspective

"*There are many humorous things in the world; among them, the White man's notion that he is less savage than the other savages.*"

Mark Twain

With no government to protect their rights as citizens, Jews want to extricate themselves from being the scapegoat "chosen people" around the world. The sheer audacity of this idea that Jews think they can have their own country, is shaking the foundation of society much like the American colonists declaring their independence in 1776. Aside from the initial reaction of "How dare they!" the underlying fear of those in power rises up, "If this group succeeds then other groups might do the same." Caucasian men, smoking cigars, in dark paneled libraries, sipping their whisky are appalled.

This segment, "Imperial Perspective," explains the magnitude of the entrenched social infrastructure of white prerogative, which the Jewish people must navigate, as they challenge the status quo.

The Rescue

**All U.S. presidents
from 1853 - 1953
will stand beside this statue
during their inauguration.**

Commissioned by Congress to create a statue to "represent the conflict between the Anglo-Saxon and Indian races," Horatio Greenough sculpted *The Rescue* to show "the peril of the American wilderness, the ferocity of our Indians, the superiority of the white man, ..."[1] The imperial perspective from the government who endorsed the sculpture ripples down to the pioneer family being portrayed. The statue includes an innocent mother shielding her baby, the family dog obediently waiting for a command and a savage Indian, armed with a hatchet. The towering white man is shown protecting his family and overpowering the Indian with only his bare hands.

In 1958, Congress thinks better of having the statue as a backdrop to inauguration ceremonies. *The Rescue* is moved to a vault in the basement. This shift in understanding (shame or otherwise) is a symbolic point on the historical time line.

Information in this section is not to characterize any one culture and declare "how bad they are." More to the point this segment shows–how far we have come. To appreciate that distance–we must go back down to the basement, look in the vault and see what else we find.

Consider the best-selling book, *Types of Mankind,* that went through twelve printings during the nineteenth century. Although now deemed "exhibit A" of American racism, during the 1900s it was a go-to source for teaching. The book, studied as a credible source, was co-authored by an American medical doctor, Dr. Josiah Clark Nott and the British lecturer, George Robins Gliddon. The textbook explained that only the White race was civilized and that "wherever in the history of the world the inferior races have been conquered and mixed in with the Caucasians, the latter have sunk into barbarism."[2] Aside from the glossing over that "mixed in" meant unwanted pregnancies from the raping of local females–here was what was taught in the schools:

Types of Mankind described Native Americans:

"He can no more be civilized than a leopard can change his spots. His race is run, and probably he has performed his earthly mission. He is now gradually disappearing, to give place to a higher order of beings. The order of nature must have its course... Some are born to rule, and others to be ruled. No two distinctly marked races can dwell together on equal terms. Some races, moreover, appear destined to live and prosper for a time, until the destroying race comes, which is to exterminate and supplant them."[3]

Seeing what had been taught in the schools for Caucasians helps us not be so dumbfounded in the coming pages of this book. Massacres were justified because they, the Caucasians, were the "destroying race." It also helps us understand why the British were so appalled at the obstinate will to survive of the Palestinian Jews. The fact that Jews refused to let other cultures "supplant them" was nothing short of annoying to those in charge.

President Teddy Roosevelt's favorite professor at Harvard taught, "white supremacy based on the racial heritage of England, [finding] non-Aryan peoples lacking in the correct "ancestral experience" and impossible to Americanize."[4] Armed with his education, Teddy gave a lecture at Oxford University where he pointed out the modern White race had covered much of the world but unlike the past Anglos–the more recent conquests had allowed native races to survive, so White gains would only be temporary. He told his white, male, Christian audience, "all of the world achievements worth remembering are to be credited to the people of European descent… the intrusive people having either exterminated or driven out the conquered peoples."[5] Teddy called the process "ethnic conquest."[6] Given this was the perspective in the training for future leaders of the British and United States empires–it's a wonder more cultures were not annihilated.

Joining in was the Pan-German League in 1891. Their posters, displayed in shop windows, read, "The world belongs to Germans."[7] And the founder of the league declared, "We want territory even if it belongs to foreigners so that we may shape the future according to our needs."[8] Fast forward to Nazi Germany, Hitler admires the British Empire, that small island of people, which controlled so much territory. "Ethnic conquest" will translate to "ethnic cleansing."

Not a thin veneer but a generally accepted American belief was in Caucasian superiority. This conviction was used to justify our decimation of the Native Americans. It was also trotted out to rationalize the United States takeover of Hawaii, Puerto Rico and the Philippines.

The fighting to occupy the Philippines included US troops

executing POWs, torturing civilians, and raping women. In charge of the troops was Medal of Honor recipient General Frederick Funston. His defense of this brutality was, "They (Filipinos) are, as a rule, an illiterate semi-savage people, who are waging war, not against tyranny, but against Anglo-Saxon order and decency."[9] General MacArthur will later explain away U.S. soldiers killing four times more Filipinos than the usual number being injured with this comment, "Men of Anglo-Saxon stock do not succumb as easily to wounds as do men of 'inferior races.'"[10]

The trickle down, of this mentality, runs from the President, to the Generals and into the troops. A veteran soldier told newspaper reporters, "The country won't be pacified until the niggers are killed off like the Indians."[11] (Philippine natives are referred to as "niggers.") The veteran goes on to contend that it was necessary "to blow every nigger into nigger heaven."[12]

Another page in the indubitable book of "Caucasian Imperialism" was the belief that natives can't run their own country. It didn't matter there was evidence to the contrary. Admiral Dewey sent two American Navy men on a fact-finding tour of the Philippine island of Luzon (Oct 1898). The men documented a Filipino government administering court justice, keeping the peace, giving appropriate police protection, holding fair elections and following through with the consent of the governed.[13] This document, that reported a functioning democracy, got buried. Secretary of War, William Taft told the Philippine audience in 1905, "I did not come to give you your independence... You will have your independence when you are ready for it, which will not be in this generation–nor in the next, nor perhaps for a hundred years or more."[14] The Filipinos wait another sixty-four years for their independence.[15]

The "inferior" country, if not conquered, could also be given away as a political gift. Those in control could dole out the governance (to include economic profits) to another country deemed fit.

In 1905, President Teddy Roosevelt, impressed with his Japanese Harvard classmates, described to a reporter his vision of the East, "All the Asiatic nations are now faced with the urgent necessity of adjusting themselves to the present age. Japan should be their natural leader in that process, and their protector during the transition stage, much as the United States assumed the leadership of the American continent many years ago."[16] In 1900, Theodore Roosevelt lined up his ducks for Japan to be the "natural leader" and said, "I should like to see Japan have Korea."[17] It didn't matter that in 1897 Emperor Gojong of Korea had wanted to prevent his country from having Japan as their "protector." Playing his cards in favor of the United States, Gojong had said, "We feel that America is to us as an Elder Brother."[18]

Teddy's perspective was for the United States to play the role of Big Brother and as such, bestow advice to be followed by Japan. In Teddy's opinion Japan was "the only nation in Asia that understands the principles and methods of Western civilization."[19] Teddy Roosevelt would never know the results of encouraging the Japanese to mirror his imperial attitude. Aside from war crime atrocities to the Chinese, the Japanese took from Korea two hundred thousand young girls as sex slaves for the Japanese troops in World War II.

Nor would Teddy ever know the future irony of his delight after Japanese torpedo boats had a surprise attack on Russian ships in 1904. Teddy wrote his son, "I was thoroughly well pleased with the Japanese victory, for Japan is playing our game."[20] When this "game" was played again in Pearl Harbor, December 7, 1941, it will be Teddy's nephew, President Franklin D. Roosevelt who will utter the immortal words, "a day that will go down in infamy."

The British Empire, into the 1920s, included 458 million people, one-fifth of the world's population. The scope of their dominion covered over 13,000,000 square miles, almost one-fourth of the Earth's land area. As such, the empire assumed they had the righteous destiny of being chosen to lead the world.

Seeing themselves as custodians over unfortunate souls, the rhetoric of protecting the natives and spreading morality was the façade for their own country's economic self-interest. Benevolence to the locals was code for keeping them pacified and not uprising. Their protection from invasions was to England's advantage of keeping their trade routes free and clear. So for the sake of this story, the British interest in the Arabian Peninsula was to keep the grain supplies that fed her armies, the oil fields that fueled her navy, and the shorter shipping route (Suez Canal) that ensured higher profits for their goods to and from India.

> Transporting the raw materials from India to England was a grueling four-month trip by ship around the Cape of Good Hope. With the opening of the Suez Canal (1869), that voyage is shortened to just three weeks.

In the next chapter, Golda is on a ship bound for an area called Palestine that has been promised to be turned over to the Jews. The Jews are showing their capabilities in running their own government. Rights and privileges (health care, education, and higher wages) of future citizens under their government will include the Arabs living in the region. The Jews, given the reins to run their country, have no intention of kicking any Arab citizens out. It can be that easy. Except…

The British, with egocentricity the size of their empire, are weighing their promises to the Jews against their economic ledger that needs oil. Wealthy Arabs can provide oil, but they want to ensure their wealth and a hold over their lower class countrymen. They can see that the masses might be swayed away by increased education and a share (with the Jews no less) in the benefits of a successful economy. The keystone to meet the combined objectives of the British and the wealthy Arabs is using the religion and terror tactics of Muslim extremists.

The tactics are the same as the P.S. on the 1903 Russian poster mentioned in the beginning of the book—*Make your visitors read this, or else your establishment will be sacked. We shall be kept informed of this by those of us who go amongst you.*

In the early 1900s, the Palestinian Arabs are a pawn for the powerful Arabs living in their palaces. One hundred years later, it is still the same.

5

POCAHONTAS

{ **Pocahontas, is the name of a ship,
not a nickname for Golda.** }

Golda is the ring leader of the small group who has decided to make the trip to Palestine, although, "trip" is an understatement. This decision is a permanent move, forsaking family and friends; they are quitting the comforts of a modern society, for a hostile territory on the other side of the world. There are many Zionists in the United States who believe in the rebirth of Israel, but they do not have the compulsion to go and live there. Golda's group is going, and their courage is admired. Golda and Morris, along with Regina and her fiancé Yossel have moved to New York City. The two women are dedicated to this cause–the men are following along. This is pretty progressive, considering the year is 1920, and women just got the right to vote.

While in New York City, Golda's Poale "family" includes the Goodmans and the Zuckermans. Golda had previously helped raise money for the Poale Zion newspaper, *Der Zeit*, of which Jacob Goodman is the editor. Jacob has now told Golda that some of the local newsstands are refusing to carry the paper because of threats from competing papers. Jacob's complaint is rewarded with Golda's typical swift response. Golda, Regina and Nina Zuckerman take the paper to the streets and sell it on the corners.

The Zuckermans also have a past connection with Golda. It is Nina Zuckerman's husband, who Golda, as a nine-year-old, had gone to hear him speak. Golda remembers, "I cannot claim to have understood everything, or that I even remember what Baruch (Zuckerman) said standing on that stage as I sat next to my sister, intent and involved in what was happening–that I cannot forget."[1] As the little girl in the audience, could Golda have imagined a day she would have a job with the Poale Zion? That job, albeit a small one, is sweeping floors.

Golda, no longer in the audience, is in the game and in her glory. Morris is not. When Golda is asked what would she have done if Morris had decided to not go to Palestine she responds, "I would have gone alone, but heartbroken."[2]

Preparations are being made for the trip. "Before we left, we sold everything,"[3] Golda said. In the pioneer spirit they purchase and pack blankets. Golda explains, "If I have to sleep on the ground, I want to be prepared for it." [4] They only make an allowance for the luxury of Morris' record player, the records and some boxes of books.

Golda and Morris make a farewell trip back to Milwaukee. It's the spring of 1921. They stop in Philadelphia to say good-bye to Morris's mother and three sisters. Not much is mentioned of this visit, but future letters between Morris and his family reveal how unhappy Morris is, and his family urges him to "come home." But for now the relationship between Golda and Morris is still rose-colored.

The couple travels to Milwaukee to see Blume and Moshe. Clara is away at college, and her future is to stay in the United States. But Blume and Moshe are full of promises that they will come to Palestine. The goodbyes are particularly painful because of recent reports about the violence in Palestine. Their headstrong daughter is going straight into the storm of

Arab riots. They wonder if they will ever see their beloved Golda again.

Golda writes of those final moments, "I had expected Mother to cry, but Father wept too."[5] Golda is moved that her father has "tears rolling down his cheeks" and looking at her mother, once such a bundle of energy now "looked so small and withdrawn."[6] It is a realization to Golda of her effect on her family. She is not a little girl telling her mother that she will fast, or a teenager running away to Denver. She is making a decision to leave the country, not because she has to go but because she wants to go. When Blume and Moshe left Russia, it was a decision between their lives or their possible deaths. Golda's decision is vastly different.

This mother and father, who have already risked so much to make it here to America, wanted their daughters to grow up, have traditional lives, marry local men, and give them grand-children. Golda has been anything but traditional. Do the par-ents feel rejected by Golda? Are they angry? Can they grasp the desire of their daughter to want to live what she believes is her destiny? Golda expresses an understanding of what Moshe and Blume are suffering. Golda writes "My parents saw their home and their family collapsing, but they did not protest."[7]

Golda later writes her explanation about leaving, "I loved America. I owed America much. I arrived a frightened little girl. When I left, I was a self-confident young woman. I was not fleeing from oppression and insecurity; I was leaving of my own accord a good, generous people. I was born under a tyranny, but brought up in a democracy. It was a country which had fought for its American dream. It still believes in tomor-row. I took what I valued with me. So I had no regrets about leaving anything behind. I was leaving to participate in the set-ting up of independence and security for my own people."[8]

The next stop is Denver to bid farewell to Sheyna and Sam and their two children. Judy is ten and Chaim is three. Sam asks Sheyna, "You want to go too?" Sheyna simply answers, "I am going."[9] Sheyna going includes taking the children with her. Sam stays behind to earn money to send them and he will join them later. Knowing how close Sam and Sheyna are to each other, Golda is deeply touched by her sister's decision.

Sam has been persecuted in Russia, was imprisoned and escaped, fled to the United States, and married his beloved Sheyna who had escaped a death from tuberculosis. A person would think, "Isn't that enough for one life?" Now he is seeing his wife and children leave for a remote land that is fraught with extremists—who would think little of murdering his family.

Back in New York City, Golda and the group will be boarding the ship, *S.S. Pocahontas*. At the same time there are reports in the newspapers of Arab riots in Palestine.

During these months, the Muslims are stirred up again to make violent attacks on Palestinian settlers. One attack in May ends in the murder and mutilation of forty-seven Jews and the wounding of a hundred. In the prior year, marauding gangs were murdering and raping Jews in their settlements.[10] Sam sends letters pleading with Sheyna to postpone her trip. He touches her Achilles heel saying that soon they could all go together as a family. But the plea to wait until the violence stops is met with Sheyna's response, "Then I must go."[11]

Regina remembers, "We had several meetings before we left,"[12] with friends and families saying, "You're crazy, you won't be able to get into Palestine. There's no more immigration."[13]

Golda also recalls, "But I was very stubborn, I said, 'Look, if we go back, each one of us settles down again.' This was it. I don't know whether we will ever decide again to go."[14]

Later Golda acknowledges, "The truth is that I didn't have exact information, (about conditions in Palestine), but I knew very clearly what I wanted. My mind is not so complicated. Once I accepted that there is no other solution for the Jewish problem but a home for the people, I decided to go there."[15]

"Only those who dare, who have the courage to dream, can really accomplish something. People who are forever asking themselves, 'Is it realistic?' 'Can it be accomplished?' 'Is it worth trying?' Accomplish nothing.... What's realistic? A stone? Something that's already in existence? That's not realism. That's death."[16] Golda Meir

Golda writes, "But I was never so naïve or foolish to think that if you merely believe in something, it happens. You must struggle for it." [17]

Golda's struggle is just beginning–the voyage ahead will be enough to try anyone's conviction.

May 23, 1921, the journey begins for twenty-two American immigrants as they set sail from New York City. First, there will be a stop in Boston, then cross the Atlantic, followed by a stop in Italy and then on to Palestine. Simple. Right?

The crew on board is disgruntled and makes it known. With the engines sabotaged, what should have been a two day voyage from New York City to Boston stretches to seven. The passengers endure gross amounts of salt in the food and sea water in the drinking water.[18] The ship is docked in Boston for nine days to make repairs.

Sheyna is receiving pleas from Sam to please reconsider and come home. Does she look at her children and worry? Does she doubt she has made the right decision? Regardless, her response to Sam is "No." Not all the immigrants in Golda's group match this fortitude. Some take this opportunity, while still docked in Boston, to let go of their dream and disembark.

Two weeks and two days after leaving New York City the *S.S. Pocahontas* leaves Boston Harbor to cross the Atlantic Ocean. Mechanical troubles continue, most probably sabotage, and four crew members are locked in irons for threatening to sink the ship. The vessel limps into a small port in the Azores Islands for more repairs, another week goes by. As they leave the Azores, their trip has already taken one month. Between the Azores and Italy, the Captain's brother goes mad, and he is chained and locked in his cabin; an engineer, whose death is listed as suicide, is found with his hands tied behind his back; a passenger dies and is buried at sea. Add to these murder mysteries is the captain's death. It will be thirty-four days of rough seas, rice and salty tea for the party of pioneers. Docking at Naples can't come soon enough.

During this ominous start Regina remembers, "… when all of them were downhearted it was Goldie who raised their spirits. We used to sing folk songs, things like that."[19] Aside from the continual death drama on board, Golda recalls, "I can remember staring at the sea for hours."[20] Fifteen years earlier, Golda had spent her days on the deck doing the same thing, leaving another life behind, in Russia.

Naples is a sigh of relief? Well, not really. Drama and disaster continue to follow the ship and its passengers.

Because the port in Palestine can't accommodate ships, the passengers have traditionally disembarked at sea, boarded small boats that local Arabs row out to the ship, and then ferry the passengers to shore. The Arabs are rioting and refusing to carry Jewish passengers. Having no means to disembark, Golda's group can't take a ship direct to Palestine. They must come up with a new plan.

The pioneers wait for days in Naples and finally book passage on a ship that will take them to Alexandria, Egypt. From there they can take a train to Palestine.

On the day they are to board the ship to Egypt, they arrive at the Naples port only to find that their entire luggage is lost. For some in the group, this adventure is becoming more than they bargained for, and the pioneer spirit meant for Palestine is being used up just getting there. There is a debate among them whether or not to stay and wait until their baggage is found. Golda tells them, "You can wait for baggage, I won't."[21]

Once on board they are to check in with an immigration official on the ship that represents the British Mandatory Authorities in Palestine. The official is a Jew named, Mindel. As he examines Golda's passport, he taunts her by asking how she expects to make a living in Palestine. Any joke will be on him because Mindel later ends up working for Golda, and she remembers that he "was forever apologizing for having sneered at us aboard ship."[22]

Fellow passengers onboard are a group of Lithuanian Zionists, tough men who have dubbed the American Jews as "soft." Having no money for cabin fare, they are sleeping on the deck. Golda, bent on dissuading the Lithuanians from labeling them "soft," suggests her group leave their cabins and join the Lithuanians on the deck. Morris must have groaned.

Arriving at Alexandria, the final leg of their journey still cuts them no slack. They take a train across the Sinai desert–through sand storms of course.

July 14, 1921, nineteen new immigrants from America arrive in Tel Aviv. Keeping their options open, eighteen of them hold on to their American passports.

There is one who cuts off any means of escape. Golda surrenders her passport.[23]

6

LINES IN THE SAND

~∽

They stepped into an utterly alien world. Golda and her group would readily admit they had no idea what they are getting themselves into—as readers, you probably don't either. These next few pages paint the political landscape of the area called Palestine and will explain the meaning of a few Hebrew words common to the Palestinian Jews.

The brief back story:

Ottoman Empire 1320-1922: The Ottoman Empire was founded by Osman who lived from 1258 to 1324. The empire ended after World War I. The Turkish Republic was established, and the rest of the lands were divided into Mandates (colonies) for European countries.

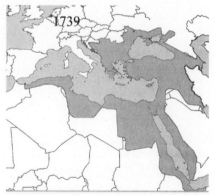

**Ottoman Empire (in dark gray,
light gray is water) - 1739**

> *"Few Europeans of Churchill's generation knew or cared what went on in the languid empires of the Ottoman Sultan or the Persian Shah. An occasional Turkish massacre of Armenians would lead to a public outcry in the west, but would evoke no more lasting concern than Russian massacres of Jews. Worldly statesmen, who privately believed there was nothing to be done, would go through the public motions of urging the Sultan to reform; there the matter would end."[1]*

Before World War I, the primary British interest in the Mideast was to secure access to the Suez Canal–their shorter/cheaper route to India. Oil-burning engines created another economic as well as strategic value–oil. With the advent of WWI, the British government worried the rulers of the Ottoman Empire would ally themselves with the Germans, giving the Germans a means of accessing these two economic advantages. Defeat of the Germans in WWI allowed the British, French and Spanish to control land in the Mideast under the auspices of Mandates from the League of Nations.

This was a fluid time, and the emerging boundaries for the Mandates will become the boundaries for the Mideast countries; Egypt, Iraq, Iran, Saudi Arabia, Syria, Jordan and Palestine. The land areas were designated for tribes of local people, Muslims. One of the tribes, albeit a small tribe, had a small portion of land, designated for them. It was called Palestine. The tribe was not Muslim. It was Jewish.

{ Yishuv: the body of Jewish residents in Palestine before the State of Israel is established. }

Churchill stated, "It is manifestly right that the scattered Jews should have a national center and a national home to be re-united and where else but in Palestine with which for 3,000 years they have been intimately and profoundly associated? We think it will be good for the world, good for the Jews, good for the British Empire, but also good for the Arabs who dwell in Palestine and we intend it to be so; ... they shall share in the benefits and progress of Zionism."[2]

What was hammered out, signed and agreed upon by the League of Nations was this: "The Mandatory (Great Britain) shall be responsible for placing the country under such political, administrative, and economic conditions as will secure the establishment of the Jewish national home...."[3] The size of the land to be governed by Jews is illustrated in the following map:

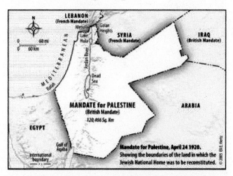

The 1920 provisional Palestine Mandate
http://www.mythsandfacts.org/, Eli E. Hertz,
Date accessed 2014

To simply state: "Golda and her group arrive in Palestine in 1921" does the current events of their situation no justice. The rest of this chapter explains the political and social unrest that greets them.

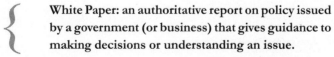

{ **White Paper:** an authoritative report on policy issued by a government (or business) that gives guidance to making decisions or understanding an issue. }

The British are becoming loath to upset the Arabs and risk losing access to oil and the Suez Canal. After the Arab riots in

1921, they issue the White Paper of 1922 that subtracts all the land east of the Jordan River from the original promise of a Jewish homeland. The area appropriated from the Jews is called "Trans-Jordan." (see map below) The White Paper also concedes to the Arab demand of limiting Jewish immigration. The White Paper declares that the principle of "economic absorptive capacity"[4] will be a factor for determining the immigration quota. It is a loophole, a means of limiting Jewish immigration.

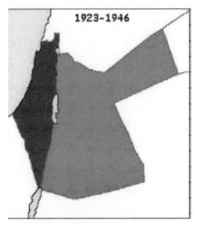

**British White Paper 1922, The division of Palestine
Darker shading (west of the Jordan River) for the Jews, lighter shading (east of the Jordan River) for the Arabs
Jewish Virtual Library External Online Map,
Date Accessed, 2014**

The above division, lopping off two thirds of the land for Arabs, prompts a huge argument among the Jewish leadership on whether to accept this or not. It doesn't matter. It never happens. The Arabs don't want even this smaller area to be under Jewish rule.

Urban legend would maintain that Arabs, from the top down, were against Jews being given an area of land to govern. This is no truer than the rumor that all whites in the southern states espouse the dictates of the Ku Klux Klan. Instances of Arab leadership understanding the need of a Jewish homeland include:

In 1918, the future King Hussein states, "We saw the Jews... streaming into Palestine from Russia, Germany, Austria, Spain, America... The cause of causes could not escape those who had the gift of deeper insight; they knew that the country was for its original sons, for all their differences, a sacred and beloved homeland."[5]

Hussein's son, Faisal, the future king of Iraq, in January 1919 states, "all necessary measures shall be taken to encourage and stimulate immigration of Jews into Palestine on a large scale... In taking such measures the Arab peasant and tenant farmers shall be protected in their rights, and shall be assisted in forwarding their economic development."[6]

King Faisal signs an agreement with the Zionist leader Chaim Weismann on the principle of a Jewish homeland in Palestine. It states, "We feel that the Arabs and Jews are cousins in race ... [and] have suffered similar oppression at the hands of powers stronger than themselves... We Arabs, especially the educated among us, look with deepest sympathy on the Zionist movement... We will wish the Jews a hearty welcome here... People less informed and less responsible than our leaders and yours, ignoring the need for co-operation of the Arabs and Zionists, have been trying to exploit the local difficulties that must necessarily arise in Palestine in the early stage of our movements." [7]

Post WWI the British and French are the "People less informed and less responsible..." as they play a geographic chess match of what to do with the Mideast. Appeasing local Arab rulers and promises of kingdoms to those who show potential to live by the rules of the European game is assisted with money. Payrolls of ten thousand pounds a month keep Ibn Saud in alliance with the British.[8] Once Ibn Saud conquers, consolidates, and becomes King of Saudi Arabia, he is no longer a chess piece to be played. The king leverages his power for the British to recognize his territorial gains and in exchange he recognizes the British territories that the British want in order to protect their trade routes to India through Iraq and the Suez Canal.

Also mollifying the Arabs to not rock the boat is President Franklin D. Roosevelt. He sends King Ibn Saud a secret note stating, "I will not undertake in my role as head of the Executive Branch in this administration any action likely to be hostile to the Arab people."[9]

> **Mufti: Sunni Islamic scholars who are interpreters or expounders of Islamic law and daily life. The term "grand mufti" is a step up from "mufti." Muftis who would buy in to extremist rhetoric of hate and violence against Jews are encouraged by the British government and the Arab families in power, to use their influence as a means of destroying the Jewish presence in Palestine.**
>
> **Any more than assuming a white Southern Baptist preacher is a pawn of the KKK, by no means are all muftis using their faith as a terrorist tool to ramp up the Muslim masses and commit acts of brutality.**

Wealthy Arabs, afraid of losing power and control over their people, encourage religious extremism with proclamations from the grand mufti to incite massacres and violence against the Jews in the region. Their goal is to stop Jewish immigration to the area and to destroy the progress of Jews already living in the area. Maybe the Arabs were chagrined the Jews could make successful farms of the swamp lands the Arabs sold them. In 1944, Jews are paying between $1,000 and $1,100 per acre in Palestine, mostly for arid or semiarid soil; in the same year, prime farm land in Iowa is selling for about $110 per acre.

The British governments, in hopes of making it too difficult for Jews to stay, directly and indirectly, use their position to encourage the mufti to lead attacks on the Jews. Having someone else chip away at the progress of the Jews is much tidier and absolves the British of direct responsibility.

The problem is–the Jews don't leave.

Attacks against Jews and their settlements increase, particularly in the years 1920-21, 1929, and 1936-39; during these years the Jews are subjected to torture, mutilation and massacres.

Student's hand chopped off during Hebron Massacre, 1929 Rechavam Zeevy (1994)

Blood running down the steps The Hebron, Safed, Jerusalem Massacre 1929–killing 140 elderly Jews

The 1929 Massacre occurs while Golda and Morris live in Jerusalem. Hearing the screams of the men, Morris runs to the street and sees old men trying to run from Arab mobs who are armed with sticks, rakes, hoes and guns. He sees one Jew felled by a rock and the mob beat him, leaving him dead.[10] This pogrom is incited by Grand Mufti Haj Amih el Husseini by distributing falsified photos that "world Jewish conspirators" had set off bombs in a mosque.[11] The mufti claim is a lie.

The determination of the British government to abide by their prior legal commitments to the Jews is worse than waning. It is reversing. The lines in the sand are subject to the winds of politics. Golda and Ben-Gurion will be faced with the game of smoke and mirrors as the British, under a guise of "diplomacy," move to reverse their position and support the Arabs. The British dismiss any massacres as "disturbances," and no one is brought to justice. In fact, this British tacit message to Arab extremists is a nod of approval for Arabs to continue trying to wipe out the Jews or at least break the Jewish resistance.

Efforts by the Jews to expose this facade must be tempered. The British are in control of the mandate and have the power to make life more difficult for the Jews. A Jewish organization in Palestine that becomes the political voice of the *Yishuv*, the Jewish people, is the *Histadrut*.

> **Histadrut: An organization founded by Jews in 1920, during the British Mandate, to represent labor, build infrastructure and business. Becoming the political voice of the Jewish citizens, it was critical as a means of providing services (hospitals, housing, schools, roads) to both Jews and Arabs since the British Mandate only covered law and order. During the years no out-of-country business would risk building in Palestine, the *Histadrut* was the number one employer and owner of businesses**

Defense for the Jews by the British is undependable and, if relied on, would have resulted in annihilation of the Jews. Golda records that Jews wanted peace and quiet, "but not the peace and quiet of a cemetery."[12] The *Histadrut* organizes and trains an underground Jewish defense force, the *Haganah*. (Later they become the basis for the Israeli Army.) The *Haganah* reports to the *Histadrut* and will be sent to defend the outlying kibbutz villages and to infiltrate specific Arab hideouts. They do not randomly shoot innocent civilians.

During a future court case, Golda is reexamined and asked, "Is it true that there was a terrible massacre and almost all the Jewish population is killed in Hebron only because there was no Jewish self-defense there?"[13] Golda replies, "Yes, that was in 1929 (sixty-seven Jews killed), and the same thing happened the same year in Safad (twenty Jews killed, eighty wounded); in 1936 there was a night of terrible slaughter in Jewish quarters on Tiberias, and all this could only happen because there was no *Haganah* in those places."[1]

{ **Hebron: During the 1967 Six Day War, Israel took Hebron from Jordan. Residents were terrified that Israeli soldiers might massacre them, a retaliation for the events in 1929. Arabs waved white flags from their homes and voluntarily turned in their weapons. It has also been learned that during the 1929 massacre, there were Arabs in Hebron who hid Jewish families.** }

Tensions continue to rise among the *Yishuv* as the number of Jews who can immigrate into Palestine is further restricted. The British arrest and imprison members of *Haganah*, raid Jewish (not Arab) homes to search for arms, and still give no protection to Jews from Arab attacks.

There are some groups of Jews who strike back. Golda records her feelings and those of Ben-Gurion about counter-terror. "The notion of attacking Arabs indiscriminately, regardless of whether or not they were the particular perpetrators of an outrage, was morally abhorrent to me. A specific attack had to be repelled, and a specific criminal had to be punished."[15]

Context and Commentary 3 will cover the efforts of the Jewish leadership to restrain any Jews that want to lash back.

Having provided the backdrop, the political stage of the region, the text returns now to Golda's story. She and her group are just arriving at Tel Aviv.

7

PIONEER AND POVERTY

T he trials of the last two months' journey are merely a prep time for what is
ahead. Golda writes, "There we were–after
that terrible journey–in Tel Aviv at last. Our
dreams had come true. The railway station,
the houses we could see in the distance,
even the deep sand that surrounded us all
were part of the Jewish national home. But as we waited there
in the glaring sun, not knowing where to go or even where to
turn, it was hard to remember just why we had come. Someone
in our group turned to me and said only half-jokingly, 'Well
Goldie, you wanted to come to Palestine. Here we are. Now
we can all go back–it's enough.'"[2] "I don't know what I had
expected it to look like, but I certainly was not at all prepared
for what I saw."[3]

Sheyna sees her daughter Judy in tears. Judy remembers, "I
started crying because I wanted to go back home."[4]

A room at the only hotel in town is small comfort for the
group. During the night, bed bugs come out to greet them,
and by morning, they are scratching the swollen red bites that
cover their bodies. A trip to the market doesn't make anything
better. Even if you aren't a stickler for cleanliness like Sheyna,
the filth in the streets and seeing flies that freely wander on the

meat, nixes any illusion of their new life being "quaint." The group is happy to accept an invitation for a meal from a couple who has also immigrated. During dinner, the hosts inform the group they have had enough, of the horrors, and the murders, even their shop in Jaffa has been destroyed–they will return to America. How many in Golda's group sat there wondering if this will be them in a few months?

Golda, Morris, Sheyna and the two children move to a two room apartment. There is no icebox. The kitchen is outside. The toilet, in the yard, is shared by forty people.[5] These are worse conditions than when they lived in Pinsk.

What made it worthwhile? Why don't they just go back and be good Jews in America? Two instances stand out.

Golda explains, "Walking down the street on our first Friday evening in Tel Aviv and feeling that life could hold no greater joy for me than to be where I was–in the only all-Jewish town in the world, where everyone from the bus driver to our landlady shared, in the deepest sense, not only a common past but also common goals for the future. …alike in our belief that only here could Jews live as of right rather than sufferance, and only here Jews could be masters, not victims, of their fate."[6]

Golda records her first trip to Jerusalem, the old city, the Wailing Wall:

"…I pictured it more or less as a monument. Until I got there. Then everything changed. And then everything made sense. I had heard, of course, that men and women…put little pieces of paper with wishes on them in the cracks of the Wall. I can't say that it had much sense to me. All of a sudden it made sense … this was the symbol of our struggle, of having been driven out from this country. But this remained, the Wall was there as a fortress of guarantee that the land will be there when the Jews come back. To me it was everything. It is almost something alive. And if it's alive, then you talk to it, you have contact with it."[7]

There are substandard conditions in this new country, but pioneers like Golda can change that with the triumph of their hard work. They have left behind the challenge of fighting off despair and the intolerable living in countries where the dominant culture enacts twisted laws against them and encourages anti-Semitism, police brutality, and bayoneting children. Here in a land that is promised back to them, there is a thread of hope for a chance to build their own country. It is all the Jews are asking for—to be given a chance.

> *"Life here is bitter, bitter. I could not live anywhere else than in this beloved, blessed land of mine."*[8]
>
> **Jewish Immigrant**

Some countries are hoping the thread of hope is a frail fiber. Increase the weight of suffering, heighten the tension of injustice, and the Jews will snap. They are wrong.

The baggage, lost in Italy, is finally delivered to their small apartment. Pots and pans, a tablecloth—Morris is the homemaker again using two of the trunks as a sofa, two more as dressers, hanging a couple of framed pictures on the walls. His books are waterlogged and torn. His one joy, the phonograph and records, are intact.

Golda is teaching English. This supports the finances but not her dream. Her objective is to join a kibbutz. She sends an application to the kibbutz, Merhavia.

A kibbutz is a small agricultural cooperative settlement, in the middle of nowhere, equipped with nothing but the will of its people, dedicated to reclaiming the desert and making it bloom once again. The tract of land has been purchased by the kibbutz members or a Jewish agency. The land is farmed and managed by the community that lives there. Everything is owned by the community; jobs are rotated each week. Men and women are equally responsible for farm work, chores, and child care. Meals are eaten in the common dining room; children are raised in communal quarters and visited by the parents. Everyone gets the same clean clothes from the same shelves. No one person is above another; equal dignity and value is given for any task to be done.

In the kibbutz, the ancient Jewish language, Hebrew, is restored, becoming their future national language. Relishing the freedom to own land (Jews were denied land ownership for hundreds of years in other countries), one kibbutznik wrote, "Our hunger for work in the soil after thousands of years of exile overwhelmed us."[9] It is within the kibbutz that workers can also realize the dignity of self-defense. Their remote locations make them vulnerable targets, and they are the first to resist Arab marauders and invasions.

Golda explains kibbutz life like this, "Look, to me the kibbutz is an ideal form of human society. I don't say they don't have difficulties sometimes, but the society is an ideal society where you share everything. You are part of a group where there is no competition, no exploitation. A human being is accepted and judged and participates in the life of the society not according to what kind of work he has but because he is a human being."[10]

Imagine Golda's surprise when their application is turned down. Golda applies again. They are turned down again. The members are not as inclined to accept couples and they feel this "American girl" will be too fainthearted for the difficult physical labor that is required of each member, men and women alike. Golda says, "I felt as though [I had to prove] that even though I had lived in the States, I was still perfectly capable of doing a hard day's work. I argued fiercely that no one had the right to make such assumptions, and that it was only fair to give us a chance to show what we could do."[11]

Golda doesn't take "no" for an answer. She sends in a third application with the demand that she and Morris be given a trial period of one month and then have their membership be determined by a vote. The kibbutz agrees.

It's hard to fathom how Morris must have felt. His "along for the ride" stance keeps him as an outsider looking in and he is lonely. If Morris thinks Tel Aviv is a low point, September of 1921, in the Merhavia Kibbutz, he is looking around at swamps, mud and a few shacks.

Golda and Morris are allowed their own room with two cots. Once again, Morris goes to work as homemaker. Creating furniture out of orange crates, he is hoping this new adventure will bring him closer to his wife. This will not be the case. The kibbutz, with its priority of community, is not designed or inclined to nurture the bonds within family. This revelation is alarming to Morris and freeing to Golda. Not tied to housework after work hours or the social pressure to be home with her husband, Golda is able to spend her evenings with the group having political discussions. Morris is becoming increasingly more isolated. Golda is becoming increasingly more engaged.

Driving herself to utter exhaustion is a point of Golda's pride. She describes one day at the kibbutz, "The hoe came up against a pile of stones. The blade sank into a kind of marsh, and I could not pull it out. I used all my strength, and was drenched in sweat. My hands were covered with blisters, which soon burst open. My skin peeled off and blood oozed from the wounds... I worked with all my strength, and strained my muscles un-til my hands and feet shivered, as though from malaria. After a day's work came a sleepless night, pains in the back and loins. And there was the troubling thought—will my physical strength and determina-tion suffice to stand the test?"[12]

Golda working at the kibbutz
From the Archives Department,
University of Wisconsin-
Milwaukee Libraries

There is never the question— "Why am I here?" At the end of the day, when exhaustion takes over and the weight of her fork feels like a ton—Golda is in her glory.

In the midst of conforming to the community, Golda finds her own ways of noncompliance. Ignoring the scoffing comments from her comrades, every evening she irons her blouse and skirt for the next day. When Golda has nursery duty, she insists the tubs be wiped out with alcohol to prevent infection after each child's bath.[13] Golda also initiates having table clothes (using sheets) for Friday evening's meal, skinning the fish before serving it for dinner, and oatmeal as a warm breakfast—all met with a solid group suspicion of Golda being too "bourgeoisie." Golda stands her ground and the community concedes.

Golda feeding chickens at the kibbutz
*From the Archives Department,
University of Wisconsin-Milwaukee Libraries*

One task, given to Golda is taking care of the chickens. Golda hates chickens, but if this is what is assigned, she will perform the duty and make improvements. Her initiatives are noticed and used in other communities. This trait will later propel her into the inner circle of the founding fathers of Israel, but for now she is surrounded by chickens.

Within a year, Golda transcends from being rejected by the kibbutz to earning their admiration and being picked to represent them at the first kibbutz convention in 1922. Attending the convention are two people she had last seen in Milwaukee, Ben-Gurion and Ben-Zvi. Golda is asked to work in the Pioneer Women organization (they provide social services for Jewish women and children in Palestine). Because of her excellent English, Golda's job also includes meeting with any visiting foreign dignitaries.

After the convention, Golda gets a visit from Berl Katznelson, akin to George Washington calling on Betsy Ross. Berl wants Golda, not to make a flag, but to reconsider a decision. The Pioneer Women had asked Golda to escort the wife of the British Labour Party on a tour of Palestine. Golda, feeling her time is better spent working at the kibbutz than touring around with a wealthy woman, had told the group "no."

Golda knows this attention from Berl is an honor and that even Ben-Gurion defers to decisions by Berl. She agrees to be the tour guide. It turns out that it is an enlightening time to see the rest of Palestine and meet Arab people in their Bedouin camps.

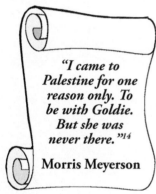

"I came to Palestine for one reason only. To be with Goldie. But she was never there."[14]

Morris Meyerson

Golda is exhilarated by her new life. Thrilled with the intellectual challenges of the convention and kibbutz debates, striving to improve her Hebrew, requested by the "inner circle" to be involved, she sees herself living for the cause to which she committed back in Milwaukee.

Morris is depressed by his new life. Suffering with the physical hardships, sullen from the lack of privacy, resenting the co-operative living that dictates only making tea in the communal kitchen and if he wants time with his wife, she is in the midst of an animated group discussion. He sees himself living a miserable life for which he has no commitment.

Morris is also suffering from malaria. He is hospitalized, and the doctor's orders include no more manual labor. Morris and Golda must leave Merhavia. Golda remembers, "I don't think I ever would have left if it were not for the fact Meyerson took ill. I hated leaving. It was a feeling of pain that still goes through me like a needle."[15]

Golda saw the decision like this, "We packed up again–for the third time in three years–and made our farewells. It was a great wrench for me to leave the kibbutz, but I consoled myself tearfully by hoping that we would both be back soon, that Morris would regain his health quickly, that we would have a baby and that the relationship between us–which had so deteriorated in Merhavia–would improve. If all this happened, I told myself, then leaving the kibbutz for a while was a very small price to pay. Unfortunately, it didn't work out that way." [16]

They leave Merhavia in 1923. Golda works as a cashier in the Office of Public Works in Tel Aviv but leaves because she is expecting their first child. Menachem is born November 1924. A job opening up for Morris means another move, Jerusalem.

During their last year at the kibbutz, Golda had wanted to have a baby. Morris, firm in his opinion on this, says–no baby at the kibbutz. He wants to be a parent in the traditional way and not have a commune raise his child. Golda, unable to change that opinion, makes a true effort to conform to the role of the "traditional" wife for Morris. Moving back to Jerusalem, having a baby, she hopes to mend her marriage. There are few efforts where Golda fails. This will be one of them.

In the spring of 1925, Golda returns to the kibbutz with Menachem and without Morris. This doesn't work either. Golda, as a mother, makes everything different. She is put in charge of the nursery and mothering five children. She misses Morris and returns to Jerusalem. Morris is still hoping Golda will "grow out of it" and return to the United States. In May, 1926, their daughter Sarah is born.

That year brings more family to Palestine. Sheyna's beloved Sam arrives and they have a baby, their son Jonah. Like Golda and Morris' children, this generation born in the Promised Land, are called *sabra*, meaning–"born in Palestine."

Moshe and Blume, now in their late fifties, also arrive that same year. They buy land and build a house. (Moshe will later construct a secret room to hide arms for the *Haganah*.) Moshe becomes a cantor in the local synagogue, a leader in the carpenter's cooperative, and he has an orange grove. Blume, still the entrepreneur, starts making lunches to sell to the workmen in the area. Blume also hasn't stopped her custom of being critical of Golda's priorities. This includes haranguing her daughter about how many cigarettes she smokes every day.

Despite the joy of family, the harsh reality is this: there is no food. Morris doesn't have steady work, and the boarder who provided some additional funds, has to leave because the room is needed for their two children. On credit, Golda can get half a pound of bones and a quarter pound of meat (the size of a hamburger in one Big Mac) as soup for her family. The scarcity of milk and bread is made worse by a neighbor who warns the milkman that he might not get his money from the Myersons. Golda tears into him, "No one will take milk from my children!" [17] Sheyna is receiving letters from Golda about the unpaid grocery bills, no heat, and now Sarah is sick and needs a special diet and medicines. Sheyna and Sam stop by to bring fruits and vegetables.

Golda writes, "The next four years are the most miserable I ever experienced … the worst in my life. We lived in more poverty than even back in Pinsk."[18] But in Pinsk, they had never gone hungry. With only two small rooms, the bathtub is in the living room. The water, drawn from a cistern, has to be boiled before drinking. Sheyna's daughter Judy, recalls, "The kitchen was very primitive and the toilet was in the backyard. It was sad there, really sad."[19]

Golda clarifies, "It wasn't the work I minded. In Merhavia I had worked much harder–and liked it. But in Merhavia, I had been part of a group, a member of a dynamic society whose success mattered to me more than almost anything else in the world. In Jerusalem, I was sort of a prisoner, sentenced–as millions of women by circumstances beyond their control–to battling over bills that I couldn't pay, trying to keep shoes from falling apart because it was impossible to buy another pair, worrying whenever a child coughed or ran a fever that our inadequate diet and inability to keep the apartment warm in winter might be permanently damaging our health."[20]

Menachem is four years old, and Golda wants to send him to nursery school but can't afford the tuition. Golda barters his tuition in exchange for her washing all the children's clothes. This means: pails and pails of water need to be heated and then scrub the clothes by hand on a washboard. "I laundered at night when the children were sleeping. The kitchen was outside and I laundered in the courtyard so I had to put a kerosene oil lamp in the window. I think there must have been fifteen or twenty children… little towels, aprons, diapers… whatever needed washing."[21]

Golda has made a supreme effort to be the wife and mother that would make Morris happy. The result, Golda is miserable. She writes, "If your husband is not a social animal like yourself, and feels uncomfortable with an active wife, a wife for whom it's not enough to be a wife… there has to be a clash."[22]

Golda has been six years in Palestine, and aside from living at the kibbutz, there is no sense of satisfaction that she is living for her cause and making the Zionist dream come true. She is back to teaching English and coming to grips with the fact that the gap between her and Morris continues to grow. At a very low point, Golda tells her friend Regina, "It isn't working out."[23]

Both personally and professionally, Golda is feeling desolate. She remembers, "But it wasn't only our actual poverty–or even my constant fear that my children would be hungry–that made me so wretched. There was also my loneliness, the sense of isolation to which I was so unaccustomed and the constant feeling that I was being deprived of just those things for which I had come to Palestine in the first place."[24] Golda's break comes in 1928.

One of the attendees from the kibbutz conference, David Remez, sees Golda and offers her a position in the *Histadrut*. The job will give Golda what she has been wanting most; back to working for the rebirth of Israel. Golda will be a secretary for the Women's Labor Council.

The job entails long hours, travel, and living in Tel Aviv. Personally, this gives her a way to break from Morris. Morris will stay at his job in Jerusalem and visit on weekends. They will never live together again, although they never divorce. Golda records in her autobiography, "…didn't regret the decision to take the job–what I do regret–and bitterly so–is that although Morris and I remained married to each other and loving each other until the day he died in my house in 1951 (when symbolically enough, I was away), I was not able to make a success of our marriage after all. The decision I took in 1928 actually marked the start of our separation, … Morris understood me only too well and felt that he couldn't make me over or change me. I had to be what I was, and what I was made it impossible for him to have the sort of wife he wanted and needed. He didn't discourage me from going back to work, although he knew what it really meant."[25]

Acknowledging that her marriage is a failure, Golda admits, "frightened me."[26]

If Golda had been a man and Morris a woman, this marriage

might have worked. Golda, the husband, out and about fulfilling her role as a founding father with Morris, the mother, at home keeping house and raising the children, much like the founding family of the United States, John and Abigail Adams. John, as he packs for Paris, can say to Abigail, "I have to go for the next few years. My country needs me." Society or family does not criticize John for leaving Abigail to work the farm, raise the children, survive brutal winters in Boston and outlive small pox epidemics.

Golda will continue to struggle with the conflicting commitment to her children versus life dedicated to a cause. This dual role she describes as, "The eternal inner division, this double pull, this alternating feeling of unfulfilled duty–today toward her family the next day toward her work–this is the burden of a working mother."[27] Golda explains, "I think that women get not so much an unfair deal as an illogical one."[28]

Golda later writes for *The Plough Woman,* "Taken as a whole, the inner struggles and the despairs of the mother who goes to work are without parallel in human experience. But within that whole there are many shades and variations. There are some mothers who work only when they are forced to, when the husband is sick or unemployed, or else when the family has in some other way gone off the track of a normal life. In such cases, the mother feels her course of action justified by compulsion–her children would not be fed otherwise. But there is a type of woman who cannot remain home for other reasons. In spite of the place which the children and the family as a whole take up in her life, her nature and being demand something more; she cannot divorce herself from the larger social life. She cannot let her children narrow her horizon. And for such a woman, there is no rest."[29]

Golda will have no rest, and she will have life no other way. She has been banging on the door of destiny, demanding her role in creating a country. Starting her new job is the answer.

8

HIT THE HIGH ROAD

David Ben-Gurion
From the Archives Depart-
University of Wiscon-
Milwaukee Libraries

"A nation must discover in itself its strength *and its* dignity *if it is to achieve its* true destiny.*"
David Ben-Gurion, Zionist and first Prime Minister of Israel

During the 1920s, the Zionist leadership is discovering its "strength" when their goals include building schools, hospitals, power plants, universities and roads. Its "dignity" is in the fact that both Jews and Arabs enjoy the improvements to infrastructure and all benefits to daily life. Its "true destiny" will be to govern itself as an independent nation.

Golda is employed by the *Histadrut* as secretary of the Women's Worker's Council. She organizes the training of women and prepares them to work in agriculture and other trades in which the *Histadrut* is establishing business. Never considering herself a feminist, Golda simply expects women to have equal pay and that, "teaching girls various trades is more important than women's rights."[1]

One man says of her, "Goldie was a prime mover, doing a variety of jobs, outstanding in whatever she did. She knew how to combine idealism and practicality. She knew how to get an idea across. And you just couldn't say no to Goldie."[2]

Traveling to Great Britain in 1930, as a delegate to the Women's Labor convention, Golda has the immediate purpose of continuing to educate the public that Britain, under the mandate, is to support Jewish citizens as well as the Arabs. In light of the recent Arab massacres of 1929 (discussed in Chapter 6, Lines in the Sand), her message is all the more important.

Golda is quick to inform her audiences that the schools, hospitals, jobs and all infrastructure being developed are for all the citizens not just the Jews. One woman clarifies their misperception when she tells Golda, "We didn't know that was what you were doing. We thought that you're chasing out the Arabs."[3] This misinformation feeds the fantasy of flowing Arab robes and the romantic image of T.E. Lawrence, the superior white man, working with deferential Arabs during WWI. Golda, dressed in her not so romantic, crisp white blouse and plain skirt, hopes to turn the discussion to the facts of successful Jewish programs and disastrous Arab violence.

Golda also goes to the international Annual Labor Conference with Ben-Gurion, and both have been scheduled to speak. The contingents of Arab delegates are shouting down any Jewish delegates. Ben-Gurion is telling Golda to not attempt to go against this tide and instead concede giving her speech.

Golda disregards Ben-Gurion's advice and takes the floor because it is her decision to speak. Regardless of the outcome she will have the facts on record about this most recent murdering spree in the previous year. It is an example of her quote, "I think I can honestly say that I was never deflected from doing something because I thought I might fail."[4]

Ben-Gurion later writes in an article, "I trembled at her daring words. Her speech shook the convention. She spoke with genius, assertively, bitterly, with hurt and sensibly."[5]

Within the team of founding fathers, Golda is proving her worth. Able to maintain a righteous stance for justice, Golda is an effective speaker on the world stage as she fearlessly confronts irrational agendas by political opportunists. She is promoted, by the *Histadrut*, to taking over the Department of Mutual Aid which means trips to Brussels, Belgium and Berlin.

There is an abrupt halt when she gets a cable from Morris.

SARELE DESPERATELY ILL. COME HOME AT ONCE.

For the last few years, Sarah has suffered with debilitating ill health. The doctors have been advising a diet regime that is not proving effective.

A family portrait
From the Archives Department,
University of Wisconsin-Milwaukee Libraries

Golda and Morris discuss the options for hours. If Sarah stays, it is quite possible she will die. Golda argues to take Sarah to the United States for medical treatment. Golda is told, "You're crazy to cross the ocean with her… the salt air is dangerous for her condition."[6] Doctors are saying, "The trip will kill her." Golda's parents pipe in with their opinion that the plan is "madness."[7] Golda decides to take the children and go.

Travel to the U.S. is a possibility because Golda has been offered a new position by the *Histadrut* to become secretary to the U.S. based group, Pioneer Women. Started in 1925 the membership will increase to 10,000 by 1936. Much of this is due to Golda's talent in building a bridge from the smell of coffee in their living rooms in America, to the aroma of a fragrant orange crop in Palestine, made possible with their support. Her success is stunning considering Golda's fund raising trips are during the Great Depression.

{ **Pioneer Women: Jewish American women's club, not wanting to immigrate themselves, they are willing to raise money to support the women, young people, and children who are living in Palestine.** }

As the ship crosses the Atlantic, Golda doesn't have speeches and fund raising on her mind. In today's terms Golda is "disconnected," and her children are thrilled to have this time alone with their mother. While keeping a close eye on Sarah's condition, days are spent reading books, talking, and singing. Menachem writes, "And Mother played shuffleboard with me for hours."[8] The threesome makes it to America and the trip becomes a beloved memory.

In New York City, the Goodmans, who had befriended Golda at the beginning of the *Pocahontas* voyage, become Golda's surrogate family. They take Golda and her two children into their home. Sarah spends the next six weeks in a hospital where her kidney disorder is properly diagnosed and treated. Golda was right to insist on bringing her to the United States. She is told if the medical treatment Sarah had been receiving back in Palestine had continued, it would have been the death of her daughter. Instead, Sarah leaves the hospital completely cured.

For Menachem, this has been six long weeks. He is unable to go to the hospital to visit Sarah. Alone in a strange new house, new people, new language, no friends; he sits in his room–reading and waiting. When Sarah is back they both go to school. Once again they are pleased with their mother's attention. Golda sits with them during their classes the first full week and translates everything from Hebrew to English. Whether this is enough time or not, it doesn't matter. Their mother must get to work.

Golda will spend the next two years traveling to various chapters of the Pioneer Women. Talking to members and new recruits she continues to broaden the membership base, raise money and educate her audience. These trips by train don't allow for even a quick visit back to New York City, Golda is often gone for weeks or months at a time.

When Golda does return, she explains again to her children why it is important for her to be gone and talk to people across the country. It will continue to be a pain for Golda's heart when she hears responses like this from her daughter Sara, "So why can't you stay home and talk to me?"[9] A day will come when Menachem and Sara will understand and support the dedication of their mother that overrides the daily needs of all else, even her children, in order to bring about the rebirth of a country for the Jewish people. But that day is not going to happen during those two years in New York City.

The months of traveling become a blur of meetings, lunches, sleeping on trains, sharing bedrooms with members of a host family, and staying up late to meet more people. It is an exhausting schedule, away from her children and feeling guilty, away from her homeland and being out of touch.

For Golda, who thrives on being in the power vortex of deciding policy, meeting Jewish women in the Chicago suburbs is not exactly the inner circle. But Golda's job is to keep telling the "story." These audiences are women who would send their money but not themselves and would be aghast if Golda suggested they let their children immigrate. So Golda walks a fine line of encouraging and cajoling their support, honoring their role in the game at stake, and subtly shifting the message to be most effective to each group across the economic strata. What always stays the same is the sincere warmth and enthusiasm that Golda uses when she speaks. It's just that by the end of many days Golda is pretty used up.

And for what? It's the Depression and some groups who pledge $165 raise only $17.10 in ten months. When one out of every four men is unemployed, thousands are wandering the country living in box cars, and millions repair their children's shoes with cardboard, it is a sacrifice when a Delaware group sends in five dollars.[10]

There is no record of Golda writing back to David Ben-Gurion and saying, "Maybe we should call it quits." Or "I will come back to the states when the economy is in better shape." Or "This simply isn't worth my time." Golda stays. She boards the next train, to the next city, and attends the next meeting.

Golda's speaking venue has moved beyond her Milwaukee days of standing on a soap box in a public square, although her speaking style, direct to the heart of her audience, will remain the same. She never succumbs to beating the drum of guilt in order to shame people into emptying their pockets. Instead, Golda can connect her audience to feel the struggle of the pioneers. And finally, in spite of any details of the hate, murder, and injustice going on in Palestine, Golda will end with giving her audience the sense of pride not pity, that all Jews play a role in this time of history.

Golda continues this connection off stage and off hours. Meeting the members to help them pack and sell produce coming from the kibbutz farms in Palestine, Golda teaches the women new songs and a dance. Golda also convinces them the utility of multitasking. For the mothers who are walking their babies, Golda encourages them to use this time to deliver the freshly packed produce.

The Labor Zionist movement formalizes as a political party, Mapai, in 1930. Golda, as its spokesperson, is up against the systems of capitalism in the United States. In spite of the economic crash, the terms Labor Zionist, Mapai Party or socialism, are not favored political beliefs in the United States. Golda will point out that for the development of their new country, capitalism will not work because no company will risk coming to their area to invest.

Golda must also explain the political perspective of being not just a Zionist but a Labor Zionist. She knows her audience traditionally sees things in the realm of Democrat or Republican–not Labor. Golda describes her efforts to explain, "What's more, the ideals of the Labor Zionism were not particularly popular anywhere in 1929, least of all perhaps in the States, and the Pioneer Women's campaign for the Women's Labor Council was an uphill road, to put it mildly."[11]

"Not particularly popular" is especially true when Golda visits her sister Clara in Cleveland.

Married to Fred Stern, Clara has one son, Daniel David. Clara will know her share of suffering when he dies of illness at the young age of eighteen. Clara will also be disillusioned with her marriage.

Within hours of Golda being their guest, Fred makes it clear that he disagrees with any form of nationalism for the Jews.[12] He wastes no time or pleasantries when he espouses his belief that Zionism is an extreme reactionary movement. He ascribes his personal success, giving no credit to anyone, as the result of his own self-efforts.

Obviously, this is a complete opposite from Golda. What she values is the results and success of her work within a collective of people. She repeats this sentiment so frequently it has become a common quote, "I never did anything alone. Whatever was accomplished in this country (the future Israel) was accomplished collectively."

Sheyna might have agreed with Golda's political perspective but not Golda's priorities. Sheyna's circumstances have given her an opportunity (which she will refuse), to temper her high-handed principles.

 Jihad: Religious duty of Muslims, an inner struggle to fulfill religious duties, an outer struggle against those who are considered enemies of Islam.

During the riots in 1929, thousands of Arabs flood into Jerusalem and the surrounding settlements. Spurred on by their mufti, this *jihad* brings the murder of more than 130 Jews. The massacre in Hebron, mentioned earlier, is a part of this *jihad*.

In the midst of these attacks, Jewish children are gathered in a refugee camp. Sheyna is one of the volunteers helping feed the children. When Sheyna's opinion on the food is questioned by a sneering nurse, Sheyna is spurred on to enroll in a dietician course back in the United States. Because Sam is temporarily stateside earning money, Sheyna must make arrangements for the two older children to be cared for while she takes the youngest back with her. Golda, seeing her sister have a conviction that overrides motherhood, writes to Sheyna, "Perhaps you understand me now?"[13]

Sheyna doesn't concede any such similarity. In a letter back to Golda, Sheyna's retort makes the point that her plans (unlike Golda's) will never be outside the desires of her husband. "Sam understands and helps me because he is all my life."[14] Sheyna, still unbending in her opinion, "knows" if Golda would be a better wife to Morris, he would be like Sam in his understanding.[15] Golda, wanting this family thorn in her side to be removed, writes back, "I ask only one thing, that I be understood and believed. My social activities are not an accidental thing; they are an absolute necessity for me. I am hurt when Morris and others say that this is all superficial, that I am trying to be modern. It is silly. Do I have to justify myself?"[16]

Judy, Sheyna's daughter, later writes, "My mother envied Golda, oh yes. I even felt it then. That's why she tried to get her own reputation. She got a job in the Hadassah hospital as a dietitian."[17]

In another twenty years, the reality of Israel will justify Golda's endeavors. For now, Golda's drive and determination is seen by the family as selfish.

It is during these trips around the United States that Golda is refining her speaking skills and learning to acclimate her message to different groups. She relinquishes some of her puritanical principles when she learns that certain groups are raising money by playing cards. Golda also dismisses any preconceived barriers and makes friends with women of the DAR (Daughters of the American Revolution). These alliances and the genuine warmth of friendships will serve as an integral part of the success of Golda's future trips to the United States.

Amidst her traveling, Golda meets Leah Biskin who becomes Golda's personal assistant. Leah moves back to Palestine and gives Golda her total commitment, service and support for the rest of Golda's life. Another woman to be a lifelong friend will be Marie Syrkin. What Leah gives Golda in generous praise; Marie gives in honest critique, feedback and intellectual insights. Marie comes to understand Golda so well that Golda trusts Marie to be her written voice and to write her biography. Golda's personal and professional life is supported by these two women.

It's 1934, Golda and her children are taking the ship back. Golda, Menachem and Sarah have been gone for two years. Golda has developed a network of Pioneer Women, some calling themselves the "Goldie Meyerson Clubs." (Golda uses her married name, Meyerson, until becoming Foreign Minister. See Chapter 15) The Pioneer Women membership has increased by thousands. Golda can be proud of what she has accomplished, but her real pleasure is from seeing the increased understanding of the Zionist cause.

"SHE WOULD NOT ACCEPT THE LOVE OF HUMANITY IF IT SERVED AS A COVER FOR ESCAPING THE LOVE OF ISRAEL."

David Remez[18]

Returning home, Golda finds Morris waiting at the dock. He is anxious to reunite with his children. Sarah and Menachem will always be close to their father. There will be no emotional reunion with Golda.

Golda has been involved with Zalman Shazar, an author, poet and political colleague. She hoped the growing relationship between them would culminate in both their getting divorces and then be married, but Golda realizes this will never be. Her true passion, her first love, her dream of Israel–takes on new responsibilities.

9

LADY LIBERTY ~ BETRAYED

"Give me your tired,
your poor,
Your huddled masses
yearning to breathe free,
The wretched refuse of
your teeming shore.
Send these, the homeless,
tempest-tossed to me,
I lift my lamp
beside the golden door!"

Just kidding.

{ Within the Statue of Liberty this poem is inscribed in bronze. For the sake of this chapter, the last line is added. }

Golda, returning from her two-year duty in the United States, is pulled from this minor league game into the major league, the epicenter of making decisions. Similar to the United States president requesting a state level person to work as one of his cabinet members, Golda is asked by David Ben-Gurion to be a member of the Executive Committee of the *Histadrut*. Taking her seat among the men who develop policy for the people in Palestine, Golda is officially a part of the inner circle. She has come a long way from scrubbing nursery clothes in the courtyard.

Golda's fluent English, and her innate ability to cope with the British, make her the natural pick to be the leading representative, the Jewish voice, to the British. More importantly, Golda has the utmost confidence of Ben-Gurion. As the liaison, Golda's job is to tell the moderators of the mandate about incidents of violence, sabotage and massacre by the Arabs. The violence is so rampant Golda writes of that time, "I kissed the children good-bye in the morning knowing that I might well never come home again."[1]

Riots in the spring of 1936, incited by the grand mufti of Jerusalem, result in farms burnt, buses assailed, trains sabotaged and 100,000 newly planted trees destroyed. Personal damage includes, attacks on Jews where hundreds are wounded and eighty are killed. The 1936 riots include two nurses being murdered in a Jaffa hospital that served an Arab population. A synagogue is set on fire while people are inside, six children are shot, a mother stabbed in the chest and another mother begs the rioters, "These are children!" The response? "They'll grow up... kill the Jews!"[2]

The British, with the covert mandate of seeing the Jews fail, will raid Jewish settlements and disarm them. Without their weapons, the Jews cannot defend themselves from Arab riots. One settlement, established in 1906 had been burnt down in 1929, raided and evacuated in 1936, and now the British are expecting these Jews to give up their weapons.[3]

Reacting to riots, some Jews attack an Arab bus. The Jews are arrested by the British and sentenced to death.

Newspaper report (partial), 1938 Massacre

When the number of Arab riots and extent of their destruction create a high enough moral outcry, the British show concern by requesting a commission. Downplaying the extent of the mob violence, the riots are referred to as "disturbances." The Peel Commission (1937) is sent to evaluate or better yet–reevaluate–the problems in Palestine.

21 SLAIN BY ARABS IN PALESTINE RAID

10 Children Among Victims as Band Attacks Jews' Homes in Suburb of Tiberias

FIRE AND STABBING USED

Six Killed as Bomb Blows Up House in Jaffa—Tel Aviv Youth Sentenced to Death

By JOSEPH M. LEVY
Special Cable to THE NEW YORK TIMES.
JERUSALEM, Oct. 3.—Twenty-one Jews, including three women and ten children, ranging in age from 1 to 12 years, were killed and three persons wounded last night on the shores of Lake Galilee, in the old Jewish quarter of Tiberias, in a massacre by stabbing, shooting and burning perpetrated by Arabs.

Aside from the physical "disturbances" to be investigated, the commission must investigate acts of economic sabotage. Hoping to cut the ability to harvest crops, the mufti declares that no Arab will go to work in Palestine. Another tactic, causing a decrease in revenue for the Jews, is to disrupt shipping. The port of Jaffa is closed in 1936 because the Arab workers strike.

To short circuit this setback of having no place to dock their ships, Golda and David Remez make plans to construct a new port in Tel Aviv. Golda returns to the United States for a fund raising trip of luncheons. When giving speeches, Golda focuses on what the Histadrut has accomplished, not the violence and suffering from the Muslim attacks. Her passionate belief in the potential of this land for Jews is infectious. She succeeds in raising the money to build the port, buy the ships and train Jews to do the work.

A Jewish activity that will be of interest to the Peel Commission is the smuggling in of "illegal" immigrants. Unabashedly, Golda is among groups who spend their nights going down to the beaches to greet new arrivals who are escaping the brutality of the growing Third Reich. Avoiding arrest by the British, local Jews hurry the refugees to safe houses.

One immigrant woman is from Pinsk, Golda's home town in Russia. Golda hears the woman explain how she was shot and tossed into a ditch with other Jews from the village. Managing to escape, she has miraculously made it to the shores of what she hopes will be her freedom. Golda relays the stories of these atrocities to British officials. The response is an echo of world opinion. "You mustn't believe everything you hear..."[4]

Golda responds not only with words but action. To show support and solidarity with the Jews who are suffering, Golda organizes a protest parade.

The results of the Peel Commission concur with the original purpose of the British Mandate—establish a Jewish national home. However, in the Peel Commission, new land concessions are made, not to the Jews but to the Arabs. The commission proposes partitioning Palestine. They suggest making 2,000 square miles a Jewish state and giving 48,000 square miles to the Arabs. The city of Jerusalem, within the Jewish 2,000 square miles, will not be controlled by the Jewish government but will be an internationally held enclave.

There is a debate and vote within the Jewish leadership. Golda, at first, is against the further partition of land and not only having Jerusalem taken from them but leaving its fate in the legal no man's land of an "internationally held enclave." Her retort to Ben–Gurion is, "Someday, my son will ask me by what right I gave up most of the country, and I won't know how to answer him."[5] Ben-Gurion is adamant that some state, no matter how small, will be better than no state at all. Golda relents.

It doesn't matter. The Arabs say "no" to the Peel Commission. If Arabs had said "yes" the group that is now Palestinian refugees would have had their country in 1937.

Do the Arabs need more land? After the Ottoman Empire, the Muslim faith dominates governments that will rule 3 million square miles in North Africa. In the Middle East, land for the Muslim people includes Saudi Arabia, Iraq, Syria, Lebanon, Turkey, Iran, Jordan, Yemen, and Oman which covers over 2.4 million square miles, mostly under populated. The designated area from the divisions of the Ottoman Empire, for the future Jewish homeland is just over 8,000 square miles. This is approximately one tenth of one percent.

It's not about land.

With the Arabs saying "no," the Peel Commission and their recommendations are now ignored by the British. Why? It's pre-World War II, and the British government, under Prime Minister Chamberlain, is increasingly desperate to garner support in the Arab area.

The British are seeing the utter failure of their gamble to let Hitler have Czechoslovakia. Since this gift of appeasement did not halt the march of the Third Reich, the British shift their foreign policy to one of encouraging Arab nationalism in hopes of Arabs not siding with Hitler. This "plan B" translates to, once again, not upholding the mandate or their former policy to give Jews their own homeland.

Are the Arabs siding with the British and pledging their support to fight the Nazi regime? No. Arabs are answering Hitler's courting call and meeting frequently at his Bavarian estates. Hitler, having the same interests as the British, wants access to Arab oil and the Suez Canal.

**Haj Amin al-Husseini (Grand Mufti of Jerusalem)
and Adolf Hitler meeting November 28, 1941**
Photographer: Heinrich Hoffmann, German Federal Archives

Haj Amin al Husseini flies the flag for the Nazis. In a broadcast from Italy, he declares that "If England and America win the war, the Jews will dominate the world. If on the other hand the victory is carried off by the Axis [Germany, Japan, Italy], the Arab world will be freed. The Axis is befriending us. Fight for its victory."[6]

"Kill the Jews wherever you find them.
This pleases God, history and religion.
This saves your honor. God is with you."
Mufti Amin al-Husseini
Radio Berlin *broadcast, March 1, 1944*

The Jews supported the British by fighting in World War I, and they will again support the Allied powers; Great Britain, United States and the Soviet Union and fight in World War II.

This morally right policy, Jewish soldiers fighting Germany, must include maintaining the *Histadrut* shadow policy of fighting for a Jewish independent nation. Superimpose these two Jewish agendas over their core desire for peace with Arabs and to include the local Arabs as part of the new nation. How does one transform this disparate interwoven landscape from a blue print of policy to a function of daily action?

A tangible example plays out when Golda is in a meeting with the British officials to represent the rights of Palestinian labor, Jews and Arabs. Being British, they offer her a chair. Golda refuses to sit until everyone is given a seat, including the Arabs. Any negotiations that resulted in better wages or conditions for the Jewish labor applies to the Arab labor, too.

**Golda speaking to a group
in Palestine**

Golda's position within the *Histadrut*, to represent labor, makes her the bearer of bad news to her own people. She tells the Jewish workers that each month, one day of their pay is to be taken and used to cover the damage done by the Arab riots and to supply an unemployment fund that would also cover Arab workers. Afraid these pay cuts will be too much of a strain; friends are accusing Golda of trying to destroy the *Histadrut*. Some are suggesting that she return to the United States and ask for money to cover the cost of damages.

Any person pursuing power might have succumbed to the pressure to win over public opinion. But this is another grain of the "true grit" in Golda. With no concern for her public image, she proceeds with what is a just path—the burden of this responsibility is on the workers. Golda has the backing of leadership, but it is Golda who bears the cries and criticisms of the people. Her moral North Star leads her to visit the factories, meet with the workers, and she points out the needs and reasons for this policy. Golda explains that requests for funds from the United States will be used only to build the country. Covering the expenses caused by riots or to pay unemployment will be met by the workers themselves.

Through the 1930s, Golda is also in her thirties. Her jobs within the *Histadrut* have included convincing visiting VIPs that the

Jews are capable of governing themselves, providing medical services for the Jewish population, ensuring fair labor conditions, and resolving unemployment. These efforts and the subsequent success are remarkable enough against a backdrop of Arab raids and *jihads*. Now add this context: The dark power of the Third Reich is overtaking Europe.

{ **Comparing Golda's struggle against "The Force" in *Star Wars* would make Luke Skywalker change his name to Luke Cakewalker.** }

Through the 1930s, in Germany, the politics are in place for another world war. Hitler is elected to power in 1933 on the promise of prosperity and getting rid of the Jews. In the next three years 150,000 Jews leave Europe and go to Palestine.

September 15, 1935, the Nuremberg Laws declare all Jews in Germany as legal outcasts. As the Jews now have no civil rights, Germans can break into Jewish shops, homes and synagogues to set a fire, destroy or steal. Murdering Jews and beating Jewish children carries no conviction in court. A park bench must be explicitly marked "Jew Bench" in order for a Jew to sit. Store signs go up in the window "We Do Not Sell to Jews," and the Germans use intimidation of their own people when a woman is forced to wear a sign saying, "I am the biggest pig of all... I only sleep with Jews."[7]

{ **World Scale Catch 22 – The Germans allow some Jews to immigrate but only when they leave their wealth behind. The British, with their selective immigration, only allow Jews with over $5,000 to come to Palestine.** }

In the spring of 1938, the Nazis take Austria. The world watches as 400,000 Jews are arrested. The world listens to news reports of gang violence and public degradation. Old Jews must use their underwear to scrub latrines with acid water, and men are forced to pull down their pants and show their circumcision to "prove" they are Jews. Jews are dragged into streets and beaten or taken to a sports field to crawl on their hands and knees and "mow" the grass with their teeth.

If the above paragraph is Scene One for a tragic play on the world stage, Scene Two, *The Évian Conference*, follows that summer. Not even Shakespeare would have thought to add this extra bitter mockery for his readers to keep in mind: The Statue of Liberty poem is written by Emma Lazarus, a Jew.

Celebrating the fifty year anniversary of *The Statue of Liberty*, President Roosevelt announces a conference with the goal of gathering together countries who will accept Jewish immigrants. The "huddled masses" of Jews in Germany who are "yearning to breathe free" see this conference as a literal life line, an amazing American example of implementing the ideals for which Lady Liberty stands.

In July 1938, The Évian Conference, held for eight days in France, is attended by thirty-two countries, thirty-nine private organizations, twenty-four volunteer organizations and 200 international journalists. Jews around the world, Golda included, are full of hope. This sentiment by a Jew explains, "The United States had always been viewed in Europe as a champion of freedom and under her powerful influence and following her example, certainly many countries would provide the chance to get out of the German trap. The rescue, a new life seemed in reach."[8]

The sense of breathless expectation is described forty years later by Walter Mondale:

At stake at Évian were both human lives—and the decency and self-respect of the civilized world. If each nation at Évian had agreed on that day to take in 17,000 Jews at once, every Jew in the Reich could have been saved. As one American observer wrote, 'It is heartbreaking to think of the … desperate human beings … waiting in suspense for what happens at Évian.' But the question they underline is not simply humanitarian … it is a test of civilization.[9]

The test is failed. The Évian Conference, hyped to portray the nobility of a civilized human race, is a charade. Characters without courage twist the plot and the torchlight of Lady Liberty shows us a tragedy. When public opinion wonders why Golda maintains her attitude that the Jews can depend on no one but themselves to protect their own people, the farce of the Évian Conference is just one of the reasons.

Golda is at the conference as the representative of the Jews in Palestine. However, she is not given the status of "delegate" only "observer." She doesn't want to cause a fuss and risk an offense that could give the gathering countries reason to not take refugees. She forgoes the political slight, but she records later, "the ludicrous capacity of the [Jewish] observer from Palestine, not even seated with the delegates, although the refugees under discussion were my own people…"[10]

The countries come to the conference, not with open arms, but armed with excuses for why they can do nothing. The Netherlands say the climate in any of their colonies is unsuitable for these immigrants. Canadians announce they only allow farmers. This is convenient knowing the Jews, not allowed to own land in their current country, will not fit this criterion. Australia claims it has no racial problems and doesn't want one to start. The United States raises their immigration quota, but this is disingenuous since the quota is already filled through 1940. One country, Santo Domingo, with its forty square miles, agrees to accept some Jewish refugees.[11]

It can be granted that countries are still in the midst of severe economic depression. Limits have been reached for giving to their own citizens. Understood. Golda doesn't ask anyone to "do" something for her people. She simply asks permission for these Jews to come to Palestine.

Golda has the opportunity to address the audience at the end of the conference. She is direct. She does not rant and shame the delegates. She simply states that the *Yishuv*, the Jewish community, is prepared to take in as many immigrants as will be allowed. At no expense to the rest of the world, the Zionist Jews will care for the European Jews. Golda tells the delegates, "We want them. We'll share whatever we have with them. Please let us only have them."[12] As Golda is speaking, the American representative stands up and leaves. He is followed by the British representative and then the French.

How does she not scream to their backs, "**COWARDS!**" or something worse…

Remembering the Évian Conference, Golda will quote Dr. Weizmann.

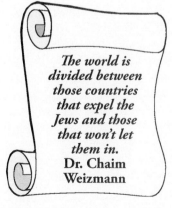

The world is divided between those countries that expel the Jews and those that won't let them in.
Dr. Chaim Weizmann

In her autobiography, Golda records her feelings, "I don't think that anyone who didn't live through it can understand what I felt at Évian–a mixture of sorrow, rage, frustration and horror. I wanted to get up and scream at them all, "Don't you know that these 'numbers' are human beings, people who may spend the rest of their lives in concentration camps, or wandering around the world like lepers, if you don't let them in?"[13]

Meeting the press after the conference, she gives this statement, "There is only one thing I hope to see before I die and that is that my people should not need expressions of sympathy anymore."[14]

The underlying message from the conference is–laissez-faire. Countries, populated with their own prejudices will not lift a finger to provide a means for the German Jews to escape. There will continue to be more "expressions of sympathy," shock and horror. The skin of some of these Jews they have just rejected will be used to make lamp shades, their fat used to make soap.

The apathetic outcome of the Évian Conference is the nod, the implicit approval for Germany to act out a show stopping sequel within the next few months. Hitler "gets the memo" and unleashes Germany to take action. It has been called "The Night of Broken Glass" or "Kristallnacht." The name doesn't do justice because the impact is more than a two-night performance.

The overt justification of this German Pogrom is retribution for a German being shot in the German Embassy in Paris by a young Jewish man. In truth, the incident provides the tiny flash point needed for the cruelty of the German people to be let loose and to implement Hitler's policy to exterminate the Jews. "The Night of Broken Glass" is the beginning of the Holocaust.

1938, Kristallnacht, Synagogue burnt down

1938, Kristallnacht, Shop windows smashed

The unfettered fury of the Reich includes: 30,000 Jewish men are arrested and sent to concentration camps; 2,000 deaths and casualties of innocent Jewish citizens; 171 Jewish apartment houses destroyed; 7,000 Jewish stores or businesses demolished; over 1,000 synagogues set on fire. Throughout Germany and Austria there is a continual exhibition of Jewish homes, hospitals and schools being consumed by fires. Jewish men, women and children are thrown out the windows of their homes or pulled to the street and beaten or hanged. On the streets Jews are dragged behind horse carts, or tied up and thrown into rivers. Jews, while riding on trains, are thrown out the window. Many Jews are simply shot trying to escape.

World outrage is in words only. A newspaper article reads, "No foreign propagandist bent upon blackening Germany before the world could outdo the tale of burnings and beatings of blackguard assaults on defenseless and innocent people, which disgraced that country yesterday."[15]

The German landlords who rent to Jewish merchants (Jews are not allowed to own the stores) are not going to pay for the damages. Because Jews are the *cause* of the destruction, Jews are billed with the amount of repairing the store windows and damage. The cost of replacing the glass is five million marks. (US dollars for the year 2013 would equal 201 million dollars) The total bill to the Jews for property damage is a fine of one billion marks (US dollars for the year 2013 equals over 40 billion dollars). This is one-tenth of the wealth of Jews in Germany and Austria.[16]

Usurping Jewish wealth not only financially supports the Third Reich; it abets their plan for The Final Solution.

Following Kristallnacht, the Intergovernmental Committee on Refugees is formed. In light of the events in 1938 and into 1939, the committee proposes that thirty-two nations each accept 25,000 refugees from Germany. Every country answers–no.

It gets worse.

The British put out another White Paper, May 17, 1939. Indifferent to Nazi atrocities, the British hand the Arabs and

Germans, nails for the coffin of any chance for a Jewish home-land. The paper states, "His Majesty's Government therefore now declares unequivocally that it is not part of their policy that Palestine should become a Jewish state." The British White Paper also declares that only fifteen thousand Jews a year will be allowed into Palestine and that policy expires within five years. After that the Arabs will decide.

Weizmann records, "We have been betrayed… Ours is the sorrow, but not the shame."[17]

During the summer of 1939, the British are evacuating their children from London. They can send their children to the countryside of England to wait out the war and have a better chance of survival than living through the Germans bombing London. Who can blame them? Parents waving goodbye to their children in train cars, not knowing if they will ever be together again, is news-reel footage that can make us cry.

WWII children executed

The government who made trains available for their own children is unwilling to provide an escape for 20,000 Jewish refugee children in Germany. The British will not permit them to enter Palestine and argue with Golda that the Arabs won't like it. The fact that the Arabs are regular guests of Hitler and openly support the Nazis is irrelevant?

The British need an alliance with Palestine in case Hitler's forces continue their march across North Africa and take control of the Suez Canal. Jews, ready to fight Hitler, sign up by the thousands–Arabs don't.

Jews are willing to fight alongside Britain, which is the country forsaking (The White Paper) its promise (The Balfour Agreement and the British Mandate) to give Jews, their homeland. Arabs who are siding with Hitler still get their one-way support in Palestine from the British. If you can follow those twisted dynamics, you will understand the brilliance of the statement Ben-Gurion puts out to his people:

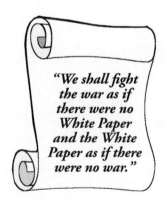

"We shall fight the war as if there were no White Paper and the White Paper as if there were no war."

In the following year, 1939, the World Zionist Conference is held in Geneva. Golda and delegates from Palestine meet with representatives from Europe. Over the years, this gathering is more than a meeting to encourage a cause. These are colleagues, friends and extended family.

The heat of the days declares August, but the air is chilled with fear of impending death. Forecasting the uncertain whispers of "if" war starts is replaced with gauging the winds of "how much" violence and torrents of "how many" will die. The cold death front pushing across Europe drops from foreboding to the futility of rescuing fellow Jews from disappearing in the twisting forces of anti-Semitism. The attendees, this small fraction of Jews, will withstand the pressure from "civilized" governments who have shattered any barometer of ethics. These Jews make a stand and proclaim their seed has value.

Having to say "farewell" is particularly painful for the attendees leaving the conference. Many of the European Jews returning home will be murdered in the next few years. Golda later writes, "…it was the memory of their spirit that gave us heart, inspired us to go on and, above all, lent validity to our own refusal to be wiped out to make life easier for the rest of the world."[18]

Two weeks later, September 1, 1939, the fear of another full scale world war is confirmed. Germany invades Poland. What the Nazi regime has started is World War II.

PART THREE

CONTEXT AND COMMENTARY

JEWISH RESISTANCE

{ This segment is background information that coincides
with events covered in the coming chapters. }

During the 1930s and through WWII, the majority of the
Yishuv are hoping that when the war is over, the reputation the Jews earned fighting against the Germans will convince
the British (and the world) that Jews deserve an independent
land of their own. The *Yishuv's* governing body, the *Histadrut*,
continues to provide the leadership and organization of infrastructure and administer the beginnings of government necessary to run their own country and protect its people.

The *Haganah*, originally trained to safeguard the Jews, is
having its role expanded. In light of the shifting British policy
to appease the Arabs, the *Haganah* role now includes implementing acts of resistance when the British try to prevent the
immigration of Jews into Palestine. In spite of British and
Arab harassment, the *Histadrut* policy remains–no retribution
and all military actions by the *Haganah* must have the approval
of the *Histadrut*.

An example of the approved military actions is blowing up
the British vessels used to intercept the ships carrying Jewish refugees. However, blowing up trains for British mining will not be
an option. Passive resistance includes the *Haganah* organizing the

coincidence of thousands of residents turning out into the streets of Tel Aviv at the same time as British soldiers are trying to search those segments of the city for unauthorized Jewish immigrants.

To the British, the *Haganah* is an illegal organization, and those who participate are criminals. If members of the *Haganah* are caught, they risk arrest, imprisonment or hanging.

There is a minority among the *Yishuv* who contend that the *Histadrut* policies and how they use the *Haganah*, are not strong enough to achieve their objectives. They are quick to point out that playing by the British rules isn't working. Their mindset has merit when considering an account of Jewish accomplishments to date that has won them no favor with the British:

1.   Bought, developed and farmed swamp/desert wasteland

2.   Built infrastructure; roads, hospitals, schools, bridges

3.   Supported all local residents; Arab standard of living has increased, Arab life span has increased, Arab immigration to Palestine to work has increased

4.   Organized leadership to run the country; David Ben-Gurion, David Remez, Zalman Shazar, Berl Katznelson, Zalman Aranne, Golda Meir

5.   Fought alongside mandate country in charge during WWI and joined British troops to fight Hitler

6.   Play nice in the sand box: don't succumb to the violent provocations of Arab extremists

A militant Jewish group, which breaks off from the *Haganah* and is active until 1948, is the Irgun. A group branching off from the Irgun, active until 1942, is the Sternists. Another subgroup, the Lehi, is active through 1948. Their policy is to

ensure every Jew has the right to enter Palestine even if that means a loss of innocent Arab life. These groups believe a Jewish armed force is the means of securing a Jewish state and is the only deterrent to Arab violence.

The leader of the Irgun is Menachem Begin, and his position is, "We fought to right the greatest wrong done in the history to any people… We fought to bring the Jewish people back to their ancient country and to build a home for homeless people. Liberty or death."[1] The Irgun membership is around 600 while the *Haganah* membership is 33,000.

Through 1948 (the year of independence for Israel), the Irgun are responsible for sixty attacks that result in 250 Arab deaths. They will target British leaders, sabotage railways, blow up bridges, and destroy the infrastructure of the oil fields. The Irgun is also responsible for acts of resistance, such as the 1944 Yom Kippur being announced with the blowing of the *shofar* (ram's horn). This is a taunt to the British who have prohibited this religious ritual since the Arab riots in 1929.

As this symbol of the Irgun shows–the boundaries are shown by the land outlined behind the gun. This was originally promised to become the state for the Jews.

The incoming reports of Jewish massacres from Europe during WWII give the Irgun more reason to retaliate. Lord Moyne, serving as the British colonial secretary, is well-known for his policies in Palestine being pro-Arabist and anti-Zionist. It is his hand in implementing the strict policy by the British that lead to the denial of docking permission for the *Struma*. This ship, carrying 781 Jewish immigrants, is subsequently torpedoed, killing all aboard but one. Two members of the Lehi assassinate Lord Moyne in November, 1944. The assassins are tried and hanged the following spring.

The *Histadrut* denounce the Jewish extremist groups, and Golda relays, "I was and always have been unalterably opposed–both on moral grounds and tactically–to terror of any kind, whether waged against Arabs because they are Arabs or against the British because they were British... my firm conviction that, although, many individual members of these dissident groups were certainly extremely brave and extremely dedicated, they were wrong (and thus dangerous to the *Yishuv*) from start to finish."[2] She goes on to point out these acts of violence "could only boomerang against us–which it usually did."[3]

When dealing with their extremist groups, the contrast in leadership of the *Histadrut* and the leadership of the mufti is an antithesis of directives. Arab governments do not discourage the policies of their extremist groups; rather they continue to use the mufti to encourage the escalation of violence.

The *Histadrut* denounce the extremist groups within their Jewish community, and this policy against the Irgun and Sternists is not mere public posturing. In an intricate balance of justice, the effort to restrain the Irgun and Sternist leads to developing a small secret group within the *Haganah* called *Sezon*.

{ **Sezon: Hebrew word for "hunting season"** }

The *Sezon* will turn over information to the British Intelligence tipping them off to plans by the Irgun and Sternists. One step further, the *Sezon* will kidnap members and leaders of the Irgun and Sternists, handing them over to the British.[4] In turn, the *Sezon* alert the Irgun and Sternists that their plan has been exposed.

The Irgun suspect Golda of selling out to the British. Their opinion is bolstered because Golda serves as the British liaison. In order to prevent innocent bloodshed, it is Golda who warns the British officials about plans of actions by the Irgun, Sternist or Lehi.

Jewish leadership is not able to prevent some of the terrorist acts by these groups. There is the bombing of the King David Hotel, July 1946. [A previous plot by the Irgun had been discovered, reported to the British and prevented.] The blast kills 91 people. And a village, Deir Yassin, is attacked in April 1948. (This attack is discussed in Chapter 12.)

Golda is convinced, if there had been no *Haganah* as a method of resistance, more Jews would have turned to the tactics of the Irgun. Golda explains, "I don't think it was possible to destroy terrorism, as long as immigration was not permitted. ... If it had not been for the *Haganah*, probably most of the Jews would have been with the Irgun. The idea of not doing anything was unthinkable."[5]

The Jewish leadership and more importantly the *Yishuv*, has evolved their strategy from one of compliance with the British Empire to one of challenging the British Empire. In a speech where Golda gives voice to the death of their old illusions, to now taking control of their destiny she states, "We have no alternative."

Golda's words declare a new chapter in Jewish history. A page is turned. Jews will take Hitler's ghastly term "Final Solution" and redefine their death sentence. The Jewish people, the *Yishuv* come to their own final solution—they will fight.

But first there is a world war and six million of them will be murdered.

Understanding the depth of the *Yishuv's* struggle during WWII the following explanations will help you.

Military Front:

Hitler's strategic offensive, fighting just one military front, the Western Front, could have won domination over all of Europe, including England. Hitler chooses to have two fronts. This "second front" overextends the reach of the Third Reich. Using resources that might have brought victory to the Western Front (Europe), Hitler instead diverts resources to invade Russia, the Eastern Front. Germany discovers it can't win a war on two fronts. The Third Reich, started in 1933, promising to rule for one thousand years, will end in 1945. (These twelve years, will witness the deaths of over 60 million people.)

Home Front:

The dimension of a war heightens the struggles and resources for managing the services of the civilian population. It is called the home front. Schools must keep teaching children, hospitals must continue caring for patients, produce must be delivered to stores, roads must be built, electricity/sewage/water services must be maintained.

10
THE JEW'S "FINAL SOLUTION" ~ FIGHT

During WWII, the *Yishuv* is fighting to defend their Jewish people in Europe and will stand with the Allied Forces to beat Nazi Germany. This is one military front. The *Yishuv* will also share the same war struggles of a home front.

For the Jews of the *Yishuv*, they must risk the drain on their resources and take on a second front, a quasi military/home front, which is waged in the shadows. This "second front" is the fight to fulfill their moral obligation to help any Jew escaping from Hitler's regime. This second front pits them against British policy and the Arab extremists. Ben-Gurion's battle cry illuminates the Jew's double bind, "We will fight the war as if there were no White Paper. We will fight the White Paper as if there were no war."

With a primordial purpose to protect her people, Golda is busy day and night.

During WWII, Golda serves on the War Economic Advisory Council and continues as the liaison between the Jewish people of Palestine and the British administration. Her job entails finding ways to improve production for farms and factories, keeping distribution of goods moving, and negotiating with the British for better wages for the Jews working on military projects. She is also the constant moral voice asking the British to protect the Jews from Arab attacks within Palestine. That is her official day job.

Golda's covert night job is supporting the "second front" of helping Jews escape Germany. The *Histadrut* keeps its priority to actively assist any Jewish refugees being smuggled in from Europe. For each person saved, it is literally a matter of life or death. Nothing else matters.

Golda had heard, two years earlier in 1936, Dr. Weizmann calling an alarm, "There are six million people doomed to be pent up where they are not wanted and for whom the world is divided into places where they cannot live, and places which they may not enter. Six million!"[1] In the coming years, Weizmann's lament "doomed to be pent up" will read, "doomed to be murdered in gas chambers," "doomed to have their corpses raided for gold in their teeth," "doomed to have their hair shaved for mattress stuffing," "doomed to have their bodies burned in crematoriums and their unburnt bones used for phosphate and their ashes for fertilizer in German flower gardens." "Doomed to be pent up" would have been good news.

In 1939, after the failed Évian Conference, Golda asks the British officials, "Let our people into Palestine. If you don't, the Nazis are bound to turn them into a factor in the war effort of the Nazis (They do become a huge resource of slave labor.). Let us bring them in, and they will be a very important help in the war effort for the Allies." The British refuse.[2]

In 1939-1940, Jewish leaders are negotiating with Nazi SS officer, Adolf Eichmann (discussed later in chapter 15) on conditions of letting Jews out of Germany. Eichmann agrees that he will not deport German Jews to the Polish death camps if Jews are allowed to deport out of Germany. Armed with this information, Golda approaches British authorities to request the papers needed to save the lives of these potential deportees. The British say "no," and the situation is made worse because the British close this loop hole by classifying the Jews of Germany as "enemy aliens."

It is worth noting a government and its people who stood up for their Jewish citizens: the Danish.

Germany views the Danish citizens as "Fellow Aryans" and, therefore, the Third Reich is less savage in its occupation of this country. The Danish government, much to the ire of the Germans, will not dismiss Jews from their government positions, will not enact anti-Jewish legislation, nor will they expropriate Jewish property. Losing patience with Danish policy, the Germans decide to deport all the Danish Jews to death camps. Learning of this plot, the Danish authorities are alerted and all 8,000 Danish Jews are hidden and in one night ferried to Sweden in an agreement with the Swedish government. The Germans find only four hundred Jews and they are sent to a work camp, not a death camp.

The Danish government continues to watch over the four hundred Danish Jews sent to the camp. They insist on inspecting the camp and this show of solidarity with their fellow citizens results in no Danish Jew being deported to the death camp, Auschwitz. Ninety-nine percent of the Jews in Denmark survive the Holocaust.

The Danish government, along with the German official, George Ferdinand Duckwitz, who leaked the information about the round-up, will later be esteemed by Israelis. They are awarded the honor "Righteous Among the Nations." (discussed in Context and Commentary 4)

Stories of suffering continue to be dismissed in world opinion.

Polish women, exchanged for German war prisoners, will give eyewitness accounts of the slaughterhouses established in Poland by the Germans. The story is considered "sensational" and disregarded in the press. Golda believes them and writes in her autobiography, "I remember distinctly the day that those first awful reports reached us about the gas chambers and the soap and lamp shades that were being made from Jewish bodies."[3]

There is no record of her response when she hears a news report from Auschwitz: 4,000 dead by shooting, 2,900 by gassing, 2,000 by phenol injections, 1,200 beaten to death, 800 suicides by walking into the camp's electric fence. What is recorded is the British response. Golda goes to the British authorities with this latest information and the request to raise the number of immigrants allowed into Palestine. Golda promises that the Jewish community will care for them, nothing will be asked of the British but to say, "yes." Instead their response is, "There might then arise shortages of housing accommodation and food… there are not unlimited supplies."[4]

Golda Meir
From the Archives Department,
University of Wisconsin-Milwaukee Libraries

Is this the sadness that is in Golda's eyes, in this photo? Not only for the deaths of her fellow Jews but for the depravity of British decisions?

When the world acknowledges the annihilation of 3,000,000 Polish Jews (1942) and it can no longer be denied that Germany is determined to have a complete genocide of all Jews, Britain does declare anyone who reaches a neutral country (Turkey) can be given a permit to enter Palestine. The fact that the British fail to inform the Turkish government for six months means any large scale transports are not authorized and organized until July 1943.[5]

In light of such blatant disregard for the lives of Jews, the leadership of the *Yishuv* continues its commitment of smuggling as many European Jews as possible into Palestine. Golda's apartment in Tel Aviv, with its balcony overlooking the sea, becomes a look out for boats carrying refugees.

In spite of a British imposed curfew for everyone, teenagers show up on the shores to carry the fugitives from the boats to the beaches. As the new arrivals dry off and warm up at bon fires on the shore, they can burn their old identity cards. Golda hears again and again as they each proclaim, "I am a Jew from the Land of Israel…"[6]

Golda will also hear their stories of another bonfire, although this bonfire is a camp in Poland. The Nazis force the Jews to undress and hand over their jewelry. Next the Jewish men and women are shot–not fatally. They are thrown onto the fire to burn alive. The children have their heads smashed against a wall and they too are thrown into the flames. This is the method of murdering 900 people and from their ashes the Nazis sift for gold.[7] These stories fuel Golda's constant quest for more ships.

Golda declares, "We must do all in our power to help the illegal immigrants. Britain is trying to prevent the growth and expansion of the Jewish community in Palestine, but it should remember that Jews were here two thousand years before the British came."[8]

"… all in our power" for Golda means raising money to buy any seaworthy ship to transport the immigrants.

Some refugee ships don't reach Palestine's shores, and the story becomes more tragic. The *Struma*, (mentioned earlier) is afloat for over two months with 781 Jews that were escaping death camps. They are refused permits from the British to enter Palestine. It is torpedoed by a Russian submarine and all are lost except one man.[9]

The British, who are overwhelmed with fighting Hitler while their London is being bombed, can still afford to have planes and patrol boats policing the shores to halt any decrepit ships with a cargo of a few hundred Jews escaping from death camps. The Arabs and their oil are that important.

This is the war for Golda; work with the British to keep improving the lives of Palestinian Jews, and disregard the British and their immigration regulations, in order to rescue European Jews. The added twist is this third dynamic of fighting alongside the British to beat Hitler. Golda is on the front line of each of these "fronts" and she must continuously measure her words carefully, keeping her senses on constant high alert. The lives of their beloved people are precariously hanging on to any thin chance that a few more passports might be granted. Golda's missteps can mean their death. An impatient reply could be cause for an official to deny entry or close a loop hole for immigrants.

Golda exists on cat naps, coffee and sixty cigarettes a day.

Questions being considered by the Jewish leaders come from the Warsaw Ghetto Jews. By 1942 they are being systematically murdered, and now they are slowly starving within the fenced off confines of the designated blocks of the city. This is the Warsaw Ghetto. Their question is beyond a cry for help. These Polish Jews know that any arrival of help is impossible. In their desperate and lost voice they are asking, "Should we surrender or die fighting?"[10]

How do you have a meeting about that? What will be on the agenda? Do you list the pros and cons? The leaders, David Ben-Gurion, David Remez, Golda Meir, and others gather in the usual room where before heated debates on policy were vehemently hammered out, but this time there is silence. It is a deathly silence because everyone knows, their decision won't matter. The Polish Jews will be murdered. A message gets through to the meeting. The Polish Jews have made their own decision. They die fighting.

Golda will later meet Zivia Lubetkin, a Warsaw ghetto fighter and survivor. Golda says to her of that painful time, "We were the parents and you the children, but on that day we felt that the parents were unworthy of the children."[11]

Recalling the memories of seeing her father simply nail boards to the back of a door to keep out violent gangs, Golda has never abided well with the feeling of helplessness. She and her colleagues are determined to find some way to support the Jews trapped within the clutch of the Nazis.

Golda asks the question, "What can we do, first of all, to let them know that we know and we're doing something about it? And second we need to do something." Golda later says, "At a time of such tragedy, there's a feeling that one should be part of it. And if you weren't, well–it's as though you weren't where you should have been."[12] It is agreed to send paratroopers behind enemy lines. Their mission is to contact any remaining Jews, support their underground resistance, assist escapees, and to let the Jews know they are not alone. The *Yishuv* will not forsake them, and every effort is being made to get them out.

*"Whom shall I send?
Send me."*

**Hanna Senesh,
poet and
paratrooper**

By cajoling the British, the Jews are given permission (tainted with restraints) to have a group of Jews become paratroopers and go behind the enemy lines in Europe. The volunteers must pledge allegiance first to the British mission for being paratroopers and, only then, can they pursue the Jewish purpose of finding/supporting any Jews. The story of each of these paratroopers could be a Steven Spielberg drama movie that ends tragically, most of them never return.

One group of paratroopers is dropped off in Yugoslavia to help rescue the Hungarian Jews that will soon be deported to the German death camp, Auschwitz. Hanna Senesh is a twenty-three year old Hungarian Jew who had immigrated to Palestine

a few years earlier. Like Golda, she has yearned to be a part of
the Zionist cause, more than just living in Palestine. Becoming
a paratrooper is her answer. She volunteers and is assigned a
group that will return to her country of Hungary. She is caught,
tortured, and executed in Budapest. Her poem, written days
before being shot by a firing squad deserves a place here:

> *Blessed is the match that is consumed*
> *in kindling flame.*
> *Blessed is the flame that burns*
> *in the secret fastness of the heart.*
> *Blessed is the heart with strength to stop*
> *its beating for honor's sake.*
> *Blessed is the match that is consumed*
> *in kindling flame.*[13]

Is this a high adventure story of a young woman wanting to be
a martyr? Read one more of her poems:

> *To die, to die in youth,*
> *No, no, I did not want it;*
> *I loved the warmth of sun, the lovely light.*
> *I loved song, shining eyes, and not destruction.*
> *I didn't want the dark of war, the night.*
> *No, no, I did not want it.*[14]

Hanna doesn't know her poems will become literature for
Jewish children and will be used in the film, *Schindler's List*. She
doesn't know the future state of Israel will honor her with a memorial, or a museum in Skokie Illinois will feature her story in a
special exhibit, and PBS will carry a documentary of her life, using her poem title, "Blessed Is the Match." All Hanna knows is
she hears the call–"Who shall I send?" She answers, "Send me."

Hanna's immediate objective, help Hungarian Jews escape,
is not achieved. But the immediate impact of her courageous
story gives courage to all Jews to keep fighting on all fronts.
Her words come true. "I know I will not be disappointed. I

want to do everything to bring this dream nearer to reality, or the reality nearer to the dream."[15]

These are the people, not numbers, that Golda is able to see when she is so distraught after the Évian Conference. These human beings are why Golda continually cajoles the British to grant more immigration passes.

The pouring in of immigrants, legal and otherwise, continues at the shores of Palestine. Earlier waves of Jews had come to the same shores, but they were a different breed, physically and emotionally. Their previous hard life had earned them a hard body ready for the rigors of physical labor. Emotionally they had suffered the strain of anti-Semitism, but they know now, they can determine their destiny. It is their choice to immigrate to Palestine.

The new immigrants of the 1940s are physically fragile from work as slave labor, escaping death camps and living through years of Third Reich brutality. The strength of their emotional fortitude is no better. Their lives have been decimated to only a decision to survive. This is the reason they come to Palestine. They can garner enough strength to exist, but they have no reserve energy or desire to build a new nation. Golda reminds the "old guard" of tolerance by saying, "The new immigrants are heroes in their way–heroes because they have remained Jews. The places where they come from, it takes a lot of heroism to remain a Jew."[16]

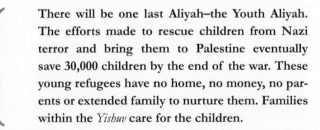

There will be one last Aliyah–the Youth Aliyah. The efforts made to rescue children from Nazi terror and bring them to Palestine eventually save 30,000 children by the end of the war. These young refugees have no home, no money, no parents or extended family to nurture them. Families within the *Yishuv* care for the children.

Years later Golda reflects on the views of the *sabra* (native born) Jews and facing their questions about the Holocaust. She states:

> *"I am afraid that our youngsters will look down upon the Jews in the ghetto because they did not fight. But in their very preservation of life, Jewish life, there was heroism. Our youngsters who have grown up in the atmosphere of modern Israel often say: 'How could six million people go to the gas chambers? Why didn't they fight?'" Golda explains, "But how do you fight under a regime of that kind? (In any case, I believe that anyone who has not been there has no right to pass judgment.) To me the very fact that people in the ghetto organized dramatic circles, music lessons, and literature classes is evidence of their heroism. What, after all, did the Germans want? Not only to kill Jews. They wanted to bring the Jew to the state where he was no longer a human being. So to me the heroism in the ghetto did not start on the day when they rose against the Germans with what arms they had, but throughout their whole life there. When rabbis went at the head of the group to the gas chambers, they went with prayer, saying 'Ani ma'ameen' ('I believe'). They did not go with bowed heads, crying. I want our youngsters to know, appreciate, and respect that."[7]*

The Jews are hoping that after the war there will be a better world. They have helped fight Hitler while millions of their people have been murdered. The Jews and their leadership have come to understand that foreign governments will not value the Jewish lives as the Jewish people do–but they do keep the belief that after all this, the Jews will now be allowed to settle in peace in their homeland.

They are wrong.

11
BETWEEN A ROCK ...

May 8, 1945: V-E Day (Victory in Europe)

The unconditional surrender of Nazi Germany is achieved. Hitler, having committed suicide one week earlier, is unable to attend.

The British are going back home. The Russians are going back home. The Germans, who started and lost the war, are going back home. Maybe their homes are bombed out, but their home is their country, their own people who will welcome them back. They can and they will rebuild.

And for the Jews? Across Austria, Rumania, Yugoslavia, Greece, Germany, France, Belgium, Luxembourg, Poland, USSR, Hungary, Italy, and Czechoslovakia 30,000 Jewish communities are gone.[1] Imagine returning to your burnt out village: Main Street, your church, school, the corner meat market and finding no one is left of your community. Imagine, every one of your family and friends being dead, not because of a bomb or because they were soldiers, but because they were massacred. Of your family, your neighborhood, you are the only survivor.

Where do these remaining Jews go to rebuild? Back to a village where they were forced into box cars bound for camps? Back to their shop that had windows shattered and merchandise destroyed by the non-Jews who lived next door? Back to a street where their baby was bayoneted or their grandfather forced to crawl and eat grass? Many Jews try and return. They are murdered by the locals who have confiscated their property.

Women, survivors of the camps, having no place to go, are being kept behind barbed wire in Austria–first they are stripped and searched by the Austrian guards.[2] In Kielce, Poland, forty-three Holocaust survivors who return are killed by neighbors.

In the post war years, these Jewish refugees, the subject of genocide for seven years, are weak, desperate and dying. Their former lives are in ashes, and they hope the Jews in Palestine will provide a place to live. Their dream, to immigrate to a desert land governed by their own people, is a cruel mirage because the British won't change the immigration policy. The *Yishuv*, still determined to take in their fellow Jews, is up against the White Cliffs of Dover.

So for this chapter–"Between a rock..." British policy is the "rock."

After WWII, the Jewish belief that Britain will uphold its pledge to create a nation for the Jews,[3] must be abandoned. Any inkling that the worthiness of the Jewish cause will prevail after all this suffering becomes the story line for *Don Quixote Part 2*.

The Jews have reasoned that showing the world the beauty they will bring back to this land would substantiate their worthiness to run their own country; building the city of Tel Aviv where there had been sand dunes, growing roses on the salty shores of the Dead Sea, founding factories, a university, and hospitals, and establishing an increased standard of living and life span for Jews and Arabs. Jews want to believe this overwhelming evidence will convince the world powers that they will be responsible, civilized citizens capable of self-government. This mentality becomes a fool's errand, and the Jews will not be fools. The Jewish community is transitioning to accept that their future is not based on the merit of their humanity.

Ben-Gurion, after WWII, is making clear that his goal is the immediate establishment of a Jewish State.[4] The *Yishuv* is progressing from being a community to a nation. Grasping this concept means no longer living as a cringing people under the colonial oppressor. Acting as a nation will include clever resistance and yet not succumbing to deeds of retaliation. This transformation in the hearts and policy of the Jews will challenge the British Empire, the Anglo-American oil interests, and the Arab states of the Middle East.

The world community is resisting this transition. In fact, the world opinion, shown with its continued passive/aggressive ambivalence to Jews in the post WWII months, would have preferred to develop relations with the Arabs without this Jewish thorn still sticking in the side of the Mideast. Golda's succinct assessment: ""We intend to remain alive. Our neighbors want to see us dead. This is not a question that leaves much room for compromise.""[5]

The next trial for the Jews will be to win in combat their right to have independence. They will need to fight off invasions, sacrifice money meant for domestic growth, and watch their sons die in battles. To prove their solidarity and determination to win back their country, Jews wanted to use plow shares. The world is demanding swords.

Jews must "evolve" or become extinct.

"This is the Voice of Israel, the voice of Jewish Resistance."

Radio broadcasts out to the streets of Tel Aviv and remote kibbutzim.

To engage in open physical conflict is up for a vote within the executive committee. Debates have gone on long enough. No shouting. No political posturing. Just a sad vote as they have to admit their dream to act as an advanced civilization has not worked. As mentioned in the segment "Jewish Resistance," the *Histadrut* castes its vote to use the force of the *Haganah* to; 1. bring immigrants into Palestine; 2. establish settlements and keep the Jewish National Fund settlements safe; 3. sabotage British property but not people.

Coming to the conclusion of being forced to fight Golda says, "If fighting for the right of Jews to enter the Land of Israel means terrorism, then we are all terrorists... Those who were killed in the gas chambers by Hitler were the last Jews to die without defending themselves. This is going to become an independent state... There may be a lot of blood that's going to flow, but this is what's going to happen." [6]

Remez, Golda's long time close friend, is in disagreement with the policy. Remez tells her, "Ben-Gurion and you are destroying the last hope of the Jewish people."[7] Remez continues to contend that civil disobedience alone is the answer. Golda disagrees. "We refuse, absolutely, to be the one people in the world which consents to having its fate decided by others."[8]

The *Haganah* troops are protecting the settlements. They arrive with barbed-wire fences and floodlights. They build trenches and concrete fortifications. They keep watch during the nights so the workers can get their sleep and tend to their crops during the day or run the factory. The result of this increased self-defense at the kibbutz is that Arab terrorists spread their attacks to the roads. Aside from disrupting business, the snipers and their road bombs kill innocent passengers in cars and buses.

For the *Histadrut*, the smuggling of arms into the country to protect their citizens demands priority over the normal growth decisions for the livelihood of a peaceful society. And yet, keeping the economy thriving is necessary to support the coming out of their new country and the coming in of refugees, thousands of them.

Over one hundred thousand Jewish refugees in displaced persons (DP) camps are waiting to flee Europe, and the *Yishuv* will not put them on hold. Golda explains, "We've seen children who didn't know how to smile, children who came to us from the camps in Germany—the few who were left after a million children went to the gas chambers. They didn't know how to sing, they didn't know what a rose was—they had never seen one grow." [9] These are the children she sees as they come to the shores of Palestine. These are the reasons she will be brutal on herself and anyone else until she can say, "And now in Israel, in the north and in the south, these children have made things grow—on sand and on rocks where nothing has grown for centuries."[10]

The plans of the *Histadrut* are to absorb any and all refugees into their Jewish community. Golda's practical implementation entails stockpiling food, preparing housing, and making available medical attention, showers and clothing—all necessary for the first day of an immigrant's arrival. Then they must have places to live, jobs to work, schools to teach them, and clinics for their medical care—within the first weeks of their arrival.

To guarantee these resources being available, the existing

settlements and Jewish communities must keep the economy going in order to make the necessary sacrifices to ensure the immigrants' transition into a new life. Meanwhile, the Jewish people are spending their time fending off Arab gangs of violence, Arab boycotts of Jewish goods and British interference.

> *"Jewish products and manufactured goods shall be considered undesirable to the Arab countries. All Arab institutions, organizations, merchants, commission agents and individuals" are called upon "to refuse to deal in, distribute, or consume Zionist products or manufactured goods."*
>
> *Arab League Boycott declaration, December 2, 1945*

British Foreign Minister, Ernest Bevin, is in charge of the Palestine Mandate after WWII. Golda spends her days in meetings with Bevin and his staff, advocating for more British protection from Arab attacks. She points out the British are raiding Jewish homes to confiscate arms that the Jews need to protect themselves while ignoring the arms used by Arabs to attack Jewish settlements.

It can be understood Bevin is in place to protect the interests of his country, and so, he writes in a top-secret letter about "the vital importance to Great Britain and the British Empire of the oil resources of this area."[11] Although in his next remark he describes Jewish refugees as "the scum of the earth."[12] That is not political, but personal anti-Semitism. When Jews are pushing to have the British fulfill the mandate, Bevin publicly scolds the Jews not to "push to the head of the queue."[13] Golda recalls, "I had no doubt that if we gave in to Bevin, we were finished."[14]

In early 1946, Bevin proposes a commission (yes, another one) to study the problem of the escalating unrest. This time it is called the Anglo American Commission and Bevin states he will oblige their recommendations.

In the meantime, daily life includes British truck patrols roaming the streets blaring messages on loudspeakers day and night. Across the harbor of Tel Aviv, searchlights and depth charges are used by the British to look for "illegal" ships carrying immigrants.

The restrictions get tighter. A curfew is placed on the community. This keeps Golda home evenings, but the continual strain of standing against warped world politics is taking its toll. Marie Syrkin, while staying with Golda, remembers several instances when Golda passes out, suffers from migraine headaches, or endures the pain of gallstones. During this time Golda's father, Moshe has died and her mother, the feisty Blume, is now quietly losing touch with reality.

What fuels Golda's fire, and strengthens her stance will be seeing the initiative of the children, the next generation. Golda records this:

> *"The time came when the [children] themselves gave us the answer. They are not strangers to casuistry and abstract precepts. … For them, matters are simple, clear and uncomplicated. When the catastrophe descended upon the Jews of the world, and Jews began coming to Palestine in "illegal" ships, as they still do, we saw these children of ours go down to the seas and risk their lives–this is no rhetoric, but literally so–to ford the waves and reach the boats and bear the Jews ashore on their shoulders. This, too, is no rhetoric no flowery speech, but the literal truth: sixteen- and eighteen-year-old Palestinian girls and boys carried the sur-*

vivors on their backs. From the mouths of Jews borne on those shoulders I have heard how they shed tears for the first time–after all they had been through in Europe for seven years–when they saw Palestinian youngsters bearing grown men and women to the soil of the homeland. We have been blessed in this youth, which sets out to offer its life not on behalf of its own particular kibbutz, or [for] Palestine in general, but for the sake of every Jewish child, or old man seeking entry." [15]

In April 1946, two ships carrying over one thousand refugees are blocked on their way to Palestine. The passengers announce they will sink their own ships and kill themselves rather than be turned back to Europe. In the meantime, refusing all food, they start a fast.

A refugee wounded resisting British arrest, deported to Cyprus, April 1946

Golda, quick to unite with the principle, organizes a fast of the *Histadrut*.

A British official tells Golda, "Do you think for a moment that His Majesty's Government will change its policy because *you* are not going to eat?"[16]

Golda replies, "No, I have no such illusions. If the death of six million didn't change government policy, I don't expect my not eating will do so. But it will at least be a mark of solidarity."[17]

Golda, in spite of her doctor's protests, is once again the ringleader. Thirteen of the *Histadrut* are committed to fast. As day one turns to day two and turns to day three, a crowd gathers in the courtyard outside to watch and wait. A request from British officials comes for them to stop the fast since the parties are now negotiating. It is Golda who says "no." The fast will continue until there is an official government statement releasing the ship.[18] The situation garners world publicity, so the British relent. It will be 104 hours, (4 ½ days) until they eat.

Golda has been going before committees and commissions (a British stalling tactic ruse), since the 1920s. Phony motive or not, each time Golda must give her best effort to educate the audience.

March 25, 1946, Golda testifies before the Anglo American Commission that Bevin had requested. One viewer remembers, "One felt that all the commission members, without exception, were hanging onto every word she uttered. In the beginning, it was her personality her commanding presence, and also that certain femininity of which she was not devoid. But once she had begun to speak, it was what she said and how she said it that mattered. It was clear-cut, lucid, precise, and based on knowledge of facts, rather than on emotions or opinions. She definitely stole the show."[19]

Golda is asked by the commission, "If the Jews could have the same privileges as a minority that you promised the Arabs as a minority would they be content?"[20] Golda responds, "No, sir, because there must be one place where Jews are not a minority. I believe that the Jews have come to this situation of helplessness and persecution and lack of dignity in their lives as Jews, not as individuals but as Jews, because of this curse of being a minority all over the world. There must be one place where their status is different."[21]

May 1, 1946–The results of the Anglo American Commission have come back. The commission recommends that 100,000 certificates be immediately given to Jewish immigrants wanting to go to Palestine. The United States government is in full agreement. Bevin rejects the plan.

Golda gives this crisp response, "You will not frighten us. We do not want to fight you. We want to build. We want to enable the small remnant of European Jewry to come to Palestine in peace. But should you persist in preventing us from doing this, Bevin will also have to send a division to fight us..."[22] Her words, "We have no alternative," is still the battle cry.

The betrayal from Britain is deeper than Bevin. Bevin is a part of the Labor Party, a party with the same ideals as the Labor Party of Golda and Ben-Gurion. When the British vote the Labor Party into power after the war, there is an expectation that British policies would soften toward the Jews. Not so. Golda's responds, "For over twenty years, British Labour supported the Jewish Labor movement in Palestine... Who could have dreamed that this covenant ... would be broken?" [23] Golda looks forward to the day a Britisher will come to the consulate of a Jewish state and have to ask for a visa.

The next month, June 16, 1946, following Bevin's rejection, the British are jolted from their sleep and from their supremacy by the sound of explosions. All the railroad bridges leading out of Palestine are blown up. The one-hundred-fifty-three detonations send a message to the British. The Jewish resistance has begun.

Two weeks later, June 29, the British react. The 100,000 troops that are usually behind the barbed wire area known as "Bevingrad" are unleashed. They are ransacking houses, gutting government buildings, and arresting leaders. By the end of the day they imprison 2,738, kill three, wound and torture dozens. No Arabs are arrested. Churchill will call this "Bevin's Dirty War" and the vengefulness of the British force is seen in one commanding officer exclaiming, "I can sweep the whole lot into the Mediterranean. I've got the force to do it."[24]

The British have their lists of who to arrest and it is the top tier of leadership. Luckily Ben-Gurion is out of the country. The objective of the British is to disrupt Jewish organization. If they can break the unity of the *Yishuv*, the British hope Jews will support more moderate leaders that will accommodate the British policy to mollify the Arabs. For an unknown reason, Golda is not arrested. Considering Golda's job as the British liaison and being a prior citizen of the United States, not being arrested is a possible ploy to cast doubt on Golda's alliance to the Jews. Regardless of the British reasons, not being arrested annoys Golda greatly.

Bevingrad–Security zone in Jerusalem
http://www.etzel.org, Date Accessed, 2014

Golda assesses the damage the next day, June 30, 1946. In the *Histadrut* offices, she sees the extent of the ransacking. Soldiers have broken down unlocked office doors and needlessly destroyed furniture. She picks up from the floor photos of children with holes poked through their eyes. Reports have come in that a fourteen year old boy was beaten by a British soldier. Someone tells the soldier the child is a survivor of one of Hitler's camps. The soldier replies, "If Hitler had finished the job, I would not have to do it."[25]

With so many in jail, the obvious question is–Who will be the leader of the *Yishuv*? The obvious answer is Golda. She has the support of her colleagues behind bars although she is rejected by the Orthodox Jews because she is a woman.

Golda's first announcement as leader cuts to the point and sets the tone, "What we want is complete independence. What happened during the war and after, proves that if we had been independent we might have rescued hundreds of thousands of Jews in Europe. We were the best possible, the only friends of the British in the Middle East, but British policy has put us in an impossible position. With the detention of our leaders and thousands of other Jews who are accused of no crime, we have reached the limit. Something of that friendship may yet be preserved, but only if we are liberated from British rule and every other foreign control, be it in the form of a Mandate or a Trusteeship."[26]

In the weeks that follow, Golda is the focal point of decisions, negotiating with the British for the release of the prisoners, talking with the Irgun and Sternist to give her time and not react with violence, debating the option of civil disobedience with Jewish leadership (many of whom still feel the British can be reasoned with), accommodating immigrants arriving by night, setting food rations, providing housing, managing world opinion, and still the Arab massacres carry on. Golda adheres to the rules of using the *Haganah* for resistance that will not harm the British or Arab people. She will report Irgun activities to British authorities in order to prevent any British or Arab loss of life.

Measures of protest and resistance are continually enlisted. The Youth Movement puts out posters and flyers to support the cause. Golda's daughter, Sarah, is one of the members and later comments, "We use to put up posters in the middle of the night, right under the noses of the British."[27] To protect members within the Youth Movement, they are sworn to secrecy.

Jewish Resistance Poster

Golda, often an author of these posters, will never question her daughter as to her whereabouts at night.

The *Haganah* policy of increased resistance isn't enough for some. The Irgun believe in "an eye for an eye." After the British raid in June, which becomes known as "Black Saturday," the Irgun leader, Menachem Begin, is a part of the proposal to blow up the King David Hotel, which houses the British administrative headquarters. Begin will always insist that the British were given a warning, and they had thirty minutes to evacuate the hotel. He claims that three telephone calls were made to repeat the warning. However, no one clears out and on July 22, 1946 the bomb goes off killing ninety-one people; British, Arabs, Jews, and wounding hundreds.

Churchill's commitment to a Jewish homeland is shaken. It can be said that the Irgun is at fault. But the Irgun will dismiss this. Their unrepentant stance would have even more credence if they knew about a confidential note within the British Foreign Office that was sent to the Control Office for Germany and Austria:

"We must prevent German JEWS from immigrating to PALESTINE."[28]

This British Policy continues to be the "rock" the Jew are up against.

The British are shocked by the King David Hotel bombing. Their retribution is to ignore the escalating brutality of Arab attacks on Jews. A one-year-old Jewish baby girl is roasted alive in front of her mother.[29]

> *In a later interview with Begin he is confronted with the comparison of Arab acts of terrorism and the Irgun's. Begin replies, "We fought to save our people. They fight to destroy a people."*
> **(Martin, 1988, p. 275)**

Golda continues to meet with the British to detail the attacks being done by the Arabs, point out their biased search for guns on the Jewish homes and settlements and not the Arabs, and explain conditions of immigrants on ships. She must assess how much information she can give British officials, how willing they will be to bend rules and who to trust.

The British High Commissioner, General Sir Alan Cunningham, is one that is sympathetic to the situation although most officials are similar to the one who once told Golda, "… if this is how the Jews are being treated by the Nazis, there must be a reason for it." [30] When a Chief Secretary says to her, "You know, Mrs. Myerson, if Hitler is persecuting Jews, there must be some reason for it."[31] Golda gets up and walks out. She will never meet with him again.

Golda, no longer the second string, has moved front and center. This attention is not going to her head. What is in her head is looking around for old friends to contact in Europe, now that the war is over. While attending the World Zionist Conference in 1945, she sees all the empty chairs. Her friends, comrades and colleagues are all dead. Their voices have been silenced, and they cannot partake in the ongoing debate of the meetings. The world leadership of Jews, lead by the elder statesman Chaim Weizmann, still wants to negotiate terms with the British. Golda disagrees. Her voice for the dead persuades those still living that the time for negotiating is over.

When Golda and Ben-Gurion are at the conference, reporters are asking about the Jewish violence against the British. Is there an exasperated look, a "huff" in her voice, as Golda explains the Jews want peace and quiet. One of her pithy responses will be, "No people in the world knows collective eulogies as well as the Jews do. But we have no intention of going down in order that some should speak well of us."[32]

Returning from the conference, this silent vote of the dead is what encourages the representatives, who are still alive, to support the *Histadrut* plan for continued resistance and not Weizmann's proposal for the plan of nonviolence. The Jewish community is outraged over the shooting of a captain of an "illegal" immigrant ship and later, two Irgun members are hung. The vote continues to be justified when reports come in that a teenage boy, putting up anti-British posters is shot, sent to jail, tied to his bed, and denied medical attention that leads to his leg being amputated and his death.

There is a rise in popularity of the Irgun and Sternists, who are openly retaliating. The perception is that people like Golda are still just talking and trusting. Golda remembers, "There were pretty nasty slogans against me saying that I was selling out to the British, and that I was a traitor. ... I remember once I went with my older sister to the theater, and all of a sudden leaflets were thrown down from the balcony ... against me. I don't believe that they would have assassinated me. I was never afraid, but it wasn't pleasant."[33]

The pressure increases when she must implement a new policy for the *Haganah*. In hopes of avoiding bloodshed, the *Haganah* are told to not resist arrest by the British. Golda receives a report that a couple of the young *Haganah* men, who complied with the policy, were then left with a gang of Arabs to be murdered. Golda will be the one to go and face the people, clarify the reasons, and be the voice of the Executive Committee.

Golda, her ability to explain and be an example of living the principles, encourages the public opinion to hold fast and not surrender to an Irgunist reaction of an "eye for an eye." The Jewish population of 600,000 unites. They do not succumb to becoming a band of fanatics. This maturing unity will later serve them well when coming up against six Arab countries bent on seeing Israel's destruction.

October of 1946, the Jewish leaders are freed from their prisons. It is four months from the day of their arrests on Black Saturday in June.

In the coming months, the Executive Committee of the *Yishuv*, learns that world leaders are backing off from the commission that would establish a Jewish nation. Instead, they are leaning toward a "province" that still doesn't allow the Jews an independent state. The Executive Committee rejects this, but they do have a meeting where they secretly vote to agree to a partition of land. Ben-Gurion has believed in the past, and now Golda is in agreement, "We must demand only one thing, and that is a Jewish state in Palestine or in a part of Palestine."[34]

The British, seeing no successful end in sight for ensuring their political agenda in Palestine, make an announcement on February 14, 1947:

> *"His majesty's Government had decided to refer the whole problem to the United Nations."*[35]

The announcement does nothing to deter violence.

The Irgun and Sternists have bombed the British embassy in Rome. This complicates efforts to allow the transport of immigrants into Palestine. Golda's response to these acts is that, "These groups take it upon themselves to decide what is best for the Jewish people. They do not bring their views before any democratic forum. They decide and act, but the consequences of their acts must fall on the entire *Yishuv*."[36]

The British, knowing they will soon leave, do not relinquish their objective. Near bankruptcy after WWII, they continue to put troops and finances behind their push to appease the Arabs. Government officials, warships, planes, and troops are used to intercede and turn back ships with immigrants bound for Palestine.

The *SS Exodus*, carrying 4,454 Holocaust survivors, comes to the Haifa port July 18, 1947. Hundreds of British soldiers, in full combat dress, board the ship. Using clubs, pistols and grenades the refugees are forcibly taken from the ship, killing three and wounding 30. Dr. Noah Barou, secretary of the British section of the World Jewish Congress, relays seeing the British soldiers beating the Holocaust survivors and one woman passenger screaming from the deck, "I am from Dachau!" Forced onto deportation ships, the refugees are returned to Germany.

SS Exodus

Golda starts a protest and declares a day of mourning. The Zionist flags are draped in black and she shouts to a crowd, the mourning is not for the Jews "but for the vanished justice and morality of Great Britain."[37] The *Histadrut* have given the passengers onboard the *Exodus* priority cards, promising each one will be in Palestine, within the following year—legally or otherwise.

Since the British allow the bodies of dead Jews to be returned to Palestine, the three passengers, killed during the struggles on the *Exodus*, won't need priority cards. Golda is one of the thousands who follow the funeral procession to the cemetery.

{ The captain of the SS Exodus will be the same captain that brings the last ship of refugees from the DP camps on Cyprus to the new State of Israel. }

World opinion leans toward the underdog and the British are embarrassed. Golda's response is, "Those responsible for British Government policy cannot forgive us for being a nation without the British Government's approval. They cannot understand that the problem of the Jews of Europe has not been created for the sole purpose of embarrassing the British Government."[38]

"She never sought solace in solace."

Description of Golda

In the weeks to come, Golda goes to Vienna to visit a post-war Jewish community. The trip includes stopping at some of the concentration camps. Afterwards, she meets with a member of the American Embassy who relays, "I think she [Golda] was wearing the same black dress she wore two years before. ... There wasn't much laughter in her then. She had gone to see some of the concentration camps and she was terribly hard hit. But she didn't talk about it that much. This was not a person who spilled her soul. She never sought solace in solace. But there was such a feeling of overwhelming sadness in her. Still she had this sense of command. Whoever she met, man or woman automatically accepted her authority. And you never thought of her particularly as a woman or a man—she was a person."[39]

The British announcement in February (1947) to turn the matters of Palestine over to the United Nations does not lead to many rays of hope. It does lead to Golda meeting with one more commission of inquiry, the United Nations Special Council of Palestine (UNSCOP).

Golda is speaking before the UNSCOP and later says of the members, "It could be said with certainty that when the eleven members of the United Nations Special Committee reached this country there wasn't one among them who knew Palestinian affairs before he was appointed to the Commission."[40] Golda, in her succinct style, explains to them, "A little bit of history. Before the First World War, there wasn't an independent Arab country in the area. What was called Palestine was referred to by many Arabs as southern Syria. The League of Nations gave the Mandate over Palestine to Great Britain. And what was Palestine then? It was all the area between the Mediterranean and the Iraq border. One high commissioner, one set of laws. That was Palestine. Then Churchill divided Palestine and made the Jordan River the dividing line, creating Trans-Jordan east of the river. So Palestine was partitioned... And we never had one single day of peace."[41]

The point Golda is hoping the council will grasp is this: When Trans-Jordan was divided off taking more than half the land from the Palestinian area, the Palestinian Arabs didn't resist or revolt because they saw themselves as **Arabs** not Palestinians. It is only when the land is going to be given to Jews that the local Arabs become **Palestinians** and protest being disenfranchised. (This is aside from the fact Trans-Jordan could have been a homeland for the Arabs in the area of Palestine.)

> Establishing new borders to grant an area to a dominant religion is not a lone request of Jews. During this same year, 1947, the Muslims in India demand an independent nation with a Muslim majority. (This is the same point that the Jews want.) The Muslims are granted their request and Pakistan is divided off from India and becomes an independent Muslim country.

Before the UNSCOP leaves Palestine, the members inadvertently bear witness to British brutality. The UNSCOP delegations are eyewitnesses to the brutal scene of the British troops forcing the refugees to disembark the *Exodus*.

The UNSCOP will recommend the land for the Jews have further partitions, the city of Jerusalem will be governed by a national trusteeship, and for the British to leave in eight months. The UN vote, to accept or reject this recommendation, will be November 29, 1947. The *Histadrut* agrees to the partition in spite of losing more land and losing Jewish settlements (putting them under Arab control) to the new boundaries. The six Arab nations veto the plan, reasoning the Jews have no right to **any** land.

The rock island of Cyprus is a British colony. It is two hundred thirty miles from Tel Aviv, and there are 30,000 Jewish refugees being kept behind barbed wire. These survivors of concentration camps are provided no tables, no chairs, and live in tents on sand and slab. The shortage of fresh water makes drinking water a luxury and bathing impossible. Committing no crime, except the will to live, the British enforce punitive punishments such as not allowing the Jews to bathe or swim in the ocean. Convicted prisoners have better living conditions.

Cyprus Island Displaced Persons (DP) Camp
Yad Vashem Photo Archive

On a first in, first out list–each person is waiting his/her turn to get their passport toward the quota allowing them to come to Palestine. The war ended in 1945, it is now 1947. Many of the refugees in the camp have been waiting two years, plus the years of their suffering in prior German work camps or evading capture. The worst hardship is on the children. Lacking adequate nutrition, they are unable to fight off disease, and many have never lived outside barbed wire.

Golda plans to go to Cyprus and ask those whose names are next on the list to leave, to allow the children to move to the front of the line and get them into Palestine sooner. Golda will need to convince the persons that are going to be skipped over, not only to let the children have priority but the children's family as well.

No colleagues offer to go with Golda on this trip. They doubt her plan will work. Her reply is, "If it was right, it had to be tried whatever the result."[42] Afraid of failure, her colleagues also know they can't ask someone to do something they wouldn't do themselves. But that is Golda's moral high ground. November 11-14, Golda goes to Cyprus.

Greeting her on the island is a group of Jewish children. They have made flowers from paper. Golda wonders if they have ever seen real flowers in their lives. Some of these children will someday approach her and say, "I was one of the children."[43] And a mother will come up to Golda, years later and say, "Meet the baby, now grown up. You helped get us out."[44] So yes. Golda convinces Jews, captive in Cyprus, to let the children and their families go first.

Imagine, people who had already suffered and survived so much, who are still living in harsh conditions, and whose futures remain unsure, give up their slots so a family with children can leave. In the following ten days, 1,420 children and their parents are released to go to Palestine. The refugees being bumped know the British won't increase the quota to ease their sacrifice. These refugees also hear the rumors going around that everyone at the camp could be held indefinitely.

Public opinion can denigrate this act of humanity. It can be reasoned, "Yes, but they knew the UN vote was coming for Jews to have their own land. So they knew they wouldn't have to wait much longer." That is probably granting the Jews more faith in the humanity of the world than they are able to muster. These same adults have just lived through WWII, they were specifically hunted down and murdered while the world stood by and did nothing. These same adults knew of the Évian Conference, the chance for countries to take them in as refugees, and the countries did nothing. These same adults are being denied the right to at the very least, live humanely–go swim in the ocean–and the world is more interested in the Nazi War trials. No. It doesn't seem they have any reason to think the world will vote to let them have their own country. They have learned to not believe the world.

Golda's words to those who must stay and wait, "I promise you that every one of you will be freed to come into a Jewish state."[45] They believe Golda.

The time for the UN vote is drawing nearer, and the world still resists allowing Jews their independence. Governments are worried that if a war breaks out, their supply of Arab oil may be threatened. Golda replies, "If we are criticized because we do not bow, because we cannot compromise on the question 'To be or not to be,' it is because we have decided that, come what may, we are and *will* be."[46] Golda goes on to explain, "It's a big mistake to think the reason for the conflict between us is territory. They don't want us here. That's what it is about."[47]

The Arabs continue to argue against allowing Jews any independent land. Arabs will ask, "Why should we suffer the crimes of Hitler?" Jews remind them, that the Jewish immigrants are being brought to Jewish settlements not Arab areas.[48]

Although the proposed new state is cut down from the original 10,000 square miles to 5,600 square miles (smaller than New Jersey's 8,721 sq. mi.), the Zionists accept the decision. They accept the terms that Jerusalem will not be a part of their state and will be protected by the United Nations. The Arabs will not accept.

"It is not fair to come to a discussion thinking that one side has to give nothing and the other side has to give large and important concessions, and without any security that these concessions will be a means of peace."

Winston Churchill discussing negotiations with the Arabs in 1921[49]

The night of November 29, 1947–the energy crackling in the air is as palpable as the static crackling on the radio as Jews tune the dial to listen to the UN vote being taken. Will there be enough votes to accept the plans for an independent Jewish state?

Golda is alone in her apartment. Menachem is in the United States. Sarah is at her kibbutz. A cigarette and a cup of coffee keep Golda company. Sitting at her kitchen table, she listens to the broadcast and counts the votes. Thirty-three are in favor (including the United States and the Soviet Union), thirteen are against and ten abstentions (Great Britain abstains). Golda can hear the cheering in the streets.

She goes to her office at the Jewish Agency building and looks out from a balcony over the crowds of people. With no one else to address the people, Golda speaks to the Arabs and the Jews: "… The partition plan is a compromise–not what you wanted, not what we wanted … but let us now live in friendship and peace together…" and then she adds, "For two thousand years we have waited… We always believed it would come… Now we shall have a free Jewish state … It surpasses human words …"[50] Golda, swept by emotion, the joyous throngs in the street below, she calls out to the crowd, "Jews … *mazel tov!*…"

The chapter started with using part of the cliché, "between a rock and a hard place." You know the "rock" of British policy. The next few months, from the UN vote, November 29, 1947, to the day of declaring independence, May 14, 1948, is the "between."

So what completes the analogy of "a hard place?"

It is the Arab Higher Executive and the Arab League, local extremists fueled by the grand mufti who provides "a hard place."

Arab guerilla forces are crossing over the Syrian and Lebanese borders. The recruits for the Liberation Army will include professional European anti-Semites left over from WWII, German prisoners of war released from camps in the Middle East, Muslims from Yugoslavia, and troops from the Polish Army still wanting to fight for any anti-Jewish agenda. Local Palestinian Arabs who are not inclined to aid in the coming riots are pressured (like the P.S. on the Russian poster) to be onboard and cooperate with the mufti's Muslims.

The day after the UN vote, November 30, a local Arab gang attacks and kills eight Jews on the road to Jerusalem. That same day, there is a public gathering in Jerusalem, and Golda appeals to the Arabs, "Our hand is offered to you in peace and friendship. Take our proffered hand!"[51] December 1st and 2nd there are Arab riots in Jerusalem; pillaging, arson, looting shops, and stabbing of Jews, in full view of British troops.

The "rock" of the British and the "hard place" of the Arabs are not going to change. If the Jews want to see their country born, they will have to fight for it.

Golda states, "I didn't know how we would make it … I only knew one thing, that we must."[52]

12
"WANDERING JEW" STATUS
~ REPEALED

*"Do the Arabs
need another
state? They
already have
fourteen. We
only have one."*

Golda Meir[1]

Nor is it a question of Holy Cities—they have Mecca, Medina, Cairo, Damascus, Baghdad. The section of Palestine, designated for the future Jewish homeland, is less than 1% of the total Arab area.

The immediate reaction of the mufti's Muslims to the UN petition is to loot, burn, and destroy Jewish shops, communities, and settlements. Golda photographs mobs in the midst of this destruction as the British police stand to the side with their arms crossed. Showing the pictures to British authorities has no effect. It is the *Haganah* men and women who are arrested for carrying guns and sentenced to three years in prison.[2] During this "in between time" of Nov 1947 to May 1948, the British are still able to spend resources on preventing the entrance of Jewish immigrants. However, the stream of Muslim invaders coming across the borders and attacking Jewish settlements—*goes unchecked.*

To avoid embarrassing the British, Arab leadership agrees only to raid but not to officially invade Palestine until the British leave, May 14, 1948. In the meantime, bands of Arab irregulars, both volunteers and mercenaries, gather in and around the borders. By January of 1948 groups are coming in from Syria and attacking the Jewish villages in the north. The commander of the Arab Liberation Army is Fawzi El Kaukaji.[3] He spent WWII in Berlin mingling with Hitler or recruiting Muslims to fight with the Nazis. By February, there are 15,000 well-equipped irregulars inside the Palestine borders.

An outside observer writes in a newspaper, "As a spectator on the sidelines and a country man of neither side, may I, through the courtesy of your columns, express my tremendous admiration of the fortitude, courage, and restraint of the members of the *Haganah* under provocation as galling as it is criminal, with little or no help from these quarters from which it could have been expected in view of repeated official statements on the subject of law and order? I can never hope to witness again, anywhere else in the world a better discipline, a greater courage, or a more admirable spirit than that which has been displayed by the Jewish people as a whole ever since Partition was approved by the UN."[4]

The *Histadrut* have their focus on the future of Arab countries being their neighbors. With their constant mantra of self-restraint, they hold on to the hope of peace with Arab countries.

Reining in the Irgun and Sternists is difficult in light of the knowledge that the British are disarming members of the

Haganah and then handing them over to Arab mobs who bru-
tally murder them. When a Sternist is caught by the British,
he is flogged. So the Sternist will catch a British soldier to be
flogged. When the British hang two Sternists, the action is mir-
rored by Sternists–hanging two British soldiers.

Golda does not gloat or justify the violence of the Sternists.
Instead she states, "The incident was terrible, and I don't want
to talk about it. They degrade the moral stature of every Jew."[5]

> Siege: a military operation in which enemy forces
> surround a town or building, cutting off essential
> supplies, with the aim of compelling the surren-
> der of those inside.

A siege is on Jerusalem, lasting from December 1947 to
July 18, 1948. Mufti's Muslims have cut the road and the water
pipelines to starve out the Jews. Ben-Gurion will insist that
Jerusalem not be lost to the Arabs.

The UN, in the November vote, makes clear that Jerusalem
is important to them, and they will guard over the city. The
truth is this; their taking Jerusalem from the Jews is a concession to appease the Arabs. It is not a declaration of desire
to protect the cultural iconic city. Evidence of this is in the
coming months when Jerusalem comes under this siege by the
Arabs–the world remains silent. Under the UN rules, Jews are
to be allowed to visit the Old City of Jerusalem and visit the
Wailing Wall, but the Arabs have banned the Jews. It will not be
for another nineteen years, the third day of the Six-Day War,
when Israeli forces take back Jerusalem and only then are Jews
free to pray at the Wailing Wall.[6]

Although Jews are banned by Arabs from the Old City area
of Jerusalem, there are thousands of Jews living within segments of the broader city borders. Throughout December of
1947, Arab snipers in Jerusalem shoot at Jews who are waiting

in line for their daily ration of water, shoot at children coming from school, or shoot at the Jews hurrying from their homes to work. Regina, Golda's friend, remembers, "We didn't' go to work, we crawled to work. Stooping, then running, because they were now shelling all the time..."[7] Food is rationed to one piece of bread, one glass of water and four olives each day. Those killed include a crippled newspaper dealer who is shot by an Arab customer. A reporter is shot and killed, and his funeral convoy to the Mount of Olives cemetery comes under machine-gun fire.[8]

Street of Jerusalem, car bomb, February 22, 1948
52 Jewish civilians killed, 123 injured
Wikipedia

Ernest Bevin is still subversively supporting the Arabs. He wants the Jews to evacuate Jerusalem, meaning the Arabs would have control over the entire city. Bevin divides the city into "security zones." This tactic of support to the Arabs limits the ability of Jews to communicate and move. The Arabs can continue to accumulate stocks of arms in their mosque. Deemed a sanctuary by the British, Arabs know mosques won't be searched. While any Jew caught with a weapon has the weapon confiscated (this includes any knife longer than four inches), and members of the *Haganah* are arrested.[9] Arabs hire British deserters, who still are in uniform, and have access to British army trucks. These trucks, filled with dynamite, blow up the headquarters of the Palestine Post and the Atlantic Hotel, killing forty-seven and wounding one hundred thirty.

The one road leading in and out of the city is under constant fire by bands of Arabs waiting to ambush any Jewish vehicles passing by. The roadside becomes strewn with blown up vehicles and dead Jews.

1948, Assembling the Convoy
www.idf-israel1948.blogspot.com

To decrease the chances of being shot by Arab snipers, travel in and out of the city has to be by convoy. These convoys are the only means of bringing supplies to the Jews of Jerusalem. The buses, reinforced with thin metal, are called "sardine tins." They have wire netting over the windows to protect passengers from the stones and bombs being thrown at them. One bus driver recalls, "I would become so frightened that the sweat would pour from my head down my neck. When you know they could shoot at you from both sides, you'd hear a sort of echo inside, plucking at your nerves. It was also a horrible sight to see the car in front of you hit a mine and blow up… You can cry, but you have to go on. The convoy must get through…"[10]

Golda is living in Jerusalem and Ben-Gurion places her in charge of the city during the siege. He knows she can shoulder the emotional weight and the physical risks. One day, as Golda leaves work; a car bomb blasts under her office window. Two times a week she must travel in the convoy to Tel Aviv to meet with Ben-Gurion. More than once, on this road under fire, a bullet passes through her window.

During one of the trips, as the bus comes around a curve where it is forced to slow down, an Arab ambush begins. Golda is in the bus and she is seated beside Hans Beyth. Hans is in charge of the Youth Aliyah, and it is his job to greet newly arriving orphans at Haifa and assign them to homes around the country. He has just been telling Golda of his wife scolding him that morning for going on this trip. The words of his wife, her fears, come true. "You could make your own children orphans."[11]

Shots are being fired at the bus. Hans Beyth shoots back, but in the gun fire Beyth is hit, falling dead into Golda's lap. It will be years later when Golda is in a hospital dying, she notices the doctor's last name–Beyth. Golda asks him if he was related to Hans Beyth. "He was my father," said the young doctor, "and I've wanted to ask you more about how he died." Golda replies, "He died in my arms."[12]

As she rides that dangerous route, do her thoughts seethe with anger toward the Arabs? Does she regret the message she had a few months ago? As acting head of the Political Department, Golda called a meeting to formulate an official policy regarding the Arabs who will be living in the new Jewish State. This policy guarantees the Arab citizens to have "full and equal citizenship and due representation in all its bodies and institutions."[13] Arab women in the new Israel will be the only Arab women in the Middle East with the right to vote. The Arab children in Israel will be the only Arab children in the Middle East with a guaranteed free compulsory education for ages five to fourteen. Golda is intending to live up to her words, "Look, we shall have to show the world how we are 'making up' for 2,000 years of suffering as a minority not by emulating what was done to us but isolating every single method of making people suffer. And doing away with each of these methods, one after the other."[14]

Golda has no misgivings, no second thoughts to change her direction.

Concerning the international inaction to the siege and shooting in Jerusalem, Golda, sends a cable to the UN–

"DOES THE WORLD INTEND REMAINING SILENT?"[15]

Later Golda remarks, "What happened to this holy city? Not one single power in the world to whom the city is holy– not one–lifted a finger to defend it from the shells..."[16] "Every single Jew who remained alive was thrown out, the only people who could not go to their holy places were the Jews. We couldn't go to the synagogues which had been there for centuries. Who worried about it?"[17]

Ben-Gurion, recognizing the spiritual importance of Jerusalem, tells the *Haganah* fighters, "We must save Jerusalem... The fall of Jewish Jerusalem might prove to be a death blow to the entire Jewish cause..."[18]

Ben-Gurion is well aware they don't have enough guns or bullets to defend Jerusalem. He knows an invasion by six countries is being planned for the day after Jews declare their independence on May 14. How will they fight? With what weapons? Is he the leader of a modern dayMasada?

{ Masada: An ancient fortification on a rock plateau on the edge of the Judean Desert. The Roman Empire laid siege to Masada. Jewish rebels and their families, unable to defend themselves but refusing to surrender, end the siege by suicide. }

In one of the few times Ben-Gurion needs to lean on someone else's strength, it's Golda he calls on. He has said of Golda, "She had faith when others wavered. She believed in the absolute justice of our cause when others doubted." [19]

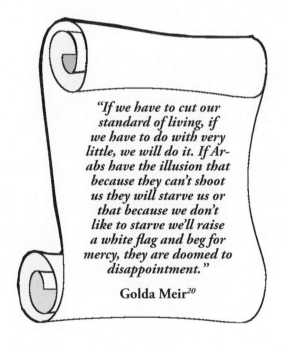

"If we have to cut our standard of living, if we have to do with very little, we will do it. If Arabs have the illusion that because they can't shoot us they will starve us or that because we don't like to starve we'll raise a white flag and beg for mercy, they are doomed to disappointment."

Golda Meir[20]

Armies are amassing around the borders of Palestine. The Arab League meets in Cairo to coordinate funding and training of Arab recruits. The drill camp in Damascus has over 20,000 men. The plan is to allow Britain to leave and attack on May 15. The Arabs expect to be rid of Jewish Palestine within the first few months after May. The secretary general of the Arab League states, "There will be a war of extermination which will be spoken of like the Mongolian massacres and the Crusades." Ibn Saud, King of Saudi Arabia declares, "With 50 million Arabs, what does it matter if we lose ten million to kill all the Jews? The price is worth it."[21]

The Arab states each have their eye on divvying up the area. Trans-Jordan is planning on incorporating the part of Palestine originally designed for the Palestinian Arabs. There is no Arab intention to have a nation called Palestine.[22]

The world watches and wonders "How will the Jews have an army by May 15th?" Another question becomes, "How will they get munitions?" On Jan 14th the United States places an embargo on the sale of arms to the Middle East although Great Britain continues to equip the Arab states with weapons, as they explain—*in accordance with its treaty obligations*. This provides the Arabs with access to the arsenal of the whole British Empire, while the Jews are barred from buying any defensive weapons.[2]

 Some of the units of the Arab Legion are commanded by British officers. Egypt, Iraq, and Trans-Jordan all have British arms and training.

After the UN vote in November, it is the Committee of Thirteen, mostly the Executive Committee from the *Histadrut*, who are running the *Yishuv* until an official government is voted in to run the state. There is a meeting to discuss their desperate situation. Jerusalem is under siege and having to use limited munitions to defend the city means the months ahead will be suicidal unless they can get arms to fight off the coming invasion and defend themselves day to day. Ben-Gurion declares he must go to the United States to plead the cause of the future of their homeland surviving.

Golda disagrees with Ben-Gurion. She tells him, "What you do here, I cannot do, but what you do in the United States, I can also do."[24] Ben-Gurion says "no." Golda insists on having a vote. The Executive Committee agrees with Golda.

The next morning, Golda is on a flight to New York City. She knows reports about the Jewish community in the United States to give much money to the Zionist cause are not optimistic. In fact, the committee has been told the most they can hope to raise is five million dollars.

Golda has been away from the United States for ten years. Her previous trip had been to help develop the Pioneer Women, middle class ladies who support Zionism. She will be seeing them again, but it isn't Pioneer Women where she will raise millions of dollars. Golda recalls, "I was terribly afraid of going to those people who didn't know me from Adam. Henry Montor (executive director to the United Jewish Appeal) being one of those people, but a great power who got things done."[25]

Golda arrives in New York City on a Friday night in the middle of a blizzard–twenty-eight inches of snow. She had not taken the time or the risk to return to Jerusalem after the meeting to pack a bag. Golda has ten dollars in her purse. Meeting her at the airport is Menachem and Golda's sisters, Sheyna and Clara.

178—Golda Meir ~ True Grit

Also at the airport meeting is the assistant to Henry Montor who is explaining to Golda that Montor doesn't think it necessary for Golda to speak at a conference of wealthy Jews that is currently in session in Chicago. This group, known for raising money for charities and causes, is anti-Zionist. Golda knows this.

What Golda doesn't know is that Clara, an anti-Zionist herself, is the one to protest and insist Golda go to Chicago and address this gathering of multimillionaires. Golda puts off the decision until the next day, except now the airport is closed due to the blizzard.

Golda's determination combines with what some might say is "divine intervention." Golda goes to the airport regardless of the weather reports. She waits.

Sitting at the airport, does she remind herself of why she is here? Is she recalling the fiery soap box speeches she gave in Milwaukee? If she is able to get to Chicago, will her speech alter the usual choices of this new audience and alter 2,000 years of Jewish history? Does she shiver and wish she had brought warmer clothes or is the shiver actually fear running through her? Fear that if she fails, if she cannot convince these people to give millions of dollars in a matter of days, that in a matter of months, every Jew in Palestine and all hope of an independent state will be pushed into the Mediterranean Sea. There will be no Jews at the shores comforting new immigrants. There will only be bodies washing up on the beaches.

There is a break in the weather. Golda boards her flight to Chicago. It is the only plane that day allowed to take off.

Arriving at the Chicago conference, Golda, now faces 800 VIJs—very important Jews. Their thick skin to appeals for money is made thicker by their minimal interest in Zionism. Henry Montor has asked they listen to this woman, so they oblige him. Montor introduces Golda as "perhaps the most powerful Jewish woman in the world today."[26]

Golda is at the podium in a simple blue dress, her hair pulled back into its usual daily knot, no makeup and no speaking notes. With her ability to never condescend nor be overawed, in her noble presence, the audience is hushed. Here are excerpts from her famous speech:

"We must ask the Jews the world over merely to see us as the front line and do for us what the United States did for England when England was in the front line in the World War. All we ask of Jews the world over, and mainly of the Jews in the United States, is to give us the possibility to go on with the struggle...

I want you to believe me, when I speak before you today, that I came on this special mission to the United States today not to save seven hundred thousand Jews. The Jewish people have lost during the last few years six million Jews, and it would be audacity on our part to worry the Jewish people through the world because a few hundred thousand more Jews were in danger.

That is not the problem. The problem is that if these seven hundred thousand Jews can remain alive, then the Jewish people, as such, are alive and Jewish independence is assured. If these seven hundred thousand people are killed off, then at any rate for many, many centuries we are through with this dream of a Jewish people and a Jewish home...

My friends, we are at war. There is not a Jew in the country that does not believe that in the end we will be victorious. The spirit of the country is such—we have known Arab riots since 1921 and 1929 and 1936, when for four years, we had Arab riots. We know what happened to Jews in Europe during this war. Every Jew in the country knows, that within a few months, a Jewish state in Palestine will be established. We have to pay for it. We knew that we would pay for it. We knew that the price we would have to pay was the best of our people. There are a little over three hundred killed now. There will be more. There is no doubt that there will be more. But there is no doubt that the spirit of our young people is such, that no matter how many Arabs come into the country, the spirit of our young people will not falter.

The spirit is there. This spirit alone cannot face rifles and machine guns. Rifles and machine guns without spirit are not worth very much. But spirit without these in time can be broken with the body.

The problem is time. The time factor is the most important factor now in this issue. Millions that we get within three or four months will mean very little in deciding the issue now. The problem is what we can get immediately. And, my friends, when I say immediately, it does not mean next month. It does not mean two months from now. It means now…

I have come to the United States, and I hope you will understand me if I say that it was not an easy matter for any of us to leave home at present—to my sorrow I am not in the front line. I am not with my daughter in the Negev, nor with other sons and daughters in the trenches. But I have a job to do.

I have come here to try to impress Jews in the United States with this fact, that within a very short period, a couple of weeks, we must have in cash between twenty-five and thirty million dollars. Not that we need this money to use during these weeks, but if we have twenty-five or thirty million dollars in the next two or three weeks we can establish ourselves. Of that we can carry on…

We are not a better breed; we are not the best Jews of the Jewish people. It so happened that we are there and you are here. I am certain that if you were there and we were here, you would be doing what we are doing there, and you would ask us who are here to do what you will have to do….

*You cannot decide whether we should fight or not. We will. No
white flag of the Jewish community in Palestine will be raised for
the Mufti. That decision is taken. Nobody can change that. You
can only decide one thing: whether we shall be victorious in this
fight or whether the Mufti will be victorious in this fight. That
decision American Jews can take. It has to be taken quickly,
within hours, within days… The time is now…"[27]*

The response is overwhelming. The total amount given is
$25 million dollars.

Montor and Golda spend the next several weeks crisscross-
ing America. Others who helped Golda raise money are Sam
Rothberg and Julian Venezky. Golda asks Sam, "Who converted you to Zionism?" Sam replies, "Hitler converted me."[28]

At the end of January, Golda is back in New York City to address the UN. She dares to ask, "Why is our buying arms for
the Jewish community in Palestine so terribly illegal when it is
perfectly legal for Iraq or Syria to buy arms from Great Britain?" [29] She continues her blunt discourse, "The USA meekly
bowed to Arab threats in order to gain what it hopes may be
strategic or economic advantages in Arab countries."[30]

At a press conference following her UN speech Golda
adds, "There can be peace in Palestine in five minutes. It depends entirely upon the attackers. The minute the attackers
stop there will be peace in Palestine. But as long as they go on,
there will have to be war, and we will have to fight back."[31]

Golda's fund raising is spurred on by the high hurdles of her
people's critical needs back home. She finds out in February that

the Arabs have succeeded in totally blocking the one road into Jerusalem. Undaunted, the Jews have blown up the mountain-side and are frantically building a road through a different pass. In March, she hears that the United States is making known they no longer are in favor of a partition. The window of opportunity for Jewish independence is closing. Golda pushes harder.

Golda is not enamored with the glamour of events and the style of American Zionism where someone tells somebody else to go to Palestine. There are times before a fund raising dinner starts, Golda looks out over a sea of mink coats and knows there are young soldiers back in Palestine on guard duty, shivering in the night, with no hat.

For one stop in Miami, Golda recalls, "I remember coming down to the patio which was so beautiful and seeing the people there dressed with all that beauty… this I couldn't take, I was sure that they couldn't care less. I was sure that when I began talking, they'd walk out of the room. Before I went in to dinner, I drank black coffee and smoked my cigarettes, tears coming out of my eyes. I thought, how can I, in this beautiful atmosphere, tell what's happening at home? I said to Montor that I was sure that when I got up and talked, they'd all walk out. But believe me, God, we ended that day in Miami with four or five million dollars."[32]

Knowing this internal struggle for Golda, the following quote about her is all the more amazing. Someone in the crowd says of Golda, "It was marvelous to watch her pulling out of an audience the noblest in them, the highest moral level, without degrading them, without making them wallow in guilt."[33]

A *Haganah* agent in Europe has notified the *Histadrut* that he can buy ammunition if he has $10 million. Golda cables this

message to him: STAY. She sends the money. For another request, $10 million to buy tanks, Golda phones him back. "Buy
the tanks."[34] Twelve fighter planes are purchased. The total list
includes 25,000 rifles, 300 machine guns, 5,000 Bren guns and
fifty million cartridges.

Yes, Golda is thrilled that the Jewish soldiers, now armed,
will not be sent out on suicide missions. But for this war and
the wars to come, there will always be such sadness that money
must be used for weapons and not hospitals, schools, roads,
factories, food and housing.

Back in New York City, Clara joins Golda at a fundraiser.
Still there is conflict when Clara hears Golda tell the crowd,
"If you side with us, I'm sure we'll win." Clara responds, "How
can you promise that?"[35] And it's not much better with Sheyna.
Golda tells a crowd, "You have a choice either to meet in Madison Square Garden to rejoice in the establishment of a Jewish
state or to meet in Madison Square Garden at another memorial meeting for the Jews in Palestine who are gone." Golda
later explains of Sheyna, "My sister wanted to choke me. She
couldn't understand how I could talk like that."[36] When Golda
says "she couldn't understand," it is a very true statement. Neither Sheyna nor Clara can understand.

At the end of March, Golda boards a plane returning to
Palestine. To honor her success, Ben-Gurion comes to the airport to meet her. He says of Golda, "Someday when history
will be written, it will be said that there was a Jewish woman
who got the money which made the state possible."[37]

Golda has raised $50 million dollars.

April 13th, Golda has a heart attack. Her doctor orders her to
rest for the next three weeks.

Golda, looking at her calendar for the next month sees this: The United States tangle the November vote and propose a "trusteeship" for Palestine. The British will pull out of Palestine. The Jews will declare their independent state. The surrounding six Arab countries will invade the country.

Golda doesn't have time to rest.

In the spring of 1948 the Arabs are fleeing the villages, whether they want to or not. The Grand Mufti, aware this mass migration will disrupt industry and farming, is telling the Arabs they must leave or else be killed by the coming invasion and bombings to the cities on May 15th. The sub-message from the mufti is clear. Any Arab staying is seen as a traitor. Once more it's a gruesome *déjà vu* of the P.S. on the Russian poster fifty years earlier: The British provide trucks to aid the mufti's plan and transport Arabs.

The British Chief of Police in Haifa reports, "The Jews are still making every effort to persuade the Arab population to remain and settle back into their normal lives in the town… Arab leaders reiterate their determination to evacuate the entire Arab population, and we have given them the loan of 10 three-ton military trucks to assist the evacuation."[38]

Rumors contend the overall Jewish policy was to drive out all the Arabs, but there is too much evidence that would say otherwise. Although, there is one credible instance, and that is for military reasons, of Jews being responsible for Arabs leaving their homes. There are two Arab areas, close to Tel-Aviv that are attacking a military supply route for the Jewish troops. Ben-Gurion gives the order to evacuate 50,000 Arabs. The calamity that follows is having them walk ten miles to an Arab Legion outpost. Several elderly people and children die en route.[39]

Golda continues her efforts to explain, "We are absolutely opposed to hurting Arabs just because they were Arabs… We have no desire to be a master race and have people of a much lower standard among us…"[40] Reaching out to the local Arabs, Golda writes pamphlets and has posters distributed. In Haifa the posters state, "Do not fear. For years we lived together in security and in mutual understanding and brotherhood. Thanks to this, our city flourished and developed for the good of both Jewish and Arab residents… By moving out, you will be overtaken by poverty and humiliation. But in this city, yours and ours, Haifa, the gates are open for work, for life, for peace, for you and your families."[41]

Golda meets with Arab leaders to explain the legislation that is being prepared to safeguard their rights. She is crushed by her inability to successfully reason with the local Arabs and convince them to stay. It doesn't matter that Arabs have a higher standard of living and a longer life here in Palestine than in the surrounding Arab countries. For these Muslim families, weighing their choice to stay or leave, they must consider the threat of the mufti retaliation against them and their families. Their own patriarchal perspective is part of the considerations too. If they stay, their women will have the right to vote and their children will be educated.

Encouraging Arabs to flee is causing more trouble than the mufti planned, and it is too late to stop the flight. The mass migration of Arabs into the surrounding countries means food and shelter is needed for thousands. (The assertion that there were millions who fled is incorrect. From the date of the UN vote in November of 1947 to after the Arab invasions in May of 1948 there are at most 590,000 Arabs who leave Palestine.) Those Palestinian Arabs could have stayed in their homes, in the area that was to become Israel.

The number of Jews that fled from Arab countries into Israel is around 500,000 to 600,000. Israel, in its limited geographic space, strained economy, and still needing to fight five more wars in the coming years, finds the means to accommodate this influx of Jews from the Arab countries.

Why are the oil rich countries of Iraq, Iran, Saudi Arabia, and Syria not able to help these original Palestinian Arabs who are made refugees by their own Arab people? These "refugees" already share the same religion, culture and language. A war, the Arab countries are starting, should mean they have to deal with the refugees their war created. Regardless, even as I write this, the Palestinian Arab's decision to leave is still a problem today.

Not all Arabs remain silent to the twisted politics. In one newspaper an Arab declares, "We left our homeland relying on the false promises of cheating military officers of Arab countries. They promised that our exile would last not more than two weeks and would be a kind of hike, that at the end of this period we would return. We are your victims, you Arab leaders."[42] Or this Arab woman when asked if she wished she had stayed behind. "Oh, of course, yes." Who did she blame? Not the Jews or even her fellow Arabs—but the Arab leaders. She understands her people are being used as pawns in their political game. The woman says, "The blood of my son is equal to all the Arab governments."[43] The prime minister of Syria, Khaled al-Azm, affirms that "We ourselves are the ones who encouraged them to leave."[44]

While offering equal rights to the Arabs, not all Palestinian Jews agree with the policy. The Irgun and Sternist are pushed to the limit by the Arab gangs committing violent atrocities. Accounts of rape, looting, and mutilation are driving the Irgun-Sternists to the brink. If the Grand Mufti's plan is to incite the Irgun/Sternists, he succeeds.

The proverbial last straw is when the mufti's Muslims murder Captain Noam Grossman, an American volunteer. His body is found hacked and slashed, his head chopped off, his penis and testicles cut off and stuffed in his mouth. His remains are identified only by his Boy Scout belt that he always wore.[45] The Irgun/Sternists, with no permission from the *Histadrut*, attack the village of Deir Yassin. On April 9th and 10th, a battle ensues and at the end 245 men, women and children are shot.

Reports conflict as to whether warnings were given and for the total number killed in Deir Yassin. Some of the captured Arab men are blindfolded and paraded through the streets of Jerusalem in the backs of trucks. It should be noted, there is no rape and there is no mutilation of the dead.

This act of retaliation is the very thing Golda and the *Histadrut* have been trying to avoid, because now, world opinion is clouded against them. The atrocities committed by Arabs, who publicly preach death, hate and slaughter in the name of Allah, are of no surprise. Their actions are accepted and carry no consequences. But the judgment on Jews who succumb to retaliation? Ben-Gurion writes to King Abdullah a letter of grief and apology. But the mufti has succeeded. They now have "evidence" of the Jews being violent. The attack on Deir Yassin fuels the flight of thousands of Arabs.

Four days after the incident, a group of seventy-seven Jewish doctors and nurses are on the road to Jerusalem (that is still under siege) to go to a hospital. It doesn't matter that this hospital treats equally both Jews and Arabs. The Arabs ambush the buses, killing everyone. British soldiers, who gave the "all clear" to the convoy, stand by and watch. Passengers who are not killed are burned alive.[46]

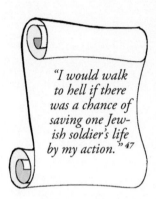

"I would walk to hell if there was a chance of saving one Jewish soldier's life by my action."[47]

Golda has made secret visits to King Abdullah of Trans-Jordan. The hope is a peace agreement or at least he will agree to not be part of the upcoming invasion. Each time she meets with Abdullah, she dresses as an Arab woman. There is imminent danger as she is driven through Arab villages. If she is discovered, she will be killed. Golda meets the king again May 10th.

Abdullah presses Golda to postpone her people declaring their independence. He exclaims, "Why are the Jews in such a hurry to have a state?" Golda responds, "We have been waiting for two thousand years. Is that hurrying?"[48]

On the last meeting, the car is stopped at ten checkpoints and the chauffeur is afraid to go any further on the return trip. He leaves Golda and the interpreter a couple miles from the nearest Jewish border at two o'clock in the morning. They are spotted by a *Haganah* scout and taken to safety.

Golda's return from her final appeal to the king is five days before the invasion. Golda tells Ben-Gurion, "The Arab world is going to declare war on you and I can't stop it."[49]

It doesn't matter that King Abdullah had leaned toward giving support to the Jews. He now bows to the leaders of his religion. He will be assassinated by a Muslim in three years.

The tensions in this drama continue to increase. If this was a fictional movie it would be deemed too improbable for anyone to believe.

It's May 12, 1948, and in two days, the Jews will declare the State of Israel. In three days Israel will need to repel an invasion from six neighboring countries. There are 600,000 Jews versus 40,000,000 Arabs. Add to this, the United States is threatening economic sanctions if the Jews move forward with declaring their sovereignty. Secretary of State George Marshall thinks the Arabs will win out and tells the Jews, "and you cannot count on any help from us."[50]

With these mounting obstacles, lives are at stake, and worst yet, the Jews could lose their one chance for independence. Golda captures the essence, "Many people have lost wars, and many people's countries have been occupied by foreign powers. Our history is much more tragic. Hitler took care of six million Jews. If we lose a war, that's the end forever–and we disappear from the earth. If one fails to understand this, then one fails to understand our obstinacy."[51]

Many within the world Jewry believe, now is **not** the time to declare independence. It is the *Yishuv*, the Jews within Palestine, who overwhelmingly say–now is the time. "We are a people which does not bow, a people which stands erect to face its tragedies. If we are criticized because we do not bow, because we cannot compromise on the question 'To be or not to be,' it is because we have decided that, come what may, we are, and we will be."[52]

"We have our backs against the wall. We don't even have a wall. We have a sea. The only friendly neighbor we have is the Mediterranean."[53]

Golda Meir

Herzl had written in 1897, after the First Zionist Congress in Basle, "At Basle, I founded the Jewish state. If I were to say this today, I would be greeted with laughter. In five years perhaps and certainly in fifty, everyone will see it."[54]

Fifty years and nine months later, "Everyone will see it" is coming true. Although, what the Jews can also see is the borders of their promised land have shrunk.

From this:

To this:

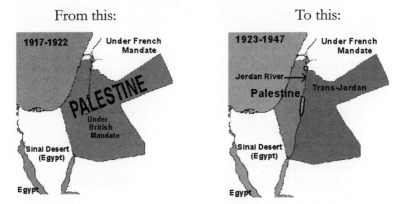

To this today.

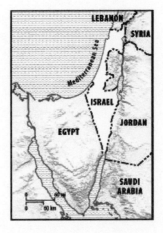

Herzl's portrait is the backdrop to the proclamation of an independent Jewish state.

**May 14, 1948, at the Tel Aviv Museum,
David Ben-Gurion reads the proclamation declaring
the establishment of the State of Israel**

www.jewishjournal.com, Date Accessed, 2014

On May 14, 1948, Ben-Gurion reads a declaration for their independence, ending with the words, "the establishment of the Jewish state in Palestine to be called Israel."[55] His voice has stayed strong through the reading. For the next segment of reading, the essence of the Jewish purpose, his voice breaks.

***"The State of Israel will be open to Jewish immigration
and the ingathering of exiles."[56]***

Ben-Gurion also declares on that day, "We extend the hand of peace and good neighborliness to all the states around us and to their peoples, and we call upon them to cooperate in mutual helpfulness with the independent Jewish nation in its land. The State of Israel is prepared to make its contribution in a concerted effort for the advancement of the entire Middle East."[57]

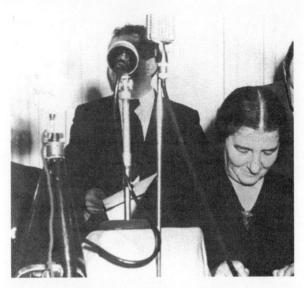

Golda signing the Declaration of Independence for Israel
From the Archives Department,
University of Wisconsin-Milwaukee Libraries

The orchestra is silent. The audience in a spontaneous burst stands to sing the national anthem, "Hatikvah" (The Hope).

♫ *To be in a free nation in our own land …* ♫

Golda is sobbing. The relief is overwhelming and she says, "I wept almost beyond control."[58] When asked why she is crying, Golda explains, "Because it breaks my heart to think of all those who should have been here today and are not."[59]

Golda, along with thirty-four others, write their signatures on this long-awaited document. With this birth of their nation, Jews have achieved a cosmic milestone.

For the school mate who had challenged Golda–"Why don't you start your own country?" Golda can now respond, "I did."

PART FOUR

CONTEXT AND COMMENTARY

AIRLIFTS AND ALTRUISM

Airlifts

After World War II, the German state and the city of Berlin are divided. Eastern Germany and a segment of Berlin are run by the Soviet Union. The Western Powers will control what is to become West Germany. The western segment of Berlin (although the city of Berlin is within East Germany), is also kept under the control of the Western Powers.

The Soviets want to be the sole supplier of food, fuel, and aid to all of Berlin, which would lead to their having control over the entire city. In a siege without shooting, all roads, rails, and canals into Berlin are blocked by the Soviets.

Western Air Forces fly to the rescue of Berliners. It will be called the Berlin Airlift. Starting June 1948 through May 1949, food and fuel for the daily needs of two million people is provided by daily flights. The number of flights and the tons of supplies attest to the international high profile priority of this mission and can leave a reader flabbergasted.

Being "above and beyond the call of duty," *The United States Armed Forces Medical Journal* reports, "Seldom, even in time of war, have persons been so rapidly removed from their homes or from established society as they were in the early phases of the airlift."[1] President Truman gives his complete political commitment. He writes in his diary, "I have listened to a rehash of what I know already and reiterate my "stay in Berlin" decision … We'll stay in Berlin–come what may."[2] Great Britain, after seven years of war, is struggling to recover its economy. In spite of severe economic depression and rationing for British citizens, the British also give support to the Berlin Airlift.

Aside from flying in the food and fuel to survive (200,000 flights will carry 2,325,809 tons of goods), support for the Berliner's economy is also a factor. Flown out from the city on otherwise empty flights are 81,843 tons of manufactured Berlin goods.

Public opinion tunes in on their televisions to sympathetic coverage. Walter Cronkite of CBS News states, "People were eating out of garbage cans. Scrounging the streets. We had fought for freedom and won famine. No man's mind is free when his body receives less than 800 calories. There is no morality on less than a thousand calories a day. There is no government on less than 1200 calories per day." [3]

The abilities of an Allied crew to forgive and forget the German atrocities are remarkable and a credit to the human spirit. One American GI writes home, "One of my guys was a Messerschmitt pilot with twenty-six kills–of American planes! It's tough to hate these people when you work with them. It wasn't long before we totally trusted them."[4]

These "Berliners" are the very people the Allied Powers have just been bombing. These are Germans who gave Hitler his rise to power. They are the reason millions of troops died in battle, lost their limbs, or suffered mental breakdowns. Their German desire for war lead to British civilians being killed going to work, London was bombed for months, children were orphaned and there are families still languishing in heartbreak as the war twisted ethics and pushed people to despair.

So why did the western world bother to help? The Berlin Airlift is implemented because the Western Powers are committed to stopping the spread of Communism. Supporting Berliners is a means to that end.

Jerusalem, like Berlin, is also a city divided. The UN has declared (Nov. 1947) Jerusalem to come under its protection. Considering the efforts of the Jews in Palestine to fight alongside the Allied Forces, surely the Allied Forces would have come to the aide of the Jews and the protection of Jerusalem?

Supporting Jerusalem during the siege or helping defend Israel in May 1948 has no political value. In fact, Western Powers are worried the Arabs, no longer supporting the defeated Germans, will now support the communist government of Soviet Russia. This political reason is partnered with the growing economic need to support the post-war manufacturing strides. The undertow of wanting Arab oil is building up to be a tidal wave.

President Truman's statement of support for Berliners, "We'll stay in Berlin–come what may" does not reverberate for the Jews or Jerusalem.

Another style of airlift is a secret; Operation Magic Carpet: June 1949–September 1950

In the Muslim country of Yemen (South of Saudi Arabia), there is a Jewish population of 63,000. In 1922, barbaric laws are instituted that all Jewish orphans under the age of 12 be forcibly converted to Islam. After the UN partition vote (1947), Muslim rioters and local police participate in a pogrom that kills 82 Jews and destroys hundreds of Jewish homes.

The airlift, Operation Magic Carpet, will transport almost the entire Yeminite Jewish community: 49,000 of the Jews are taken to Israel. Although kept secret until months after the airlift, British and American planes make 380 flights to assist the Israeli effort.

~

Altruism

"And so we must know these good people who helped Jews during the Holocaust. We must learn from them, and in gratitude and hope, we must remember them."
Elie Wiesel

Five years after their independence, in 1953, the Israeli government authorizes a means of remembering the six million murders of their people. A Holocaust memorial, *Yad Vashem* (Hebrew for "a place, a name") is established. Included in this museum is an area, The Wall of Honor, which commemorates those non-Jews who took risks to help save the lives of Jews during World War II. Bestowed on the honorees is the distinction of "Righteous among the Nations."

The review and acceptance by the commission (headed by a justice of the Supreme Court of Israel), for who receives this honorary title is rigorous. Evidence must include repeated and/or substantial assistance, no financial gain to the nominee for their help, and no pressure to convert to Christianity.

Recipients of the "Righteous among the Nations," are examples of altruists (*altruism*–other-ism) in the purist form. They each knew their decisions were endangering their own family members by helping Jews. "Under the Nazi policy of kith and kin, the rescuers' relatives, including even their youngest children, could be killed because of their actions. This meant, those who shared the rescuers' genes could be killed because of the rescuers' actions. The Nazis thus attempted to use biology to deter rescuers, but they did not succeed."[5]

Like a dog whistle to the heart, altruism hits a note not everyone will hear. As of 2011, there are over 24,000 names listed who did hear and answered this call. They are people who put the lives of others, often unknowns, as a priority, no matter what the cost. These are the "Righteous among the Nations." One example is Irena Sendler.

Irena Sendler, 1942

Irena, a Catholic social worker in Warsaw Poland, is 29 years old when World War II breaks out. The Warsaw Ghetto, a sixteen block area, seals off almost 400,000 Jews who will die from disease, starvation, fighting, or being sent to death camps. (These are the Polish Jews who will send a message to the *Histadrut* asking for guidance of whether to fight or surrender.) In 1942, the Nazis deport 250,000 of the Jews in the Ghetto to the death camp, Treblinka. An underground organization, Zegota, is formed to assist the remaining Jews. Irena Sendler is in charge of rescuing the children.

Under the guise of inspecting sanitary conditions, Irena smuggles children out in suitcases, coffins, potato sacks, body bags, sewer pipes, a tool box and the underside of an ambulance. The children are given hiding places in homes, orphanages and convents. In hopes of reuniting the children to their families, Irena keeps records of the children hidden in a jar in her neighbor's back yard. Her ingenuity will save over 2,500 children. And yet Irena doesn't see herself as a hero. She explains, "I could have done more. This regret will follow me to my death." (Jewish Virtual Library, Irena Sendler)

In October of 1943, Irena is arrested by the Gestapo. During interrogations, her arms and legs are broken. She will not reveal the other members of the Zegota underground network. Sentenced to death, Irena is taken to the forest to be shot. The Zegota, through bribes, waylays the firing squad, and Irena is rescued. In hiding until the end of the war, Irena then gives the lists of children's names to Jewish representatives.

As the children she helped become adults, Irena's role in their rescue brings her the highest honor given by the Jewish people to non-Jews. In a ceremony October 1965, the *Yad Vashem* recognizes Irena Sendler as "Righteous among the Nations."

Irena Sendler (1910-2008), seated to the left, dressed in black, pictured with children she saved from death in the Warsaw Ghetto, WWII

Photo credit: Mariusz Kubik, Warsaw, Poland, February 15, 2005, (Wikimedia.org)

"Every child saved with my help is the justification of my existence on this Earth, and not a title to glory."
Irena Sendler

Irena Sendler died May 2008. She was 98 years old. She reminds us of the power of our own decisions.

13
THE PRICE OF INDEPENDENCE

"We're trying to do something that no other nation has had to do before: fight a war, make preparations for absorption of large numbers of immigrants and make preparations for setting up a state."[1]

Golda Meir

May 14, 1948, President Truman is the first to officially recognize the State of Israel. Golda has a particular pleasure in this. It is the country where she grew up, the country where she first read about the Declaration of Independence–and now she has now signed a declaration for her own country.

Golda remembers of that day, "From my childhood in America, I learned about the Declaration of Independence and the geniuses who signed it. I couldn't imagine these were real people doing something real. And here I am signing it, actually signing a Declaration of Independence. I didn't think it was due me, that I, Goldie Mabovitch Meyerson, deserved it, that I had lived to see the day. My hands shook. We had done it. WE had brought the Jewish state into existence. Whatever price any of us would have to pay for it, we had re-created the Jewish national home. The long exile was over. Now we were a nation like other nations. Masters–for the first time in twenty centuries–of our own destiny."[2]

The British officials have left. No White Paper from them or any other government will rule over the Jewish people ever again. The barbed wire of the Cyprus camps can no longer detain the refugees from coming to their homeland. The UN cannot hand over authority to any third party or restrict immigration into the State of Israel.

Dancing in the streets that night is well deserved. Golda watches from her balcony. Knowing the next day, Egyptian planes will be flying overhead, both Ben-Gurion and Golda felt "like someone in mourning at a wedding." [3] Golda says, "Not only was I not gay, but I was very frightened–and with good reason. Still, there is a great difference between being frightened and lacking faith…"[4]

Within less than 24 hours of Israel declaring itself an independent nation, it is attacked from the north by Lebanon and Syria, from the south by Egypt and from the east by Trans-Jordan and Iraq. From their west, the Mediterranean Sea, they will not be invaded nor is there any support coming on ships from the rest of the world. Like a young gladiator's first contest, Israel enters the world arena, forced to fight to stay alive.

This article in the *New York Post* best describes the full gamut of day two for the independent Israel:

> *"Imagine an area of 8,000 square miles in all. Make it 270 miles long and seventy miles wide at its widest; border it on three sides with enemy nations, their armies totaling between 70,000 and 80,000 troops; place within it 600,000 people from more than fifty nations, whose last experience with self-rule dates back 1,887 years; sever its sea and air communications; besiege one-sixth of its number in a land-bound enclave; sack its former government; give it a name; declare it independent—and you have the state of Israel, one minute past midnight, May 15, 1948."*[5]

It's five o'clock in the morning, Golda sees four Egyptian planes in the sky. She hears the bombs dropping. The gut wrenching of that sound is swung 180 degrees when she watches a boat-load of Jewish immigrants arrive at the port of Tel Aviv. The first visa goes to a survivor of the Buchenwald concentration camp. The visa simply states, "The right to settle in Israel is hereby given." [6]

The joy of hearing a phone operator answer, "From the Minister of Transport of the State of Israel"[7] is tempered with the somber reports of the invasion. The desperate circumstances of the Israeli soldiers, outnumbered and outgunned, means Golda must return to the United States to raise more funds for munitions. Golda receives the first passport issued by Israel.

She would rather have forgone that honor and stayed. There is no guarantee that Israel won't be wiped off the face of the earth before she returns. Her children, grandchildren, everything she has believed in and helped manifest into reality for thirty years is now under fire. It could all be annihilated while she is away.

> *For me to have to leave Israel at the moment the state was established was more difficult than I can say. The very last thing I wanted to do was go abroad [but] no one knew better than I what that kind of money would mean to Israel, how desperately we needed the arms it would buy ... My heart sank at the thought of tearing myself away from the country but there was no real choice at all.*[8]

Once again, taking no time to return home and pack, Golda boards a plane with just her purse. The U.S. customs inspector will wonder about the head scarf he finds in her handbag. Golda can't explain that it was from her visit to King Abdullah just a few days prior.

Making the rounds of speaking engagements, Golda is a different woman than five months earlier. She is no longer representing a cause. Golda is representing a country. She is the emissary of the State of Israel. Aside from her successful speeches to raise money, she is constantly stopping in mid conversations to exclaim, "We have a state; imagine, we have a state."[9]

At one of the gatherings, a woman in attendance reflects back to a day in Boston twenty some years ago, when she was a part of Golda's group, and says, "I should never have gotten off that ship."[10]

June 11, 1948–The tide for the Israeli army has turned. The Israelí soldiers are driving the Arab armies back and out of Israel. UN truce #1 is agreed upon.

July 10, 1948–Arabs resume war

July 18, 1948–UN Truce #2

July 27, 1948–"Nation Day" (the anniversary of Herzl's

death), a parade, Israeli flags are waving, Israeli planes are flying overhead, Israeli citizens are cheering

Golda, still in the states, has received a request from Ben-Gurion to be the Minister to Soviet Russia. Friends are thrilled.
Golda is aghast. Her response, "At last we have a state. I want
to be there. I don't want to go thousands of miles away."[11] As
if banished to Siberia and the barren landscape of diplomacy
(not her forté), Golda accepts the appointment.

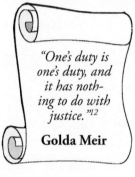

"One's duty is one's duty, and it has noth-ing to do with justice."[12]

Golda Meir

While still in New York City, Golda is in a car accident. She is hospitalized for a fractured leg and more
seriously, a number of blood clots.
Bureaucratic rumors rise up that this
is a "diplomatic illness," a means of
stalling. Ignoring the doctor's orders
for bed rest, Golda flies back to Israel
to make ready for her return to Russia.

During Golda's preparations for her trip to Russia, she will
make time for her daughter's wedding. The ceremony, in Sheyna's backyard, includes Morris and Regina. It is a poignant moment as this elder generation of pioneers, each with his or her
own story of commitment to the cause, steps back to honor
this day for their children. It is a glimpse of the future. Sarah, a
western Jew, is marrying Zacharia, a Yeminite Jew.

It is September 3, 1948 and Golda, the Minister to Soviet Russia, is ready to leave. The entourage includes the newlyweds.

For Golda, having her daughter and son-in-law be given positions within her group makes the pang of leaving her new country a little more bearable. There is no alleviation for the uncertainty of what lies ahead in the slippery diplomatic relations with Russia.

It is a twist of politics that plays to Israel's advantage, in the spring of 1948 when Andrei Gromyko (Russian representative to the UN) told the UN Security Council, "It would be unjust to deny the right of the Jewish people to realize their aspiration to establish their own state."[13] It is this Soviet support that nudged President Truman's State Department. Not wanting to be outdone, the United States rushed to acknowledge Israel on the day of their independence. Stalin's official recognition of Israel, minutes after the United States, is a ploy to get Great Britain out of the strategic region of the Middle East.

As the Israelis fly to the country of Golda's birth, the country she illegally escaped forty-two years earlier, Golda isn't reveling in a spirit of triumph. Golda is mulling over what they will find. Hebrew has been a forbidden language for its Russian citizens since the Revolution, and few synagogues are open. Decades of government persecution and the physical destruction of Jewish homes, synagogues and communities has included criminal charges for practicing Zionism. Incarceration means being sent to forced labor camps in Siberia. Golda is wondering what is left of the remnants of Russian Jews.

Arriving in Moscow, Golda will play the political game, but no one should think her diplomatic black dress, pearl necklace and hat is anything more than a costume. She will comply with the formal wear of the western world, but her public appearance includes speaking Hebrew. Someone suggests to her that she speak English. Golda responds, "But I'm not an Englishman or an American. I'm an Israeli."[14]

The Soviet officials don't allow foreigners and diplomats to mix freely with the locals–Jews or otherwise. Golda's attempt to break the ice is to have Friday evenings as an open house and invite ambassadors to drop in. Many countries have not formally recognized the State of Israel meaning their representatives cannot attend. The only people to show up are the foreign press corps. Golda, not satisfied with this superficial level of impact, extends the open house invitations to everyday Jews. It is her hope to connect with her people. It will cost her grief. It will cost Russian Jews their lives.

Any Russians displaying too much interest for the Jewish delegation suffers dire consequences. An expression is being coined on the streets of Moscow–"Golda's Prisoners."[15] For one man, known only as Hefetz, it is fatal.

Hefetz is born in Jerusalem. He leaves in 1926 to help fight the Spanish Civil War. He is wounded in Spain and escapes to Russia. Now in 1948, using stolen money, Hefetz manages to contact Golda. He is starving, cold, and in rags. Golda, remembering her own times of despair, attempts to have Hefetz granted permission to return to Israel. When the Soviets learn of Hefetz's visit to Golda, he is "severely punished." When Hefetz makes a second visit, and Golda hears about the punishment, she confronts Russian authorities and gets nowhere. Hefetz commits suicide[16]

> Russian Jews remember just forty-three years earlier the arrests in 1905. Rumors were spread by the government that the czar had granted a constitution. This ruse exposed those who wanted a constitution. Anyone seen rejoicing in the streets, was swept up in mass arrests.

Golda, attempting to reach out to her people, is sending information bulletins informing local Jews about Israel and the Israeli Embassy. Being careful to not write anything that would appear *anti-Soviet* doesn't matter. The Israelis are ordered to stop. Trying another means to mingle, Golda attends the State Jewish Theater. Golda stands in the halls during intermission, but only a few Jews dare approach her, and even then, they dare not engage in a conversation–just a comment.

Within the embassy staff, many have families in Russia and would like to use this opportunity to get in touch with them. Having no news since before the war, "Are they still alive?" remains a valid question. No one from the embassy is granted permission to travel. Even Golda will not be allowed to visit Pinsk. When the Israeli delegation requests permission for Russian Jews to emigrate they receive the same stone wall response.

At an official gathering, Golda meets the wife of the Russian Minister of Foreign Affairs, Mrs. Ivy Molotov. Mrs. Molotov is openly delighted to meet Golda and speaks in Yiddish. She tells Golda, "Yes, I am a Jew." She has heard about Golda visiting the synagogue and expresses "Jews want so much to see you." [17] This camaraderie is dangerous ground even for someone who is the wife of a high ranking government official. Mr. Molotov is unable to prevent the subsequent arrest of his wife (charges of treason), and being sent to Siberia. She is there for two years, and finally is able to return only after Stalin's death.

Golda's visits to the synagogue have not gone unnoticed by the Russian officials. For her first visit, she finds a gathering of three hundred people. After the service, the Jews are outside and they crowd around her. Golda becomes separated from her group. An elderly man whispers to Golda in Yiddish, "Don't talk to me. I'll walk ahead. You follow."[18] Arriving at Golda's hotel, he says to her in Hebrew, "Blessed are we that we have lived to see this day."[19]

A few weeks later Golda attends the synagogue to celebrate Rosh Hashanah, Jewish New Year. Golda's group is met by a crowd, over fifty thousand people. They are singing in Yiddish, "Golda, long life to you. Happy New Year!"[20] During the service, Golda is sitting in the women's gallery. Women come up and touch her and kiss her dress. Golda remembering of that day: "I am sure that not only I, but everyone who was a member of this first mission, inwardly asked forgiveness a thousand times from these Jews for having dared to doubt their spiritual strength and their Jewish ties with the whole past, present, and future of the Jewish race."[21]

After the service, when the crowds part to make way for Golda someone takes a picture of her in the throng of people. In the years to come Golda will pass people on the streets of Israel and they tell her, "We have the picture." [22]

1948, Golda Meir, Rosh Hashanah, outside the synagogue
From the Archives Department,
University of Wisconsin-Milwaukee Libraries

On that day, swept up by the crowd Golda says, "I wanted to say something, anything, to those people to let them know that I begged their forgiveness for not having wanted to come to Moscow and for not having known the strength of their ties to us. For having wondered, in fact, whether there was still a link between them and us. But I couldn't find the words."[23] Golda calls out to them in Yiddish, "Thank you for having remained Jews." She hears her words echoing as they are repeated through the crowd.[24]

Explaining this outpouring of adoration, Golda writes, "I knew that they would have showered the same love and pride on a broomstick, if it had been sent to them to represent Israel."[25] Later, Golda speaks about the risk these Jews are taking. "Arrest, torture, or Siberia is their option." Golda remembers, "it was something which shattered and overwhelmed me at the time I witnessed it and which has inspired me ever since." [26]

The next visit to the synagogue is for Yom Kippur, the Day of Atonement. Again, thousands of Russian Jews have come to the service. At the end of the service, the worshipers traditionally finish a prayer with the words, "Next year in Jerusalem." Golda says, "The words shook the synagogue as they looked up at me. It was the most passionate Zionist speech I had ever heard."[27] The centuries of their dream and desire had been accomplished.

Officers of the Red Army with their soldiers are also at the synagogue. Disturbed by this flood of veneration, the government retaliates: the Yiddish newspaper is closed down, the Yiddish theaters are shuttered, the Yiddish publishing house is closed, and books by Jewish authors are taken from the shelves of libraries. Jewish community leaders are arrested.

It doesn't matter that the Jews of Russia follow the Communist Party line. The line they cross is to have an interest in

Israel and Israelis. Russian Jews are forced to make the choice of exile and ruin or deny their identity of being a Jew. It is January 1949, and in five months there will be no Jewish organizations left in Russia.[28]

14

ALL IN A DAY'S WORK

Golda leaves Moscow on April 20, 1949. Ben-Gurion needs her to be his Minister of Labor.

Golda's new job description: *Oversee construction of public housing, road building and public works projects. Provide work and houses for incoming refugees/immigrants. Wrangle the votes for funding from her political colleagues having their own priority projects.*[1]

Internally wired to take policy to a pragmatic level, Golda is able to see the big picture and then strong arm into place the procedures that will alleviate the sufferings of masses. When someone described Golda's motive as "philanthropist," they heard Golda's swift retort to correct them, "It was because I was indignant."[2]

Her outburst of indignance will play out when she is Labor Minister. She is visiting a housing project and sees the window over the kitchen sink is above eye level. Golda exclaims, "What? Are you crazy? Are you idiots? A woman stands in the kitchen five hours cooking, and you are forcing her to see the wall and not the Sea of Galilee?"[3] The builders lower the windows. Or the contractors don't want to install indoor toilets because they assume the immigrants don't know how to use them. Golda instructs the builders that the housing is to include toilets.[4]

For this next phase of her life, Golda writes, "My seven years in the Ministry of Labor were, without doubt, the most satisfying and happiest of my life."[5] Golda fulfills her passion. "What in fact most concerned and interested me–the translation of socialist principles into the down-to-earth terminology of everyday life."[6]

Implementing an "everyday life" for the current Jewish population in Israel is challenging for a new country just finishing a war for its independence. An exacerbating factor is the tsunami of immigrants flooding in to Israel every day. The population doubles in the next two years.

The Israeli parliament lost no time in implementing the "Law of Return." The doors of Israel were now open to all Jews, anywhere in the world. Golda explains, "The period since we won our independence has been the first–for many, many centuries–during which the words "Jewish refugee" are no longer heard. There is no such thing anymore because the Jewish state is prepared to take every Jew, whether he has anything or not, whether he is a skilled worker or not, whether he is old or not, whether he is sick or not. It doesn't make a particle of difference."[7]

The first year brings at least two thousand immigrants per day. After that it is a steady stream of one thousand per day for several years. During the years 1948-1970 emigrants from Europe will total 598,375. Emigrants from Arab countries will exceed 560,000. The Israeli government will not enact any constraints on the "Law of Return." Golda is adamant: "Israel without them is not worth having."[8]

December 1, 1950, Immigration Camp
Source: Jewish National Photo Collection

Here's the challenge: One out of every three Israelis is a brand-new immigrant. These immigrants will be coming from seventy-two different lands, including; Aden, Lebanon, Syria, Iraq, North Yemen, Egypt, Libya, Tunisia, Algeria, Morocco, Greece, Yugoslavia, Soviet Union, Bulgaria, Romania, Hungary, Czechoslovakia, Poland, Sweden, Netherland, Italy, Germany, Switzerland, Belgium, France, United Kingdom, Spain, China.[9] Jews have the common bond of their faith but, what the new arrivals don't have in common is; culture, language and economics.

Over the last years, meeting the needs of the incoming trickle of illegal immigrants has been a small scale forecast for the current situation. Golda points out, "For the most part, the new immigrants come destitute, many of them broken in body and spirit. They have to be fed, clothed, given a physical examination, their sanitation needs attended to, their sick cared for. They must be given food, shelter, a roof over their heads. All in one day, the first day. Afterwards, we need schools, hospitals, work, houses, especially houses."[10] Disease is also a factor; tuberculosis, infantile paralysis, dysentery, trachoma, just to start.

When Golda arrives back from Russia there are over 200,000 people living in tents, usually more than two families per tent and probably not from the same country. By the end of her seven years as Minister of Labor, not one family will be living in a tent.

Different from the Jews who had come from Europe, thousands of the immigrants are coming from Arab and Asian countries. Most of them are not skilled workers, and they are poor. Golda believes the gap between the European Jews and the *others* can be. solved with vocational schools and education. Golda establishes training programs for 80,000 men and women and 400,000 will have jobs.[11] Over 200,000 low-income apartments are built, all with balconies.[12] (This is when Golda tells the builders to lower the kitchen windows and put toilets in the bathrooms.) When European Jews suggest that the non-European Jews not be allowed to enter Israel, or at least wait– Golda responds, "All Jews will always be welcome in Israel."[13]

Golda must also stare down her colleagues who wish to slow down the immigration rate in order to stabilize the country with a better standard of living. Golda responds, "I readily confess that I have no need for a Jewish state with a high standard of living but without a large, unlimited, Jewish immigration. I need a Jewish state for one thing only: that the gates of this state should be open without restriction to all Jews who understand what this state means for them and will want to come here in the wake of such understanding.[14]

 Knesset: The legislative branch of the Israeli government.

By May, 1949, one month into her new job, Golda has presented to the Knesset the "Myerson Plan" of 30,000 housing units to be built. By August, she has a plan in place for roads

"Let her own works praise her." **Inscribed on a brooch that Golda wears.**[16]

to be built connecting all of Israel. The "Green Public Works" program involves reforestation, terracing, and reclaiming soil along the roads. The roads, named after Golda, are called the "golden wegen." Golda uses these roads–visiting all the new housing, factories and immigrant tent camps.[15]

Refugees, before arriving, have been moving from camp to camp and country to country making their way to Israel. They encourage each other with the words, "Don't worry, our Goldie will take care of these refugees."[17] When they arrive they are met with simple food and living in a tent. Their frustrations, albeit unrealistic expectations, lead to demonstrations. Golda will hear their protest chants "bread and work."[18]

The jobs for unskilled laborers will be construction road crews or work in the orange groves. When the housing is built, it includes running water, electric and indoor plumbing. Golda asks one couple, in a new house, why did they come to Israel? The woman responds, "Because I was afraid to stay in Poland. I don't care about Zionism."[19] Golda comments to her staff as they leave, "Not one word of gratitude."[20]

Any instance of immigrants being less than grateful doesn't deter Golda's passion. She will never take this as an excuse to stop fighting for a just standard of living as a benchmark for all the immigrants. This is remarkable considering that keeping this maxim makes her very unpopular among the Jews already present. They will accuse her of being "anti-labor"

{ **Mifda: Hebrew word for "ransom" or "redemption"–a debt of honor for a man at work to help others** }

To help finance housing, food, clothing and health care the workers must agree to the rationing of their clothing and food. In order to give jobs to the thousands of new immigrants, keep a standard of self-respect and not have large scale unemployment–the established workers will need to cut back on their own hours, share jobs, and pay a mifda to the unemployment fund. Much like Golda's trip to Cyprus, she must go to the workers to garner their support for policies that ask them to sacrifice.

There is another mifda that Golda is proposing. In order to pay for the damage done by Arab riots, the *Histadrut* workers will have their pay for one day of each month, docked. A friend tells Golda, "Golda you are destroying the Histadrut. You are demanding something that is impossible."[21] As Golda tours factories, she is talking with the workers, convincing them that abiding by a mifda is the moral high ground, and their sacrifices are for the good of the country.

The suggestion is made that Golda go back to the United States and ask them for money rather than take it from workers who are themselves barely getting by, let alone getting ahead. They have waited and worked for years to have their own country, and now they still have to sacrifice? But Golda will not go and ask American Jews for this support. Yes, she will ask for money to build the country, and if needs be, to buy arms to protect the country but not money to "pay doles to the poor."[22] Ben-Gurion shares this perspective.

Not all of Golda's colleagues agree, and there is continued pressure for her to go along with their priorities to build factories and improve agriculture at the expense of bringing in immigrants. Golda holds fast to the core moral national policy–the right of return. She reminds her comrades, "The issue before us is simple and cruel; as long as we lack the courage to face it and decide "yes" or "no," unequivocally, we shall not solve it. We must answer the following question: Is there any connection between our talk in favor of immigration and our deeds for such immigration? Let me word it differently: Is there any connection between our talk and our treatment of the immigrant? Are we only for an abstract, collective immigration, numbering 100,000, 200,000, 400,000, or also for the entry of actual, flesh-and-blood immigrants, each an individual?"[23]

Golda can make these statements because she is free of self-interest. Her disregard for popularity is an unshakeable pillar that supports her constant incorruptible stance. She is unafraid of the truth and will point out any hint of self-interest in others when they try to twist decisions to their benefit for profit or politics.

Assuming Golda will include the fight for women's rights as part of her platform would be accurate, although her support is not in the traditional style. Golda brings no message of sympathy or coddling to the discussion. Doing so, would play into the argument that women need this type of support, and Golda never thinks that is true. Golda's plans include women having vocational training programs in any industry or farming. When there is a need for more workers in these positions, Golda will not return to any *traditional* positions being for men only. When asked if she feels handicapped being a woman minister she answers, "I don't know—I've never tried to be a man."[24] Ben-Gurion's famous quote about her being "the best man in my cabinet," she finds insulting and wonders why a woman would be measured against the male gender.

Golda confronts her colleagues in the Israeli Cabinet when they are discussing a series of assaults on women. Their answer is to not allow women on the streets after dark. Golda shoots back, "Men are attacking the women, not the other way around. If there is going to be a curfew, let the men be locked up, not the women."[25]

The conservative Jewish sector attempts to prevent political positions going to women and the orthodox bloc is howling because there is a bill being passed that will require women as well as men to give a one year commitment to the military. When the conservatives use religion to justify limiting the roles of women, Golda confronts them with this response, "You will not force your way of life on us."[26]

Golda shows no tolerance for any religion to be used as a means of sanctioning inequality in government policies. She will turn to her own people and say, "You will not terrorize a legislative body with demonstrations of hysterical women or by mob violence."[27] Her clear vision can detect any divergence from social justice, and she will take a straight shot at religious patriarchy. In the discussion of the military service bill, Golda asks the question, "Religious families have sons as well as daughters. If army life is degrading, why are they not concerned for the morals of their sons?"[28]

When Golda finally heads home after these long days, she will have dinner with her maid and chauffeur.

Her home is always a hub of gatherings and Golda does the cooking. From the days of living at the Kibbutz, her habit of bringing hot tea and cookies out to the men on watch continues to the men guarding her home. Golda, will sit with them, drink tea, and smoke another cigarette. She hates being alone.

Golda in her kitchen
*From the Archives Department,
University of Wisconsin-Milwaukee Libraries*

As for her children, Golda has accepted their choices to follow the desires of their heart. When Sarah decided to quit school and go to a kibbutz, Golda's only question was, "Are you going to the settlements because you want to fulfill a national mission or simply because you don't want to study?"[29] Later, Sarah will take a year of absence from the kibbutz to study English literature. To Golda's delight, Sarah stays with her. Over the years of Sarah's own growth, she has come to understand Golda's choices and says of her mother, "For such a mother it's worthwhile."[30]

For Menachem, Golda has supported his love of music. Money spent on music lessons and Golda carrying his cello to classes, when Menachem was too little, has now paid off. There are evenings Golda can sit on her balcony in her housecoat, smoking cigarettes, looking at the sea, listening to Menachem play his cello.

There will be grandchildren, and Golda will enjoy the job of grandma. When Golda is asked about her grandson the question is, "Your grandson, Gideon Meir, age seven, says that you are the best gefilte fish maker in Israel. What is your recipe?" Golda responds, "My grandson … I'm afraid he's maybe not very objective about me. I'm not very objective about him, either."[31]

For another of Golda's grandchildren, it is a different and less easy story. Menachem and his first wife Channa, have a daughter, Meira. She has Down's syndrome. At the time (1950s), this often results in the child being institutionalized. Golda and Menachem felt this to be best for the child. Channa says "no:" and keeps Meira home. Within six months after Meira is born, the parents are divorced. Golda will never have contact with Meira and never makes public mention of her. The press respects Golda's privacy. Menachem explains, "Mother didn't consider the child as her obligation in any way–especially since Channa wouldn't have anything to do with my mother."[32] Channa will explain that Golda's ignoring of Meira is due to Meira's affliction, not the divorce.

While we are on the subject of the personal side of Golda, it is clear that she is not one to fuss over her own appearance. She never uses make-up (not even on TV), never dyes the gray out of her hair, although she does use a pomade to keep any fly away strands of hair in place. She wears plain clothes, and carries with her an equally plain black handbag. An historian that will call Golda vain[33] can only support this opinion with the fact that Golda keeps her nails manicured, and before retiring for the night Golda washes and brushes her hair. This nightly ritual might be seen as a means of relaxing rather than vanity. Her Spartan appearance against anything frivolous is typical of the old guard pioneer women of that time. When other women will fuss, "I wish I were thinner." The response is, "Wish for better things."[34]

In 1951, Golda is back in the states. She receives a message that Morris has died. She immediately flies back to attend his funeral. Golda writes in her autobiography, "… my head filled with thoughts about the life we might have lived together if I had only been different. It was not a bereavement that I either could or wanted to talk about with other people, even my own family. Nor am I prepared to write about it now, except to say that although we had been apart for so long, standing at his graveside, I realized once again what a heavy price I had paid—and made Morris pay—for whatever I had experienced and achieved in the years of our separation."[35]

In this same year, Sarah is pregnant, the baby is stillborn, and there is fear for Sarah's life. Blume, Golda's mother dies. David Remez, who had been Golda's friend, lover, and confidant, also dies in 1951. Golda, as she states about Morris, keeps quiet about her personal matters and writes or discusses little of her private thoughts except to record the event.

In 1952, as Minister of Labor, Golda introduces the first national insurance bill, and declares, "no one would be neglected, no widows and orphans will hunger for bread, no people will be cast out in their old age."[36] She pushes for paid annual vacations, restrictions on night work, factory safety regulations, and protection of youth laws, old age pensions, unemployment, workers' compensation and disability insurance. Golda's support for the dual job of mother and career is seen in having mothers in government service be able to work reduced hours and yet receive the same pay. She ensures a three-month paid maternity leave given to both Arab and Jewish women, and they can't be fired from their jobs. Maternity grants are issued for women to have their babies in a hospital. [37]

In St. Louis, 1953, Golda falls and dislocates her shoulder. She continues suffering with gall bladder attacks, migraines that would take out a lesser person, and in a few years, she will be struggling with cancer. Golda is a public person, but at the time, information about her health is private. Her stays at the hospital are kept out of the press.

Throughout these beginning years, building the State of Israel for its citizens means the Arab citizens, too. Golda brings the first maternity leave check to be issued, to a new Arab mother.[38] To rebuild Arab housing and rehouse the Arabs who had been displaced by the fighting, over $28 million dollars (adjusted for the year 2013 this equals over $240 million) are allocated for this effort. [39] In 1953, the Land Acquisition Law is passed to specifically handle the Arab claims. Two-thirds of all Arab claims are paid compensation, given back their property, or given other property in its place. This never happens for the Jews in any Arab country. Golda also mentions in her biography, "and not one of them was asked to a take a loyalty oath before his claim was honored."[40] For Golda and most Jews, it is a point of pride to show the rest of the world that Jews and Arabs can live peacefully together.

It takes almost two thousand years to fulfill the dream–the rebirth of Israel. Golda never gives up her hope to have peace with the Arabs. The next chapter will challenge her resolve.

15

REVEREND GOLDA

Golda's career path:
Minister to Soviet Russia–1948-1949
Minister of Labor–1949-1956
Foreign Minister–1956-1966
Prime Minister–1969-1974
Did anyone make a joke and call her Reverend Golda?

Golda has been serving as Minister of Labor for the last seven years. She is enjoying this niche and not looking to change. It doesn't matter. Ben-Gurion asks her to fill the post of Foreign Minister (similar to the US Secretary of State). She must have groaned as she said, "I don't want to go."[1] Ben-Gurion has also "requested" that his cabinet members hebraicize their last names. Golda Meyerson becomes Golda "Meir" meaning "illuminate."

Many of Ben-Gurion's people agree with Golda and don't think she is a good choice for the post of Foreign Minister. Golda's style is informal and she is loathe to oblige protocol. Ben-Gurion gives his response to any doubts saying, "She's the best man in my Cabinet."[2] Golda packs up her belongings and moves to the foreign minister's official residence. It is June of 1956.

One month following Golda becoming Foreign Minister, Egypt "nationalizes" the Suez Canal and blocks passage of international ships. This action affects the economies of major western countries and causes their alarm bells to go off. Britain, France and Israel start planning a push back. All the while Israel has been combating continual Arab terrorist raids. In one month alone, October of 1956, the murders include; a mother and daughter, four Israeli archeologists, a tractor driver, three watchmen, six students, and five young Israelis.[3]

Along with the decision of waterways being blocked, Egyptian President Nasser abolishes civil liberties for Jews and 1,000 Egyptian Jews are arrested, 500 Jewish businesses are seized, Jewish bank accounts confiscated, while Jewish lawyers, engineers, doctors and teachers are not allowed to work in their professions. Thousands of Jews are ordered to leave the country but only with one suitcase and a small amount of cash.[4]

On the Egyptian radio they are broadcasting, "Weep, O Israel, because Egypt's Arabs have already found their way to Tel Aviv. The day of extermination draws near. There shall be no more complaints or protests to the United Nations or the Armistice Commission. There will be no peace on the borders because we demand the death of Israel."[5]

> Fedayeen: Arab terror squads recruited and trained by Egyptian army officers. Their objective is to shoot any Jewish man, woman or child and blow up any bridges, schools, buses, reservoirs, railroad tracks and wedding day celebrations. During the 1950s hundreds of Israelis are killed.[6]

President Nasser of Egypt states: "Egypt has decided to dispatch her heroes, the disciples of Pharaoh and the sons of Islam and they will cleanse the land of Palestine... There will be no peace on Israel's border because we demand vengeance, and vengeance is Israel's death."[7] Egypt is also amassing weapons along the Israeli border and terrorist attacks are encouraged into Israel from the Egyptian controlled Gaza strip.

Golda responses to Nasser's proclamations, "Peace will come when Nasser loves his own children more than he hates the Israelis."[8]

Golda explains her government's firm reaction to Nasser's remarks, "We take what Nasser says seriously. We must."[9] She expounds, "There was a man in a Czarist Russian village who always knew in advance which night the horses were going to be stolen—because he was the thief. When Nasser warns that there's going to be a war with Israel, how does he know? He's the thief."[10]

The Suez War, also known as the Action in Sinai, will start Oct 26, 1956 and includes Britain and France. Within the coming weeks, the Israelis push the Egyptians from the Gaza Strip and off the Sinai. By November Ben-Gurion is announcing to the Knesset their victory.

International shuffling for a ceasefire with Egypt includes France, Britain, US and the Soviets. Played out against the backdrop of Cold War intrigues, Golda's effort as Foreign Minister is to make sure the UN understands that the Sinai doesn't become a base again for Egypt's armed aggression against Israel. As part of the pressure on Israel to withdraw their troops, the UN promises to watch over the Sinai with UN troops.

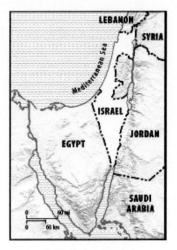

**Israeli borders after
Sinai Campaign, 1956**
*http://www.mythsandfacts.org/,
Eli E. Hertz, Date accessed 2014*

**Israeli borders
after withdrawal, 1957**

Golda, as Foreign Minister, is the one who must go before
the UN and agree to the Israeli withdrawal from the Sinai. She
remembers, "To stand before the United Nations and say we
will withdraw–that was not my finest hour."[11] In her speech
to the General Assembly, Golda maintains her usual frank assessment. Here are a few of the points she relays: "For eight
years, Israel has been subjected to the unremitting violence of
physical assault, … intent to destroy our country economi-
cally through blockade, through boycott, and through lawless
interference with the development of our natural resources.
… Since 1948 my country has had no respite from hostile acts
and loudly proclaimed threats of destruction."[12] "We desire
nothing more than peace, but we cannot equate peace merely
with an apathetic readiness to be destroyed. If hostile forces
gather for our proposed destruction, they must not demand
that we provide them with ideal conditions for the realization
of their plans. Nor should it be permitted that the sincere
desire for peace shared by so many, should be used as shelter

for such preparations."[13] "The Arab states unilaterally enjoy the 'rights of war,' Israel has the unilateral responsibility of keeping the peace."[14]

Golda would take little comfort in the credit she will later be given. "At crucial moments when the threat of sanctions (against Israel) loomed, the refusal of the foreign minister to be bludgeoned or persuaded by the fears of American friends had been decisive in preserving some, if not all of the gains of the military campaign."[15]

After Israel withdraws and the UN tells Israel's Arab neighbors "To desist from raids across the armistice lines in the neighboring territory"[16]–gangs under Egyptian direction, continue to wreck havoc and raids within Israel. President Nasser tells them, "You have proven, that you are heroes upon whom our entire country can depend. The spirit with which you enter the land of the enemy must be spread."[17] In spite of full cooperation of Israel to withdraw troops, there is no compliance by Egypt.

When the sand settles, the Egyptian Army marches back in to the Sinai and declares martial law, releases all the fedayeen from prison, and fires every official (or they are taken out and shot) who had not resigned when the Israelis came. The Egyptians announce they will punish every Arab who collaborated with the Israelis during the four months' occupation. It is one more example of the P.S. on the Russian poster.

The next few years, the Israelis experience continued Arab raids coming from the Egyptian and Jordanian borders. The Syrians are bombarding settlements in northern Galilee from the area known as the Golan Heights. There are massive military buildups again in all the Arab neighboring states and Egypt's troops are back in the Sinai. The dogs of war are forming their packs again at Israel's borders.

As Foreign Minister, Golda's job includes explaining the needs of Israel to the world audience. The list starts with, secure borders, defense against Egypt, Syria and Jordan's continual infiltrating and attacks, and free passage through the Suez Canal that Egypt had closed. Golda continues to express Israel's readiness to negotiate face-to-face with Arab neighbors who refuse direct negotiations with Israel.

It's hard to imagine the shriek of injustice against Israel if the Israeli government claimed they will not recognize their Arab neighbors. In reference to the twisted one way streets of the UN Golda remarks, "We are members of the United Nations; so are the Arab states. It seems to me that the United Nations should make the kind of situation impossible in which one member state does not recognize the existence of another."[18] The UN, bowing to Arab belligerence, is seen in the aforementioned quote of the UN to the Arab countries to stop raiding. Rather than using the word, Israel, the UN uses of the words "neighboring teritory".

A Wikipedia search of 'States, that have never recognized Israel, lists; Iran, Iraq, Kuwait, Lebanon, Libya, Qatar, Saudi Arabia, Syria, United Arab Emirates, Yemen.

Normally, neighboring countries form natural alliances because of geography and history. The Foreign Minister is responsible to pursue the solutions of their common social/economic interests while developing political bonds and support within organizations like the UN. Israel's Arab neighbors refuse any bridge and will not attend any meeting where Israelis are seated. So, Golda goes to Africa.

In her usual pragmatic style, Golda is intent on creating practical assistance to the African countries who are struggling to come out from under years of colonialism. Golda acknowledges that these efforts will help to garner UN votes for issues important to Israel, but more importantly, Israel freely gives valuable insights from its own experience of developing as a poor state. Golda says, "Tell them about the mistakes we made. So they won't repeat them."[19] When the Israeli teams arrive, they come not only to teach but to pitch in and help. One African's comment is, "For the first time I've seen a white man work with his hands."[20]

Over the next few years, Israel sends thousands of experts to Africa: engineers, teachers, and doctors, specialists in agriculture, sanitation, port management, social welfare, irrigation, transport, conservation cooperatives, and civil administration. The Israelis also set up special courses in Israel. African government leaders and students who want to study cooperative farming or road construction can come to Israel to live and learn. Many of these students can attend because of Israeli funded fellowships.

Golda will continue to offer her country's assistance to Arab neighbors. "We've sent our experts in agriculture and building to over eighty countries, and we'd be more than happy to share our knowledge with those around us. God knows– and the people in our neighboring countries know–how much they need this help. They have the same problems we have, the same lack of water, the same desert, exactly the same."[21]

 Where other countries might have "helped" the developing countries by letting their own citizens set up companies and then "give" jobs to the locals, the Israelis allow very few of their citizens to go to Africa and make a profit for themselves.

Golda is not prone to the posturing and politics expected of a Foreign Minister. Her work in Africa, having a means
to implement tangible projects, is a saving grace for Golda's
personality. "The programs with Africa were a logical extension of principles in which I had always believed, the principles that have a real purpose to my life."[22] Golda will log over
100,000 miles during the next few years as she visits, Ghana,
Nigeria, the Ivory Coast, Sierra Leone, and Liberia. Her informal, motherly approach leads a Nigerian official to say to her,
"Your Foreign Ministry is mislabeled "foreign." To us it is a
Friendly Ministry."[23]

1960, Golda Meir dancing with Mrs. Jomo Kenyatta in Kenya

*From the Archives Department,
University of Wisconsin-Milwaukee Libraries*

This friendship translates to being made an honorary chief for one tribe and "Grand Officer" for another. She becomes a member of a secret women's society, parties are given in her honor and they dance the *hora*. When there is a famine in 1962, Golda sends shipments of goods. When Belgium leaves the Congo, Golda sends in Israeli doctors, nurses, and the Israeli Army medical corps to help with the shortage of medical services. When Golda is sitting under a mango tree in Ghana, little girls come out to comb her hair. When Golda is sitting at the General Assembly for the UN, African delegates will line up to shake her hand.

Headlines in African newspapers read: "Israel Understands Us" or "Israel is like Us."[24] Golda can chastise the students (on scholarship) coming to Israel from Africa when she finds out they have servants to clean their room. Golda criticizes their laziness. The students concede. This isn't political. This is personal. She is making friends; sharing Israel's learning experience and encouraging their own self-confidence to not have the downcast look of the beholden. The number of countries having Israeli diplomats in Africa rises from 1 to 30 within five years. Across Africa, baby girls are being named, Golda.

A country she doesn't visit, in spite of an invitation from the area Jews, is South Africa. Because of apartheid, Golda will not go. When supportive resolutions for South Africa come up in the UN, Israel will vote against it.

In 1963, Golda is attending Zambia's independence celebrations. The dignitaries are invited on a trip across the border into Rhodesia (what is now known as Zimbabwe) to visit the Victoria Falls, twice the height of Niagara Falls. This is a glorious occasion until they get to the border crossing where the police tell the whites and blacks to form separate lines to show their passports. Golda tells them, "No, thank you. I can do without the falls."[25]

Interference from Arab nations is affecting Israel's interactions with Africa. In 1955, there is a conference of Asian and African nations. Israel, as one of those nations, is expecting to be invited. Arab states threaten to boycott the conference if Israel participates. Conceding to Arab wishes, Israel is not invited.

Arab opinion continues to pressure Muslim countries such as Pakistan and Indonesia, to not open diplomatic relations with Israel. The political squeeze is on the African countries to kick the Israelis out. By 1973, almost all of the thirty African states that had developed ties with Israel and benefited from Israeli's support will cave in to the strong arm tactics of the Muslim "brothers." The African countries sever ties with Israel.

Golda has years of experience addressing the UN. This time she is standing before the UN Security Council to answer charges of "illegality" brought against Israel by the government of Argentina. Argentina feels they have had their rights violated. Here's why:

One of the architects of the Holocaust, Adolf Eichmann, a former SS Lieutenant Colonel for Hitler, has been living freely in Argentina. In 1960, Israelis discover his whereabouts, and although Eichmann is unwilling, he is taken to Israel to stand trial. Eichmann is found guilty and in the only death sentence ever handed out by an Israeli court, Eichmann is hanged.

Golda explains, "I am absolutely convinced that only the Israelis were entitled to try Eichmann on behalf of world Jewry, and I am deeply proud that we did so."[26] (Would the United States have tolerated charges that we had no right to kill Bin Laden?)

Foreign Minister Golda works an 18 hour day. She is able to accomplish the successful negotiating of tariff concessions that are financially beneficial to Israel and loans through joining the European Common Market. The head of the Economic Desk writes, "Without Golda's hard work and skill, we would never have gotten such an agreement."[27]

Trying to keep up with this pace, Golda's chief of staff suggests that she take a vacation. Golda asks, "Why? Do you think I'm tired?" "No," he replies, "but I am." Golda responds, "So you take a vacation!"[28]

Golda's tough persona has lead to suggestions that she will hold a grudge at the expense of her people. It should be remembered that, while she is Foreign Minister, diplomatic relations with Germany, less than twenty years after the Holocaust, are established. Thousands of Israelis are protesting the decision. Golda acknowledges the emotional struggle of her people, "This means for every Israeli a debate between the head and the heart."[29]

Meeting the German Ambassador, Rolf Pauls, Golda warns him, "You have a most difficult task before you. This is a country made up, to a large extent, of the victims of the Holocaust. There is hardly a family that does not live with nightmare recollections of the crematoria, of babies used as targets for Nazi bullets, of Nazi "scientific" experiments. You cannot expect a warm reception. Even the women who will wait at table, if you ever come to me for a meal, have Nazi numbers tattooed on their arms."[30] Golda will later describe Pauls as "one of Israel's staunchest and best friends."[31]

Golda's tenure also includes improving relations with the United States.

Golda Meir with Eleanor Roosevelt, UN 1956
*From the Archives Department,
University of Wisconsin-Milwaukee Libraries*

A woman that Golda does reach toward, and the woman's hand is likewise extended, is Eleanor Roosevelt. When Golda is in New York City, she has lunch with Eleanor. They are informal, friendly and simple. They lack airs but not authority. Driven to fix the injustices of the world, they push themselves and anyone around them to get things done. Both Golda's and Eleanor's staff could use a replacement shift to take over when their "boss" is still going strong. Each of their staffs has asked their lady boss, "Why do you keep going?" and the answer is an echo of each other. Golda and Eleanor have both been heard to say, "They expect me."[32] [33]

Golda describes Eleanor, "Her interest is human beings, her hobby is human beings, her preoccupation is human beings, and her every thought is for human beings…"[34] And Eleanor says of Golda, "a woman one cannot help but deeply respect and deeply love."[35]

One of Golda's achievements as Foreign Minister is to shift singular support for buying arms from France to include the United States. President Kennedy publicly states, "Madame Foreign Minister, I wish to tell you, I'm aware of your problems, and the United States has the willingness and capability to assist you if attacked." Golda was impressed by his words and later said, "I felt that we were talking to a friend."[36]

Kennedy never comes through with supporting the promise. So later when he says, "Mrs. Meir, nothing will happen to Israel. We are committed to you." Golda replies, "Mr. President, I believe you one hundred percent. I just want to be sure we're still there by the time you come to honor your commitment."[37]

Golda Meir and President John F. Kennedy, December 1962
From the Archives Department,
University of Wisconsin-Milwaukee Libraries

Later Golda hears an overly dramatic rendition of her appeal to President Kennedy for arms to defend Israel. She responds, "If I had spoken to Kennedy so beautifully, I would have gotten more arms."[38]

In the early 1960s, Golda is diagnosed with lymphoma. She is in and out of the hospital for pneumonia, phlebitis, kidney stones, cardiovascular complications, migraine headaches, cancer and collapsing from exhaustion. Her battle with cancer will not become public knowledge until after her death.

In 1965, Golda gives her notice to retire from the position of Foreign Minister. On her last day in January 1966, she rides home on the bus.

Golda Meir Collection,

From the Archives Department,
University of Wisconsin-Milwaukee Libraries

16
MADAME PRIME MINISTER

"If we are still alive, it is because of the price we paid and the greater price we were prepared to pay. But we don't want to raise our grandchildren to prepare for another war.[1]
Golda Meir

To untangle the amalgamation of wars, the following list lines up Golda's position during the time of each war occurring in the first 25 years of Israel's existence. If the war information starts to feel like a violent rendition of the movie "Groundhog Day," there is a reason for that. The scenario, along with the key players and the causes keep repeating themselves.

Minister to Soviet Russia–1948-1949	1948–War for Independence
Minister of Labor–1949-1956	1950s–Fedayeen, Muslim terrorist attacks
Foreign Minister–1956-1966	1956–Suez War
Sec.-Gen., Mapai Party 1966-1968	1967–Six Day War
Prime Minister–1969-1974	1968-1970 War of Attrition
	1972–Munich Olympic Massacre
	1973–Yom Kippur War

As you see in the above list, Golda's retirement after her Foreign Minister position, doesn't last but a few months. From

1966 through 1968 Golda serves as Secretary-General for the Mapai Party (offshoot of the Labor Zionists) that supports Prime Minister Levi Eshkol.

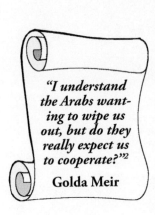

"I understand the Arabs wanting to wipe us out, but do they really expect us to cooperate?"[2]

Golda Meir

In 1967, the Israelis have been weathering Arab raids in the south and east from the Egyptian and Jordanian borders. From the Golan Heights, the Syrians are bombarding settlements in the north. The *déjà vu* feeling of the pre-Suez War story line is a reality as reports come in of military buildups along Israel's borders, Egypt moving troops into the Sinai desert, and a blockade on waterways. UN peacekeeping forces are kicked out and an Egyptian/Jordanian military alliance is signed. Nasser's threat that he will attack Israel is backed up with a line of tanks.

Israel makes the decision to risk world condemnation with a preemptive strike rather than risk losing thousands of lives of their people when Arabs strike first.

June 5, 1967 starts what will be called the Six Day War. The Israeli Defense Forces (IDF) must face three fronts: the Egyptians in the south, the Jordanians in the east and the Syrians from the Golan Heights in the north.

On the third day of the war, Israeli troops free Jerusalem. For the first time in nineteen years, Jews can visit the Western Wall (Wailing Wall). Golda is en route to the airport, for another fund raising trip to the states, but she stops first at the Western Wall.

Israeli soldier at the Western Wall, 1967
(No credits listed) www.thecuttingedgenews.com

Golda recalls, "I went to the Wall together with some soldiers. There in front of it stood a plain wooden table with some
submachine guns on it. Uniformed paratroopers wrapped in
prayer shawls clung so tightly to the wall that it seemed impossible to separate them from it. They and the Wall were one.
Only a few hours earlier, they had fought furiously for the liberation of Jerusalem and had seen their comrades fall for its
sake. Now, standing before the Wall, they wrapped themselves
in prayer shawls and wept, and I too, took a sheet of paper,
wrote the word "shalom" on it and pushed it into a cranny
of the Wall, as I had seen the Jews do so long ago. As I stood
there, one of the soldiers (I doubt that he knew who I was)
suddenly put his arms around me, laid his head on my shoulder, and we cried together. I suppose he needed the release and

comfort of an old woman's warmth, and for me it was one of the most moving moments of my life."[3]

Golda explains,

"According to the 1947 UN resolution, Jerusalem was supposed to be internationalized. Maybe only a Jew, or a non-Jew who knows the Bible well, understands what it means to have a Jewish state without Jerusalem. **But we accepted.** *(author emphasis) What happened to this holy city? It was shelled by the Arabs. Not one single power in the world to whom the city is holy—not one—lifted a finger to defend it from the shells. (referring to the siege of Jerusalem 1947/1948) We were the only ones who did. But the Arab Legion in 1948 was stronger than we were in this area, and they occupied the Old City.*

"Every single Jew who remained alive was thrown out; the only people who could not go to their holy places were the Jews. We couldn't go to the synagogue which has been there for centuries. Who worried about it? Did anybody say: But look, in this place there is the Mosque, there are the Christian holy places, there are also Jewish holy places; how is it that Jews are not allowed to go to their holy places? Did it give anybody a sleepless night? Are Jewish holy places less holy than Moslem holy places?"[4]

As a small measure of comparison for non-Jewish people: Tell Catholics that visits to the Vatican are for Protestants only. Tell the British they can't ring Big Ben. Tell a Texan he can't touch the Alamo. For the Jewish people to be denied, by the Arabs, visiting Old Jerusalem and the Western Wall is denying them a two thousand year old foundation of their Jewish structure and spirit.

Golda leaves the Western Wall and by the time her plane touch-es down in New York City, the Six Day War is a done deal. An audience of 18,000 at Madison Square Garden is waiting to hear her speak. She makes no stop at the hotel to freshen up, no quick nap to relieve jet lag, and combing her hair can wait. She tells an ecstatic audience these sober words; "Again, we won a war–the third in a very short history of independence. The last thing Israelis want is to win wars. We want peace."[5]

She uses the opportunity to prepare the audience and diplo-mats for what is to come: Israel will be pressured again to make concessions to the Arabs and withdraw to pre 1967 borders without the assurance of peace. Golda reminds them, "Is there anybody who can honestly bid the Israelis to go home before a real peace? Is there anyone who wants us to begin training our ten-year-olds for the next war? You say no. I am sure that every fair-minded person in the world will say no, but–forgive my im-pertinence–most important of all the Israelis say no." [6]

At the end of the Six Day War, the northern villages are free of Syrian shelling and Israeli or Israeli bound ships have passage through the Straits of Tiran. Jerusalem is reunified and under Israel's authority. Golda later visits the Golan Heights and sees the Russian-built Syrian bunkers connected with underground networks of tunnels, dormitories for officers, supply rooms and ammunitions. From these enclaves in the depths of the mountain, Syrian gunners have been shooting at Israeli farmers for nineteen years.[7]

{ Within Israel, the majority of Muslim citizens support the defense of their country during the Six Day War. They volunteer as blood donors and replace the laborers who are called up to the front. }

Ceasefire Lines after the Six Day War, 1967
http://www.mythsandfacts.org/, **Eli E. Hertz, Date accessed 2014**

Israel, agrees to the pre-1967 borders

Israel will agree to pre-1967 borders in hopes of a peace agreement that will be enforced. In spite of this concession, the Arabs have the Khartoum Summit Conference the following month and make this statement, "No peace with Israel, no negotiations with Israel and no recognition of Israel"[8]

The matter of Arab refugees, the living casualties of the Arab wars against Israel, continues to be a matter of contention. After the Suez War in 1956, Golda had wondered how it is that Israel is capable of absorbing Jewish refugees, hundreds of thousands from Arab lands, and yet Arabs refuse to absorb the Arab refugees from Palestine or allow the land of Transjordan (now called Jordan), taken from the region of Palestine, to be used for these refugees.[9]

After the Six Day War, Golda continues to wonder, "For nineteen years, from 1947 to 1967, the Palestinians were on the West Bank (of the Jordan River), which was administered by Jordan from the Eastern Bank, which was Jordan, and on the Gaza Strip, which was administered by Egypt, I would like to understand why there was no Palestinian entity at that time, why there was no Palestinian people? Why did they not set up a state of their own? The vast majority of Palestinians were on the Eastern and Western Banks. In Jordan, they became Jordanian citizens, were elected to parliament, and served as prime ministers and foreign ministers. If they didn't like the monarchy, why didn't they establish a republic? If they did not like the name "Jordan," why didn't they call it Palestine?"

As Foreign Minister Golda asks: "Why did the West Bank Palestinians accept ... annexation [by Jordan] ... without an uprising of explosives and mines? Why did they awaken as a Palestinian entity only after the Six-Day War?"[10]

In spite of the continued armed conflicts, wars and invasions, Golda still hopes for improved relations with her neighbors. "It will be a great day when ... the young Jew from this side of the Jordan (river) on his farm will cross the Jordan, not with tanks, not with planes, but with tractors and with the hand of friendship as between a farmer and farmer, as between a human being and human being. A dream? I am sure it will come true."[11]

The dream is tougher to come true when Russia continues to support Arab intransigence with arms deals and uses their UN Security Council votes to veto any efforts that would resolve the Arab refugee problems. Golda, while speaking at the UN, will confront the Russians. Addressing the UN, she is no longer labeled an "observer." Nor is she just a spokesperson for the Zionist cause. In fact, her office is higher than Foreign Minister.

Golda is about to be voted Prime Minister of Israel. She will be the first female head of state to rule in a Western nation. Long before Margaret Thatcher, Hillary Clinton, or Angela Merkel, entered the male dominated arena of politics, Golda has weathered greater storms; the survival of her people, the survival of her country. Golda is the original titleholder of the designation "Iron Lady."

On February 26, 1969, Golda is in a car on her way to Tel Aviv. News on the radio is announcing Israel's Prime Minister Eshkol has died of a heart attack. Golda tells her driver to turn the car around and return to Jerusalem.

The Mapai Party (Labor Party) is factious. Golda, seen as the "consensus candidate," is asked to run for the office of Prime Minister. She is seventy-one years old. At Eshkol's funeral, Golda is in tears. She later explains, "I didn't know whether I was crying for Eshkol or for me."[12] Golda writes, "I only knew that now

1969, Golda when informed that she is the next Prime Minister

From the Archives Department, University of Wisconsin- Milwaukee Libraries

I would have to make decisions every day that would affect the lives of millions of people–that is why I cried."[13]

The final tally for Golda to be Prime Minister, 293 in favor, 33 against, and 17 abstentions is clearly a vote of confidence. One month after the vote, Golda's approval rating in Israel is 61%. Within three more months it is 89.9%. Golda has hardly named her cabinet let alone accomplished what would garner such admiration from her countrymen.

Fueling the Israeli euphoria and the exuberant adoration of Golda are the victories of fighting for their independence, fending off Arab terrorist attacks, winning the Suez War and most recently, the tour de force victory of the Six Day War. Having beaten "Goliath," the Israelis relish a "David" persona that includes the irreverent flair of their new leader being a witty grandmother, smoking her cigarettes and wearing sensible shoes.

"Don't be so humble–you're not that great."

Golda Meir

From the Archives Department,
University of Wisconsin-Milwaukee Libraries

Golda's no nonsense exterior plays out as one observer notes, "She runs her Cabinet like a frontline officer, thumping the table for order, and making blunt and rapid decisions. She listens to everyone, but she interrupts if they ramble. She has an open mind, but it's like arguing before a judge. When she makes a decision, it's made."[14]

Golda's style disarms diplomats and the press. She tells a visiting senator to sit down while she cooks him some breakfast. Her maid and driver are having lunch with Golda along with Katherine Graham, the publisher of the *Washington Post*. Golda asks Katherine, "How is your mother?"[15]

Her quick wit continues to catch headlines and make for great stories. In her first international press conference as Prime Minister a journalist asks, "When your appointment was first mooted, you said you'd be a stopgap. Do you expect to be a stopgap?" Golda responds, "Did I say I was a stopgap?" Journalist, "You didn't, but others did." Golda replies, "They should be asked the question."[16]

Golda is the guest of honor for a dinner, at the Brooklyn Museum, in New York City. In the Grand Hall, with the backdrop of priceless paintings, Golda is assuring the museum curator, "I promise not to stand in front of any work of art, in case I get shot."[17] Notables, like Billy Graham, ask Golda her secret of Israel's success when helping Africa. Golda tells him, "We go there to teach, not to preach."[18]

Pithy comments include the politics of the Soviets. She explains, "We don't exactly regard the Soviet Union as our staunchest friend. And you can consider this an understatement."[19] In fact she particularly skewers the Russians when she hears of new Soviet arms being delivered to Egypt. Golda exclaims, "I am especially impressed when we are told that a partner to the search for peace in the area is the Soviet Union, since its contribution to peace in the Middle East has been, thus far, outstanding."[20] Golda can respect the political finagling between the US and the Soviets although she explains, "Not at our expense."[21]

Israelis are also enjoying postwar growth frenzy in their economy. Aside from the rewards of their own industrious efforts, continued donations to Israel Bonds and the United Jewish Appeal provides jobs and makes possible the building of hospitals, schools and universities.

One cloud around this silver lining is the need to keep buying arms. There is no relief from conflicts with the neighboring Arabs. In September 1968, Egyptians initiate the War of Attrition. Localized fighting continues over the next few years, along the banks of the Suez Canal. The skirmishes, sometimes escalating to a full-scale battle, will cause the death of 1,424 Israelis [22] and approximately 5,000 Arabs (This is an approximate number from various sources. Official figures from Arabs were never disclosed.) Hostilities end in 1970 when Egypt and Israel accept a renewed cease-fire along the Suez Canal.

Social clashes within Israel are also on the increase. New immigrants are impatient for an increased standard of living and have little tolerance for Golda's egalitarian beliefs. The ultra-orthodox Jewish sect continue to be aghast at anyone driving a car on the Sabbath, females at the beach wearing bikinis, and the fact that the leader of Israel, the Prime Minister, is a woman.

With years of practice, Golda knows how to perform on the world stage. She keeps up her visits to the United States that now includes a yearly shopping trip to Washington for more arms. The House Foreign Affairs Committee applauds as she enters their chamber, and speaking at the National Press Club,

Golda is greeted with a standing ovation. Her message to the world Jewry, keeping them integrated to Israel is, "It's our Israel. We work together. It is not just a figure of speech when we say we have a partnership. … And we won't let you people down. That we promise."[23]

1969, Golda visiting her grade school in Milwaukee
From the Archives Department,
University of Wisconsin-Milwaukee Libraries

Golda's tie with America includes a visit to her elementary school in Milwaukee. Remembering her awe of the five story "skyscraper" in Milwaukee is now a chuckle. When she travels back to New York City, the mayor tells Golda, "Madam Prime Minister, New York is yours."[24]

The UN is having a twenty-five year anniversary celebration. Golda has been asked to speak. What a contrast from so many times she sat on the sidelines as other countries debated what will happen to her people. What hasn't changed is Golda. Her pioneer pragmatic spirit is in full force. As Golda walks to the podium, the audience hears the solid sound of her black down to earth shoes, they see she is wearing a plain blue suit and her hair, pulled back in a bun, is the same style since her days at the kibbutz.

In her address to the UN, Golda acknowledges the strides toward international order by the UN, although, she doesn't succumb to any sentimental rhetoric. Her laser vision that zaps injustice in midair is still heard in her candid comments. Here are some excerpts from her speech:

"Mr. President, the whole Middle East is a dramatic demonstration of the emergence of peoples into national independence. Once the domain of colonial powers, it is today an area inhabited entirely by independent and sovereign countries ... Unfortunately, the Middle East has for twenty-two years been the scene for the cynical flouting of solemn agreements. International order, the integrity of the United Nations itself, depends upon the scrupulous observance of international obligations. Unless the members of the august body respect the sanctity of agreements, no treaties can be binding and no pacts can be maintained. ... Any member state that disregards ... agreed covenants imperils the peace as well as the United Nations. For this reason ... let me recall the sad record of broken covenants in the Middle East. From the initial violation of the Charter of the United Nations by the concerted Arab invasion of the new state of Israel to the present day, the sequence of events follows the same disastrous line of agreements made and instantly broken.

The Arab states violated the armistice agreements of 1949, they nullified the arrangements concluded in 1957, they unilaterally destroyed the cease-fire resolution of 1967 by embarking on a "war of attrition" against Israel, and now Egypt is undermining the American peace initiative by flagrantly violating the cease-fire standstill agreement.

"Despite what has happened, we still trust that, for the sake of all our peoples, the Arab leadership will join

*one day in guiding our area from the present turmoil to
the horizons of peace.*

*"No people is an island. We are bound to each
other by the problems of our region, our world. We can
make of these ties a curse or a blessing.*

"Each nation, each land must decide."[25]

Golda quietly leaves the podium with no fanfare or response to the thunderous applause.

The UN applause doesn't translate to holding countries accountable. Until terrorism strikes closer to home, continued reports of carnage in Israel are met with a yawn of western world indifference. A wake-up call for the United States won't be until September 11, 2001.

Marie Syrkin, Golda's biographer, records this personal explanation of Golda's impact as a speaker long before becoming Prime Minister. "I had no conception of the moral force which

she represented. I permit myself to write personally because it seems the most direct way of communicating the impression she made. She became the spokesman of Palestine's struggle, not because of superior eloquence–Palestine teemed with orators as any party conclave could demonstrate–but because of temperament and character, a union of intellectual directness and moral elevation which so desperate a cause required."[26]

*From the Archives Department,
University of Wisconsin-Milwaukee Libraries*

An associate of Golda's said, "The woman radiated force. She radiated authority and strength and conviction ... Golda was undoubtedly an example of superiority of the spirit, of the mind over the body. Otherwise there's no explanation for how she carried on."[27]

Golda's pace continues to be 18 hour days, and the staff is still waiting for her to take a vacation. Her burden of ill health, while constantly smoking cigarettes, includes cancer treatments every Monday. She rarely cracks under pressure; however, family can be her Achilles' heel. On one occasion her tight schedule might preclude her going to the airport with Sheyna to meet their sister Clara coming in from the states. Golda throws her ashtray and screams at her two aides, one of them being her close personal assistant, Lou Kader.

If a quick exam is done of all great leaders, similar outbursts occur. Considering the perplexity and diverse number of concerns, combined with understanding the impact of their decisions, the term "weight of responsibility" should be measured in tons. Golda comes back to both of her staff and apologizes.

In January of 1970, Golda reviews a report on the state of the country. Harvests have improved 50 to 100 percent, and 2,250,000 new trees have been planted. Road systems have been repaired with more construction underway. Seventeen new bus routes are added for villages. Free textbooks for all government schools are available. (It is interesting to note: the text and examples that were in Arab books are kept the same except for examples that encouraged hatred–e.g. *If there are eleven Israelis and four are killed, how many are left?*) New schools are built, seventeen vocational training schools start that include free food allotments and daily allowances for students. Twenty additional rural clinics, two new mobile clinics, ninety-one government clinics, and twenty-three mother-child welfare stations are up and running. Free immunizations are given to children and adults against smallpox, infantile paralysis, dysentery, typhoid, typhus and cholera. (This service is free for any residents of Jordan or other Arab lands) Kids who only knew barbed wire fences are going to summer camps.[28]

For the Arab citizens of Israel, their death rate has dropped from 20 per 1,000 to 5.9, one of the lowest in the world. Israel has a higher standard of living than any other Middle Eastern country. This standard includes: education, housing, health, and landownership, electricity, running water, along with political and individual freedoms. Arabs and Jews have the same benefits, equal pay, and can maintain their own culture and traditions. Hebrew and Arabic are the two official languages in Israel.[29]

"It is easier to make a revolution than to uphold the values for which it was made."

Golda Meir[30]

Golda would like to keep with the struggle of upholding the values of Israel. The Arabs keep bringing her back to war. The War of Attrition has been going on for years and there is evidence of a military buildup again by their neighbor, Syria. First Golda must face the 1972 Munich Massacre.

It's September 5, 1972, Israeli athletes are taken hostage by a Palestinian Muslim group called "Black September." The egregious lack of security and gross mishandling of the hostage situation, intentional or otherwise, results in all eleven Israeli Olympic athletes being murdered by the terrorist group.

Golda, as Prime Minister, appeals to other countries to condemn these criminal acts. For the last several years, there has been no strategy of confrontation from the international community against this increasing tradition of terrorism. Golda has said, "This thing has spread like an infectious disease the world over. Can it be possible that governments ... should acquiesce in this state of affairs on the presumption that they will emerge unscathed? Is it possible that there is no power in the entire world, in dozens of countries in Europe, North America, and elsewhere ... to put an end to this?"[31] Aghast, Golda must watch the Israeli athletes, now blindfolded hostages, become victims to Muslim terrorists in Germany.

Aside from a discussion about failed security, and bumbled rescue attempts, here is the message of indifference that follows:

On September 6th a memorial service is held in the Olympic Stadium. The Olympic Flag is flown at half-mast. The rest of the flags, for the competing nations, are also flown at half-mast. Ten Arab nations object and their flags are raised back up. In the following days, the Olympic Games continue and at a sports event, the crowds are honking noisemakers and waving flags. Some spectators unfurl a banner that reads, "17 Dead, Already Forgotten?"[32] Security officers remove the sign and those responsible are escorted out.

When the three surviving Arab terrorist attackers are released by West Germany in a suspiciously convenient plane hijack, Golda and the Israeli Defense Committee authorize the Mossad to track down and kill those who are responsible for the Munich Massacre.

> Mossad: Formed in December, 1949 at the recommendation of Prime Minister Ben-Gurion. The organization is responsible for intelligence collection, covert operations, and counterterrorism. They are also tasked with protecting Jews and bringing Jews to Israel from countries where they are officially forbidden to leave. The Mossad director reports to the Prime Minister.

Attending a memorial service in Israel, Golda says, "Whoever looks on passively when Jews are being murdered and Israeli planes hijacked … is dreadfully mistaken if they think the matter ends there. For if an Israeli plane is hijacked, then no plane in the world is safe anywhere, and if Arab assassins are allowed to think that Jewish blood can be spilled with impunity, then the lives of people everywhere are in jeopardy."[33]

In an interview, Golda tells the world, "Thanks to your inertia and your acquiescence, terrorism will increase and you too will have to pay the price."[34]

Golda's words have come true.

Golda's visit to Pope Paul VI, 1973
From the Archives Department,
University of Wisconsin-Milwaukee Libraries

It is after the Munich Massacre when Golda visits Pope Paul VI and he lectures Golda, "It's hard to understand how the Jewish people, which should be merciful, behave so fiercely."[35]

Golda stays respectful, but her response is a clear rebuttal: "Your Holiness, do you know what my own very earliest memory is? It is waiting for a pogrom... Let me assure you that my people know all about real harshness and also that we learned all about real mercy when we were being led to the gas chambers of the Nazis."[36]

The following spring, 1973 is Golda's 75th birthday. Honors and gifts are given. Most noteworthy on the political front, Golda receives a cable from the German chancellor, Willy Brandt and King Hussein sends her a string of pearls.

A few days after her birthday, it is the 25th birthday of Israel. Golda announces she will retire in the coming fall. She sets the date to leave office–October.

She should have said September.

17
YOM KIPPUR ~ A DAY OF WAR NOT ATONEMENT

Becoming Prime Minister, Golda was asked if there are any nonnegotiable points with the Arab states. Golda responded, "Yes. For instance, our being thrown into the sea. That is not negotiable. When the Arabs want to live in peace with the State of Israel, we will negotiate everything."[1]

Every day, Arab guerrillas are committing new acts of terror. The battles in the War of Attrition include bombs thrown into crowded buses of Jews and into market places where women are shopping for food. Sanctioned by Muslims, the Cairo radio broadcasts, "The Arab people are firmly resolved to wipe Israel off the map …"[2]

Golda authorizes air strikes to check these Egyptian aggressions. This action is denounced by the US State Department as a threat to international peace and the weapons Golda has requested are being held as ransom unless she stops the strikes. There is no denouncing of the Egyptian raids or of their moving missile sites into the truce zone.

Golda says, "We don't know how to explain this very simple thing–we want peace for ourselves, peace for our neighbors. Is that so difficult that it can't be explained?"[3] Concurrent with this declaration, Arab demonstrators are setting fire to Israeli flags and shouting, "Long live Al Fatah. Israel is a death trap for the Jewish people."[4] Egyptian President Nasser is quite frank as to why there will be no peace. Nasser explains, "If Ben-Gurion came to Egypt to talk to me, he would return home as a conquering hero. But if I went to him, I would be shot when I came back."[5]

In September of 1973, armed Arab terrorists board a Russian train bound for Vienna. They take hostage the passengers that are Jews. It's a specific train that transports Soviet Jews who are immigrating to a layover in Vienna where they are able to fly to Israel. The terrorists demand of the Austrian government to give them free passage to an Arab capital in exchange for releasing the five Jews and a customs official.

Austria's chancellor, Bruno Kreisky, obliges the terrorists' demand and his mollifying even goes one step further. He closes down the station. What had been a gateway for Jews to leave the Soviet Union is slammed shut. Golda asks Kreisky why he agreed to terrorist demands and then gives even more, he responds, "We belong to two different worlds. I will never be responsible for any bloodshed on the soil of Austria."[6]

Golda's efforts to negotiate with Egyptian President Nasser had started when Nasser took office in 1956. In March of 1969 Golda declares, "We are prepared to discuss peace with our neighbors, any day and on all matters."[7] Nasser's reply, three days later is: "There is no voice transcending the sounds of war, and there must not be such a voice–nor is there any call holier than the call to war."[8] Nasser decrees Egypt will forge, "a road toward our objective, violently and by force, over a sea of blood and a horizon of fire."[9] King Faisal of Saudi Arabia weighs in with his opinion, "All countries should wage war against the Zionists..." [10]

Any Arab peace proposals are only a ploy. Their premise for peace talks start with the demand of Israel returning to old borders. This smoke screen requirement covers the fact that even when they had those borders, Arabs still waged war on Israel. Golda explains, "Now they say we should be going back to the '67 borders, but that's where we were, so why was there a war?"[11] "And we had '47 borders. ... We didn't like them very much, but we said yes to them. But there still was a war. And after the '48 war they said we should go back to the '47 borders. But that's where we were ... and that's where they wanted to get us out from ... They still nurture a hope that at some time we'll disappear."[12]

When politicians (National Security Advisor Henry Kissinger, Secretary of State William Rogers) from western countries are vying to add "Mid-East Peace Plan" to their resume, they suggest Golda soften her stance toward Nasser. After all, he keeps losing to Israel. Golda responds, "We're told over and over that he is humiliated. Humiliated as a result of what? He wanted to destroy us, and–poor man–he failed. Somehow, I just can't bring myself to feel too sorry for him."[13] Golda also responds, "We are told that we should consider Nasser: He is weak, frustrated. What are the Arabs frustrated about? For the third time they tried to destroy Israel and were not successful. I am sorry; I have no tears for their frustration." [14]

Aside from witty quips, Golda's frustration is real and the loss of life on either side is no joke. Golda will later say of Nasser, "What we hold against Nasser is not only the killing of our sons, but forcing them for the sake of Israel's survival, to kill others."[15]

Golda must contend with many of the current diplomats who are much like the naive commissions sent to Palestine years ago. They are clueless about the background of the region or the history of the Jews. One diplomat, when visiting Golda in her home, attempts to garner good graces by telling Golda he had neighbors that were Jews and the mother made him chicken soup. Golda is not impressed.

Golda must also contend with the pressures from within her government. Any peace concessions that Golda agrees to (demands of Arabs and the super powers) could bring about a vote of "no confidence" against Golda and topple the Labor Party. The gap in government could open the opportunity for another war.

In 1970, Nasser dies of a heart attack, and Anwar Sadat becomes president of Egypt. Sadat makes clear that all peace agreements will be started with this precondition: that Israel commit itself in advance to yield every centimeter of land taken from Egypt, Syria, and Jordan in the 1967 Six Day War—including Jerusalem.[16]

Considering the premises of the previous wars that included; Jerusalem is barred to Jews when it was under Arab control, Arab countries use cease-fire periods to improve military positions, and there are no assurances of any lasting peace in the future; Sadat's offer is a nonstarter.

As a result of the pressure from the Soviets and the United States to comply with peace agreements and not require secure borders, Golda could have given a short retort, "Would you agree to that?" Golda instead responds to criticism saying, "Everybody tells us that there is no such thing in the world today as secure borders. Yet I haven't seen any people stepping back from their borders and say, 'We don't care what our borders are.'… They tell us there will be international guarantees. … Does any other people depend on international guarantees? No. But we should. And if we don't, we're stubborn or intransigent or not accommodating or we don't care about public relations."[17]

Golda's efforts toward lasting peace with the Arabs will continue to be stymied and President Sadat's wife, Jehan Sadat, could have told Golda why. Jehan explains, "I do not agree with those among us and among you who assert today that Sadat tried to achieve a real peace before 1973. Sadat needed one more war in order to win and enter into negotiations from a position of equality."[18]

The "one more war" is the Yom Kippur War.

The international, political maneuverings for the Yom Kippur War (October 6-25, 1973) can fill volumes. For more information on the details of the Yom Kippur War please refer to the books listed in the bibliography, or of course, just Google it.

For the months leading up to the Yom Kippur War, Golda needs to stay stubborn against the pressures of world politics. There are no signs the **US policy** to appease Arabs for their oil and keep Russian influence out of the Middle East, will change. There are no signs the **Russian policy** to appease Arabs for their oil and keep US influence out of the Middle East, will change. There are no signs the **Arab policy** will change their perspective and recognize Israel.

This is a world scale political merry-go-round with a "peace-plan-song" as the kaleidoscope music. Golda can't thumb her nose at this spectacle. She is trying to appease the

US in order to get arms and not have her country annihilated. Golda's efforts to mitigate will mean she doesn't stick by her quote: "I think I can honestly say that I was never deflected from doing something because I thought I might fail."[19] Golda deflected and it cost her country dearly.

Yasir Arafat, chairman of the Palestine Liberation Organization interrupts the merry-go-round with this honest statement of intent, "We don't want peace, we want victory. Peace for us means Israel's destruction and nothing else."[20]

Listen to what Arafat says and the music stops. The problem is the US, Russia and neighboring Arab countries want to keep the merry-go-round going as a means of accomplishing their own political agendas.

Golda knows Arafat speaks the truth. She has been saying all along the Arabs simply want to wipe Israel off the map. No concessions are really going to bring peace, because the Arabs want victory, not peace. She says, "Why should we talk about giving back these territories? There is no one to give them to even if we wanted ... We can't send them to Nasser by parcel post."[21] And to Kissinger, dreaming of détente (easing of tensions, especially between nations), Golda says, "I didn't just get up one day in 1967, after all the shelling from the heights, and decide to take Golan away from them. They say this is their territory. Eight hundred boys gave their lives for an attack the Syrians started. Assad (President of Syria) lost the war, and now we have to pay for it because Assad says it's his territory."[22]

> Reminder: In the spring of 1967, Israel saw the military buildup on her borders by Syria and Egypt. Western governments, give their righteous warnings to give the situation a "breathing spell"[23] and not strike. The Jews ignore the western political agenda. (The question that begs to be asked is: Would these governments have allowed that kind of buildup on their borders?) On June 6, 1967, Israel strikes first and the Six Day War is over in ... six days. Now we fast forward to the early 1970s.

In the years following the Six Day War, Golda becomes cautious. She needs to keep US politics on her side to ensure a supply of weapons for her country because Soviet Russia is keeping the Arabs up to date with the latest munitions. Israel is denied weapons by the US because US sycophants, such as Kissinger, are eyeing the Nobel Peace Prize. Extolling peace plans that give no guarantees, they strong arm Israel to share the US hope that Arabs will behave, and the military buildup on the borders will disappear. In 1973, Golda points out the intelligence she is receiving of the positioning of weapons that are closing in on Israeli borders. The US initially denies it and only later confirms the reports are true, but by then, of course, it is too late.

In the months before the Yom Kippur War, US officials, once again, advise Israel against a preemptive strike. Golda agrees but adds, "This time it has to be crystal clear who began the war, so we won't have to go around the world convincing people our cause is just."[24] Opinions about Golda's decision must consider the real threat of the US withholdig weapons.

> Since the early 1960s Germany has been helping supply Israel with weapons but wants its support to remain secret so as not to offend the Arabs. When the weapon supply becomes public in 1965, Germany stops selling weapons to Israel.

On October 6, 1973, Yom Kippur, Golda is informed by a source that Egypt and Syria will attack at sundown. Golda's chief of staff, Lt. Gen. David "Dado" Elazar, wants to launch a preemptive air strike. Moshe Dayan, the Minister of Defense advises, **no**. Golda tells them, "None of us knows now what the future has in store for us, but there is always a possibility that we'll need someone's help, and if we'll strike first, no one is going to help. I wish I could say yes because I know the meaning of it, but, with a heavy heart, I say no."[25] Syria and Egypt attack Israel on Yom Kippur, a good strategic decision because so many Israeli troops are home on leave for the holiday.

The first week of fighting is grim, and there are times it looks like Israel will lose. The Israeli spirit is also losing the image of one of its heroes. Moshe Dayan, riding the wave of success from previous military battles has enjoyed being a "war hero" celebrity. Dayan has reassured Israelis that the borders are secure. Seeing the tragic results of his advice to not launch a preemptive strike he has a "melt down" and announces, "Golda I was wrong about everything. We are headed to catastrophe."[26]

Golda hearing news of the Yom Kippur War
From the Archives Department,
University of Wisconsin-Milwaukee Libraries

Lou Kaddar, Golda's secretary, finds Golda in the hall. Lou has seen Golda's doggedness through times of extreme pressure, but now Lou sees a gray old woman, almost broken. Lou understands how dire their position is when Golda tells her, "Dayan is talking about surrender. You must arrange for me, tonight … you must go to the house of a friend… He's a doctor. I'll make him give you some pills so that I can kill myself so I won't have to fall into the hands of the Arabs." [27]

It won't be necessary.

Golda pulls from within, one more time, to be the pillar of strength her people need. Self-recrimination and quaking with fear must wait. Ben-Gurion's words again come true. "She had faith when others wavered. She believed in the absolute justice of our cause when others doubted."[28]

Golda keeps Dayan out of the public eye, while deciding to present to Israelis a sanitized press release about the situation. An Israeli news editor later records, "Dayan was beaten and defeated. It's lucky for us that Golda wouldn't let him appear on television. He would have announced our surrender."[29] Later, when the Israeli public is demanding Dayan be dismissed, Golda will not allow him to be "thrown under the bus."

The invading forces are pushed back. More than 3,600 Israelis die in less than three weeks. And now Golda must face the wrath of her people. The country's illusion of being a young, invincible nation is shattered, and their prime minister will bear the blame.

A soldier sits across the street from Golda's office with a large sign[30] reading:

"GRANDMA, YOUR DEFENSE MINISTER IS A FAILURE AND 3,600 OF YOUR GRANDCHILDREN ARE DEAD."

The Knesset holds an investigation and exonerates Golda's decisions. This does little good to help her sleep. Golda will go to her grave acknowledging she made the mistake. The world, the Israelis and Golda will never know if Plan A, strike first, would have resulted in (Golda's fear) the US withholding weapons. In grief, Golda says, "It doesn't matter what logic dictated. It matters only that I, who was so accustomed to making decisions... failed to make that one decision. It isn't a question of feeling guilty. I, too, can rationalize and tell myself that in the face of such total certainty on the part of our military intelligence ... it would have been unreasonable of me to have insisted on a call-up. But I know that I should have done so, and I shall live with that terrible knowledge for the rest of my life."[31]

Popular opinion had previously hailed their grandmother Prime Minister for her no nonsense style. They loved her cavalier meetings of cabinet members where Golda congregated a select few in her kitchen to hash out policy. The Jewish people had joked about the informality of no votes, no meeting minutes and no leaks to the press. Not a hint of derailing the nonchalance, they instead had dubbed Golda's group the "Kitchen Cabinet."

The Israelis' image of Golda and their own self image is shattered in the Yom Kippur War. A journalist writes of a grief stricken Israel, "The state has gone through a devaluation. A devaluation in leadership ability, devaluation in spirit, in values, in morale, in faith."[32] Golda, protecting Dayan, creates more exploding angst. Leaving her office one day a woman yells, "Murderer." Golda's approval rating is down to 21 percent.[33]

In the final days of the Yom Kippur War, an Israeli victory becomes obvious. This is the turning point for political maneuverings by various world leaders to start stepping up to the plate for another bat at the elusive Middle East peace plan. Keeping Golda out of the loop, Kissinger is calling the plays as a self-anointed umpire with US rules to the game. Kissinger, not including Golda in cease-fire strategies, is the point-of-contact for the Russians. He also allows Sadat, who started and lost the war, to continue the Arab policy of refusing to have direct negotiations with Israel.

For Golda, it is another *déjà vu* all over again being told decisions about her people without her input. Golda responds, "They compromise, and Israel loses. Sadat must, I think, be given time to enjoy his defeat and not to immediately, by political manipulations, turn it into a victory. For God's sake, he started a war, our people are killed, his in the many thousands are killed, and he has been defeated."[34]

Kissinger is pressing Golda to comply with offered concessions because the Arabs have begun an oil embargo against the United States, and it is causing gas shortages and high prices for American citizens. The embargo was started in October because the US was supplying Israel with arms. Kissinger had dragged his feet getting military supplies to Israel in hopes of Israel not having too grand of victory that would humiliate the Arabs. (These are more factors for why Golda had not wanted to give the OK for a preemptive strike.)

Coming to Israel, after a meeting in Egypt, Kissinger overplays his cards and jokes to Golda, "When I reach Cairo, Sadat hugs and kisses me. But when I come here, everyone attacks me." Golda quips back, "If I were Egyptian, I would kiss you too."[35]

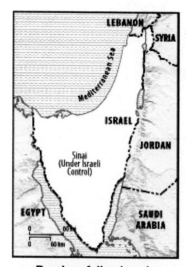

**Borders following the
Yom Kippur War**
*http://www.mythsandfacts.org/,
Eli E. Hertz, Date accessed 2014*

**After the Israel-Egypt
Peace Treaty, 1979**

Golda becomes accustomed to the world's cynicism once again and keeps low expectations for fair play from the United Nations. Golda reflects, "A strong people does not have to demonstrate the justice of its demands. Nobody ever asked Nasser, 'Why did you mass your army in the Sinai Desert in 1967? Why did you fill it with tanks and bombers and guns and 100,000 men?' Nobody ever asked Sadat or Syria's Assad, 'Why did you attack Israel in 1973?' Only a weak people has to prove the justice of its cause. And when, however it tries to do so, it's never enough."[36]

Golda consistently has asked for Arab recognition of Israel's right to exist as a basis for any "real" peace not a mere stop-gap ceasefire that gives Arabs an opportunity to rearm. Golda refers to Kissinger's tactics of keeping himself in the middle as "running to Mommy America" and it only undermines a true peace process. In her first foreign press conference (1969) as Prime Minister, Golda had made these statements and now after the Yom Kippur War, it still holds true:

> *"Nobody has ever proved to us why it is so outlandish for us to expect—after three wars—a peace settlement, a signed peace settlement, something that usually takes place between the parties of any war. The only peculiar aspect of our situation is that the party that is asking for this contractual agreement is not the party that lost the war but rather the one that won it. ... Secondly, nobody has yet been able to prove to us that anything else will create that hope, the basis for that hope, that the war fought in 1967 will be the last war, which is what we want. We don't want to win wars any more. We just don't want wars, that's all."*[37]

Kissinger brings to Golda a list of Israeli prisoners of war being held in Syria. Golda relents to concessions to the Syrians in order to get the prisoners back home. Critics who condemn giving in to any Syrian demands should understand that Golda is well aware that captured Israeli soldiers are being tortured and killed. The Syrian military and government disregard the rights of Prisoners of War as stated in the Geneva Conventions. The Syrian Defense Minister, Mustafa Tlass boasts about atrocities committed against captive Israeli soldiers of the Yom Kippur War: "I gave the Medal of the Republic's Hero, to a soldier from Aleppo, who killed 28 Jewish soldiers. He did not use a military weapon to kill them but utilized the ax to decapitate them. He then devoured the neck of one of them and ate it in front of the people. I am proud of his courage and bravery, for he actually killed by himself 28 Jews by count and cash."[38]

Coming to a final cease-fire agreement with Syria is nearly derailed when Palestinian terrorists, supported by President Assad, take four Israeli teachers and ninety schoolchildren hostage. The terrorist demands are for Israel to release dozens of imprisoned guerrillas. The end result, of this assault, is three of the kidnappers are killed and twenty of the children are dead.

Golda is deluged with pressure from both Israeli citizens and her government to break off all discussions with Damascus. She replies, "It would be illogical to renounce the cure and allow the fever to pursue its deadly course. We had all better get back to the peacemaking."[39] It is an example of her ability to maintain course for the higher purpose and it's possibly paying off.

A peace agreement is hammered out. On November 11, 1973, for the first time since the independence of Israel, there is direct, simple contact between an Israeli and Egyptian general. They shake hands and sign the papers.

The civil turmoil on the home front continues to swirl. Disparate voices, each with its own opinion about land concessions, defense spending and bringing home prisoners of war compete with the adjoining chorus of equally discordant views from the incoming immigrants. Still struggling with lower economic levels, they are angry that more is not being done for them. These coalitions want more money spent on domestic issues not defense.

The "open door" to unlimited immigration has come at a price. Imagine the strain on the economy if a country the size of New Jersey (or half the size of Switzerland), not only fights five separate wars, is also accepting 161 people per day, in the first 25 years of existence. The diversity of cultural, economic and social expectations for these new arrivals makes Golda's beginning days in Milwaukee, 8,000 Jews divided into forty nine synagogues, a memory of child's play.

In Zion Square, a crowd of over 5,000 protesters are burning an effigy of Golda.

Seeing this, does Golda have a wry smile? None of the protestors will experience government retaliation.

The Yom Kippur War is one misstep from Golda's six decades of living the motto "do justice and let the skies fall." There was no justice nor did the skies fall. Golda did.

Golda's long journey is coming to an end. The final chapter is called "Forgiving Golda." At first glance, the word "Forgiving" is a verb, to forgive Golda. But at the second glance, "Forgiving" is an adjective. That is the focus of this final chapter, "Forgiving Golda."

18

FORGIVING GOLDA

D ue to the Yom Kippur War, the October elections are postponed until December. What is also postponed is Golda's retirement. Being in the midst of peace negotiations and a frazzled government, she is asked to run for the office of Prime Minister again. The election is far from a sure thing. Golda has taken tremendous heat from political opponents for shielding and keeping Dayan and for concessions in the cease fire of the war. In spite of low public opinion, Golda garners another victory for the Labor Party and once more is elected Prime Minister.

Envisioning a few years of no wars, Golda is pleased that in her new budget more money will be spent on domestic programs than on defense. The problem is–Golda is spent.

In the spring, 1974, Golda announces she will resign. She tells her colleagues, "I beg of you not to try to persuade me to change my mind … It will not help."[1] Golda tells her son, "I am very tired. Please remember that I have really had enough."[2] Both Sarah and Menachem agree that the time has come for their mother to retire. The public is still unaware that Golda has weekly treatments for cancer.

After Golda leaves office she has the pleasure of seeing the next person to become Prime Minister is a not an immigrant like herself, Ben-Gurion, Sharett or Eshkol. Yitzhak Rabin is a *sabra*, a native born Israeli. For Golda, it is a sign of her destiny being achieved.

During days of retirement, Golda's memoirs are published. Substantial book sales, not only make her wealthy but more famous and popular than ever. Around the globe she is voted the most admired woman in the world. Golda, the unofficial ambassador of her people, is on trips to have tea at 10 Downing Street with the Prime Minister of England or lunch at Pennsylvania Avenue with President Ford. She receives gifts from King Hussein and greetings from West German officials.

Golda greeting Margaret Thatcher, 1976

From the Archives Department
University of Wisconsin-Milwaukee Libraries

How Golda is able to show heads of state a warm generous spirit when their countries had played key roles in causing the death of Jews and Israel's betrayal, is understood only by knowing that Golda is forgiving. Her actions and attitude are setting the stage for her country to move forward.

Golda is accurately portrayed making tough decisions as the "Iron Lady" and demanding no less of her people. Golda has asked Jews to relinquish their ticket of leaving the Cyprus Camps to a child, forego a day's wage each month to unknown immigrants, and give millions of dollars to fight for an independence that could be lost. An advisor to Golda said of her, "She revealed the strength of a warrior without fear. She gave us a sense of hope and the opportunity to do what was necessary to turn things around."[3] What is necessary now, will be for Israelis to grasp this newest opportunity of establishing peace. No longer writing the emotional chapters to fight for the right to have their nation, the Israelis must be pioneers of a new era to "turn things around."

Golda's ability to show grace and not bear grudges is tested when the Labor Party becomes even more fractious and is defeated in 1977. Menachem Begin, with whom Golda had her differences, becomes the next Prime Minister, and it is Begin who gets a call from Egyptian President, Anwar Sadat. Sadat wants to visit Jerusalem.

In November of 1977, Sadat, who wouldn't even come to the phone during the Munich Massacre, announces to his parliament that he is willing to go "to the ends of the world" in his quest for peace.[4] Knowing Golda will doubt his sincerity, he has written her a note of assurance stating, "You must take my word seriously. When I made my initiative in 1971, I meant it. When I threatened war, I meant it. When I talk of peace now, I mean it."[5]

Sadat's note is dated after the Yom Kippur War, and his message supports Golda's reservations that Egypt never did have intentions of peace until, as Sadat says, "**now**." Sadat pays

Golda a compliment when he later says, "I prefer dealing with a strong leader like Golda." [6]

Being a "strong leader" holds true for her years after public office. Golda extends her friendships to include the governments of England, Germany, Jordan and any of the African countries. In her efforts to safeguard the future of Israel, can the list include her acceptance of Egypt?

After the near fatal misstep of the Yom Kippur War, can Golda dare trust what Sadat's note has said, that he truly does **"mean it"**? To forgive in politics, could cost her people their lives. If Golda takes the lead and shows grace, how will she withstand any backlash from disappointed Jews if efforts go awry? Given Golda's sense of humor, does she chuckle knowing she could meet Sadat in the reception line and with her famous glare, coldly say, "You are late."

There are no quotes of Golda gloating over this turn of events that vindicate her years of balancing how much *to be or not to be* compromising with the Arabs. In a few months, she will be joking with Anwar Sadat, President of Egypt.

{ "Our World" is the first live global television broadcast (June 25, 1967). The program is to showcase artists of different countries. As the contribution for the United Kingdom, the BBC commissions the Beatles to write a song with a message that will be understood by everyone. The Beatles hit the world stage with the song, "All You Need is Love." }

Preparing for Sadat's visit, Israelis turn to the future. Taxi drivers attach Egyptian flags to their antennas. Street vendors are selling T-shirts with the pictures of Sadat and Begin above a caption "ALL YOU NEED IS LOVE."[7] Sadat's plane lands in Tel Aviv and he steps out to a red carpet, trumpets, and a line of generals who had sent their men to die in the war Sadat started. The generals shake Sadat's hand.

When Sadat comes to Golda he says, "Madam, for many, many years I wanted to meet you." Golda's quick response, "Mr. President, so have I waited a long time to meet you. Why didn't you come earlier?" Sadat answers, "The time was not yet ripe."[8]

**President Sadat sharing a joke with
Golda Meir and Shimon Perez**

*From the Archives Department,
University of Wisconsin-Milwaukee Libraries*

Golda continues the banter with Sadat, "Why didn't you tell me when I was prime minister that you wanted to come to Jerusalem? I would have had you here in a moment." Sadat's quick response, "But I didn't ask you to resign."[9]

When Sadat and Begin are nominated for the next Nobel Peace Prize, Golda is asked about her reaction. Golda, still with a sharp wit, banters, "I don't know about the Nobel Prize, but they certainly deserve an Oscar."[10]

{ Sadat's negotiation with Israel delivers him the Nobel Peace Prize from the world, but Egypt's membership to the Arab League is suspended. Sadat is assassinated in five years by a Muslim from an extremist Islamic group. }

Golda's role in fixing Israel to the world map is done. When her people ask, "Whom shall I send?" Golda will no longer answer, "Send me."

On December 8, 1978 Begin and Sadat take the world stage to accept the Nobel Peace Prize.

On the same day, it seems a wink of irony that Golda will take from them the world headlines. She is on one more trip and as usual, she didn't pack.

December 8, 1978 Golda Meir dies.

From the Archives Department,
University of Wisconsin-Milwaukee Libraries

EPILOGUE

"I know you're tired but come, this is the way."

Rumi

Throughout time, visionary humans have believed peace on this earth is possible. Even when they are weary and their dream is shredded with contrary evidence, they still believe: all people can live together in peace.

Recording the lives of Golda Meir and Eleanor Roosevelt, I understand how these women were visionaries and ahead of their time. They honestly believed peace was possible. Their practical policies and projects were a natural extension of protecting life and the dignity of all people. Equally pragmatic was their constant efforts for confronting passive violence or resolving the fears of those who desperately insist that injustice is justified.

Decades have passed since Golda and Eleanor have left us. The ideal of peace is distorted by a balance sheet of rights and wrongs. It is only a distraction. There is a way ~

Out beyond ideas of wrongdoing and rightdoing, there is a field. I will meet you there.

Rumi

BIBLIOGRAPHY

(1942, November 12). *New York Times*, p. 9.

Amdur, R. (1990). *Golda Meir–A Leader in Peace and War.* Fawcett Columbine.

Atkins, A. (2011). *Eleanor Roosevelt's Life of Soul Searching and Self Discovery.* Flash History Press LLC.

Barasch, M. I. (2005). *Field Notes On The Compassionate Life–A SearchFor the Soul of Kindness.* Holtzbrinck Publishers.

Brad, M. G. (1999). *The Complete Idiot's Guide to Middle East Conflicts.* MacMillan.

Bradley, J. (2009). *The Imperial Cruise.* Bay Back Books/Little, Brown and Company.

Burkett, E. (2008). *Golda.* Harper Perennial.

Churchill, W. (1922). *British White Papers,* June 3,1922.

Claybourne, A. (2004). *Golda Meir–Leading Lives.* Heinemann Library.

Colón, D. (2010). *Rasputin and the Jews–A Reversal of History.* Colón, Delin.

Dobrin, A. (1974). *A Life for Israel–The Story of Golda Meir.* The Dial Press.

Dranzler, B. (2010). *The Accidental Anarchist.* Crosswalk Press.

Fromkin, D. (1989). *A Peace to End All Peace.* Henry Holt and Company.

Gilbert, M. (2006). *Kristallnact: Prelude to Destruction.* Harper Collins.

Gilbert, M. (2011). *The Story of Israel.* Carlton Publishing Group.

Gold, D. (2004). *Hatred's Kingdom—How Saudi Arabia Supports the New Global Terrorism*. Regnery Publishing.

Herzl, T. (2006). *The Jewish State*. Filiquarian Publishing, LLC .

Hitzeroth, D. (1998). *The Importance of Golda Meir*. Lucent Books.

Jewish Virtual Library. (n.d.). Retrieved from www. JewishVirtualLibrary.org.

Laskier, M. (1995). Egyptian Jewry Under the Nasser Regime, 1956-70. *Middle Eastern Studies, Volume 31, Issue #3*, 581.

Mann, P. (1971). *Golda—The Life of Israel's Prime Minister*. Coward, McCann & Geoghegan.

Martin, R. G. (1988). *Golda: The Romantic Years*. Charles Scribner's Sons.

Meir, G. (1975). *My Life*. G.P. Putnam's Sons.

Meir, G. E. (1973). *A Land of Our Own—An Oral Autobiography*. The Jewish Publication Society of America.

Meir, M. (1983). *My Mother Golda Meir, A Son's Evocation of Life With Golda Meir*. Arbor House.

Mondale, W. F. (1979, July 28). Evian and Geneva. *New York Times*.

Munich Massacre. (n.d.). Retrieved from www.wikipedia.com.

Naamani, I. T. (1974). *Israel—A Profile*. Praeger Publishers.

O'Brian, C. C. (1986). *The Siege—The Saga of Israel and Zionism*. Simon and Schuster.

Perl, W. R. (1989). *The Holocaust Conspiracy: An International Policy of Genocide*. SP Books.

Reeves, R. (2010). *Daring Young Men—The Heroism and Triumph of the Berlin Airlift, June 1948-May 1949*. Simon & Schuster Paperbacks.

Robinson, J. H. (1908). *Readings in Modern European History, vol. 2*. Boston: Ginn and Company.

Shenker, I. a. (1970). *As Good As Golda–The Warmth and Wisdom of Israel's Prime Minister*. The McCall Publishing Company.

Slater, R. (1981). *The Uncrowned Queen of Israel*. Jonathan David Publishers.

Syrkin, M. (1955). *Way of Valor–A Biography of Golda Myerson*. Sharon Books Inc.

Syrkin, M. (1969). *Golda Meir–Israel's Leader*. G.P. Putnam's Sons.

Syrkin, M. (1976). *Blessed is the Match – The Story of the Jewish Resistance*. The Jewish Publication Society of America.

Syrkin, M. e. (1973). *Golda Speaks Out*. Weidenfeld and Nicolson.

Tuchman, B. W. (1994). *The Proud Tower–A Portrait of the World Before the War 1890-1914*. Random House Publishing Group.

Wallach, J. (2005). *Desert Queen*. Anchor Books.

Wiesel, E. (1996). *All Rivers Run to the Sea*, Elie Wiesel: Memoirs. Schocken.

Wolf, L. (1912). *The Legal Suffering of the Jews in Russia–A Survey of Their Present Situation, and a Summary of Laws, 1912*. T. Fisher Unwin.

ENDNOTES

Part One

[1] (Robinson, 1908, pp. 371-372)

[2] (Robinson, 1908, pp. 371-372)

[3] (Robinson, 1908, pp. 371-372)

Chapter 1

[1] (O'Brian, 1986, p. 98)

[2] (Hitzeroth, 1998, p. 12)

[3] (Meir G. , 1975, p. 14)

[4] (Meir G. , 1975, p. 13)

[5] (Meir G. , 1975, p. 13)

[6] (Bergreen, 1990, p. 10)

[7] (Martin, 1988, p. 13)

[8] (Martin, 1988, p. 7)

[9] (Meir G. , 1975, p. 74)

[10] (Meir G. , 1975, p. 21)

[11] (Meir G. , 1975, p. 25)

[12] (Martin, 1988, p. 13)

[13] (Meir G. , 1975, p. 320)

[14] (Martin, 1988, p. 15)

Chapter 2

[1] (Martin, 1988, p. 15)

[2] (Martin, 1988, p. 9)

[3] (Martin, 1988, p. 17)

[4] (Martin, 1988, p. 17)

[5] (Meir G. , 1975, p. 28)

[6] (Meir G. , 1975, p. 29)

[7] (Martin, 1988, p. 77)

[8] (Martin, 1988, p. 77)

[9] (Martin, 1988, p. 27)

[10] (Meir G. , 1975, p. 26)

[11] (Meir G. , 1975, p. 30)

[12] (Meir G. , 1975, p. 30)

[13] (Meir G. , 1975, p. 35)

[14] (Meir G. E., 1973, p. 23)

[15] (Meir G. , 1975, p. 36)

[16] (Hitzeroth, 1998, p. 28)

[17] (Martin, 1988, p. 33)

[18] (Martin, 1988, p. 35)

[19] (Meir G. , 1975, p. 37)

[20] (Hitzeroth, 1998, p. 28)

[21] (Meir G. , 1975, p. 41)

Chapter 3

[1] (Martin, 1988, p. 38)

[2] (Martin, 1988, p. 50)

[3] (Meir G. , 1975, p. 43)

[4] (Meir G. , 1975, p. 44)

[5] (Hitzeroth, 1998, p. 32)

6 (Martin, 1988, p. 49)

7 (Hitzeroth, 1998, p. 33)

8 (Martin, 1988, p. 47)

9 (Martin, 1988, p. 47)

10 (Meir G. , 1975, p. 52)

11 (Hitzeroth, 1998, p. 37)

12 (Hitzeroth, 1998, p. 48)

13 (Martin, 1988, p. 69)

14 (Martin, 1988, p. 69)

15 (Martin, 1988, p. 65)

16 (Martin, 1988, p. 64)

17 (Shenker, 1970, p. 5)

Chapter 4

1 (Martin, 1988, p. 63)

2 (Martin, 1988, p. 63)

3 (Martin, 1988, p. 57)

4 (Martin, 1988, p. 68)

5 (Martin, 1988, p. 68)

6 (Hitzeroth, 1998, p. 41)

7 (Hitzeroth, 1998, p. 41)

8 (Hitzeroth, 1998, p. 42)

9 (Meir G. , 1975, p. 83)

10 (Meir G. , 1975, p. 83)

11 (Meir G. , 1975, p. 61)

12 (Martin, 1988, p. 72)

13 (Martin, 1988, p. 72)

14 (Hitzeroth, 1998, p. 43)

15 (Martin, 1988, p. 81)

16 (Martin, 1988, p. 83)

17 (Martin, 1988, p. 88)

18 (Hitzeroth, 1998, p. 47)

19 (Martin, 1988, p. 87)

20 (Martin, 1988, p. 87)

21 (Hitzeroth, 1998, p. 47)

22 (Martin, 1988, p. 73)

Part Two

1 (Bradley, 2009, p. 232)

2 (Bradley, 2009, p. 32)

3 (Bradley, 2009, p. 33)

4 (Bradley, 2009, p. 44)

5 (Bradley, 2009, p. 330)

6 (Bradley, 2009, p. 330)

7 (Tuchman, 1994, p. 243)

8 (Tuchman, 1994, p. 243)

9 (Bradley, 2009, p. 110)

10 (Bradley, 2009, p. 110)

11 (Bradley, 2009, p. 110)

12 (Bradley, 2009, p. 110)

13 (Bradley, 2009, p. 101)

14 (Bradley, 2009, p. 253)

15 (Bradley, 2009, p. 91)

16 (Bradley, 2009, p. 317)

17 (Bradley, 2009, p. 309)

18 (Bradley, 2009, p. 309)

19 (Bradley, 2009, p. 320)

20 (Bradley, 2009, p. 214)

Chapter 5

1 (Martin, 1988, p. 92)

2 (Martin, 1988, p. 88)

3 (Martin, 1988, p. 98)

4 (Martin, 1988, p. 98)

5 (Syrkin M. e., 1973, p. 31)

6 (Martin, 1988, p. 96)

7 (Syrkin M. e., 1973, p. 31)

8 (Martin, 1988, p. 98)

9 (Martin, 1988, p. 97)

10 (Meir G. , 1975, p. 69)

11 (Martin, 1988, p. 97)

12 (Martin, 1988, p. 97)

13 (Martin, 1988, p. 97)

14 (Martin, 1988, p. 98)

15 (Martin, 1988, p. 79)

16 (Burkett, 2008, p. 29)

17 (Shenker, 1970, p. 5)

18 (Meir G. , 1975, p. 71)

19 (Martin, 1988, p. 101)

20 (Martin, 1988, p. 19)

21 (Martin, 1988, p. 103)

22 (Martin, 1988, p. 104)

23 (Martin, 1988, p. 111)

Chapter 6

1 (Fromkin, 1989, p. 25)

2 (Fromkin, 1989, p. 519)

3 (Naamani, 1974, p. 25)

4 (Churchill, 1922)

5 (Naamani, 1974, p. 27)

6 (Naamani, 1974, p. 27)

7 (Wallach, 2005, p. 225)

8 (Wallach, 2005, p. 152)

9 (Martin, 1988, p. 247)

10 (Mann, 1971, p. 115)

11 (Mann, 1971, p. 115)

12 (Martin, 1988, p. 281)

13 (Meir G. E., 1973, p. 50)

14 (Meir G. E., 1973, pp. 50-51)

15 (Meir G. , 1975, pp. 148-149)

Chapter 7

1 (Martin, 1988, p. 106)

2 (Hitzeroth, 1998, p. 46)

3 (Hitzeroth, 1998, p. 50)

4 (Martin, 1988, p. 107)

5 (Hitzeroth, 1998, p. 51)

6 (Meir G. , 1975, p. 81)

7 (Martin, 1988, p. 113)

8 (Martin, 1988, p. 111)

9 (Martin, 1988, p. 120)

10 (Martin, 1988, p. 123)

11 (Hitzeroth, 1998, p. 53)

12 (Martin, 1988, p. 120)

13 (Martin, 1988, p. 114)

14 (Hitzeroth, 1998, p. 58)

15 (Martin, 1988, p. 134)

16 (Hitzeroth, 1998, p. 56)

17 (Syrkin M. , *Golda Meir–Israel's Leader*, 1969, p. 85)

18 (Martin, 1988, p. 138)

19 (Martin, 1988, p. 138)

20 (Meir G. , 1975, p. 102)

21 (Martin, 1988, p. 143)

22 (Martin, 1988, p. 197)

23 (Martin, 1988, p. 144)

24 (Hitzeroth, 1998, p. 58)

25 (Meir G. , 1975, p. 12)

26 (Martin, 1988, p. 112)

27 (Hitzeroth, 1998, p. 59)

28 (Martin, 1988, p. 157)

29 (Syrkin M. , *Golda Meir–Israel's Leader*, 1969, p. 87)

Chapter 8

1 (Martin, 1988, p. 156)

2 (Martin, 1988, p. 157)

3 (Martin, 1988, p. 169)

4 (Martin, 1988, p. 170)

5 (Martin, 1988, p. 170)

6 (Martin, 1988, p. 177)

7 (Martin, 1988, p. 177)

8 (Martin, 1988, p. 177)

9 (Martin, 1988, p. 187)

10 (Martin, 1988, p. 189)

11 (Meir G. , 1975, p. 131)

12 (Meir G. , 1975, p. 132)

13 (Syrkin M. , *Golda Meir–Israel's Leader*, 1969, p. 90)

14 (Syrkin M. , *Golda Meir–Israel's Leader*, 1969, p. 90)

15 (Syrkin M. , *Golda Meir–Israel's Leader*, 1969, p. 90)

16 (Syrkin M. , *Golda Meir–Israel's Leader*, 1969, p. 90)

17 (Martin, 1988, p. 215)

18 (Martin, 1988, p. 201)

Chapter 9

1 (Martin, 1988, p. 206)

2 (Martin, 1988, p. 209)

3 (Syrkin M. , *Golda Meir–Israel's Leader*, 1969, p. 155)

4 (Martin, 1988, p. 239)
5 (Slater, 1981, p. 41)
6 (*New York Times*, 1942, p. 9)
7 (Martin, 1988, p. 208)
8 (Perl, 1989, p. 37)
9 (Mondale, 1979)
10 (Meir G. , 1975, p. 158)
11 (Burkett, 2008, p. 91)
12 (Slater, 1981, p. 43)
13 (Meir G. , 1975, p. 158)
14 (Meir G. , 1975, p. 158)
15 (Gilbert, *Kristallnact: Prelude to Destruction*, 2006, p. 42)
16 (Mann, 1971, p. 106)
17 (Martin, 1988, p. 219)
18 (Meir G. , 1975, p. 165)

Part Three

1 (Martin, 1988, p. 147)
2 (Meir G. , 1975, p. 196)
3 (Martin, 1988, p. 248)
4 (Martin, 1988, p. 249)
5 (Martin, 1988, p. 249)

Chapter 10

1 (Mann, 1971, p. 97)
2 (Mann, 1971, p. 119)
3 (Meir G. , 1975, p. 166)
4 (Martin, 1988, p. 236)
5 (Syrkin M. , *Blessed is the Match–The Story of the Jewish Resistance*, 1976, p. 98)
6 (Martin, 1988, p. 250)
7 (Martin, 1988, p. 250)
8 (Shenker, 1970, p. 53)
9 (Naamani, 1974, p. 42)
10 (Martin, 1988, p. 237)
11 (Martin, 1988, p. 238)
12 (Martin, 1988, p. 237)
13 (Syrkin M. , *Blessed is the Match–The Story of the Jewish Resistance*, 1976)
14 (Syrkin M. , *Blessed is the Match–The Story of the Jewish Resistance*, 1976, p. 54)
15 (Syrkin M. , *Blessed is the Match–The Story of the Jewish Resistance*, 1976, p. 26)
16 (Shenker, 1970, p. 58)
17 (Shenker, 1970, p. 58)

Chapter 11

1 (Hitzeroth, 1998, p. 68)
2 (Martin, 1988, p. 260)
3 (Syrkin M. , *Golda*

Meir–Israel's Leader, 1969, p. 122)

4 (Syrkin M. , *Golda Meir–Israel's Leader,* 1969, p. 120)

5 (Shenker, 1970, p. 12)

6 (Martin, 1988, p. 264)

7 (Martin, 1988, p. 281)

8 (Shenker, 1970, p. 12)

9 (Shenker, 1970, p. 44)

10 (Shenker, 1970, p. 44)

11 (Martin, 1988, p. 279)

12 (Martin, 1988, p. 279)

13 (Martin, 1988, p. 259)

14 (Martin, 1988, p. 279)

15 (Hitzeroth, 1998, p. 71)

16 (Martin, 1988, p. 262)

17 (Martin, 1988, p. 262)

18 (Syrkin M. , *Way of Valor–A Biography of Golda Myerson*, 1955, p. 152)

19 (Martin, 1988, p. 260)

20 (Syrkin M. , *Way of Valor–A Biography of Golda Myerson*, 1955, p. 149)

21 (Syrkin M. , *Way of Valor–A Biography of Golda Myerson*, 1955, p. 149)

22 (Martin, 1988, p. 263)

23 (Martin, 1988, p. 263)

24 (Martin, 1988, p. 265)

25 (Martin, 1988, p. 266)

26 (Martin, 1988, p. 268)

27 (Martin, 1988, p. 224)

28 (Martin, 1988, p. 273)

29 (Martin, 1988, p. 273)

30 (Martin, 1988, p. 277)

31 (Syrkin M. , *Way of Valor–A Biography of Golda Myerson*, 1955, p. 160)

32 (Shenker, 1970, p. 12)

33 (Martin, 1988, p. 253)

34 (Syrkin M. , *Golda Meir–Israel's Leader,* 1969, p. 156)

35 (Syrkin M. , *Way of Valor–A Biography of Golda Myerson*, 1955, p. 169)

36 (Syrkin M. , *Way of Valor–A Biography of Golda Myerson*, 1955, p. 169)

37 (Martin, 1988, p. 286)

38 (Syrkin M. , *Way of Valor–A Biography of Golda Myerson*, 1955, p. 171)

39 (Martin, 1988, p. 287)

40 (Hitzeroth, 1998, p. 71)

41 (Martin, 1988, p. 289)

42 (Syrkin M. , *Way of Valor–A Biography of Golda Myerson*, 1955, p. 173)

43 (Meir G. , 1975, p. 202)

44 (Meir G. , 1975, p. 203)

45 (Martin, 1988, p. 278)

46 (Martin, 1988, p. 298)

47 (Shenker, 1970, p. 12)

48 (Martin, 1988, p. 284)

49 (Fromkin, 1989, p. 520)

50 (Martin, 1988, p. 291)

51 (Syrkin M. , *Way of Valor–A Biography of Golda Myerson*, 1955, p. 183)

52 (Martin, 1988, p. 343)

Chapter 12

1 (Shenker, 1970, p. 33)

2 (Martin, 1988, p. 293)

3 (Syrkin M. , *Golda Meir–Israel's Leader*, 1969, p. 171)

4 (Martin, 1988, p. 294)

5 (Martin, 1988, p. 275)

6 (Meir G. , 1975, p. 105)

7 (Martin, 1988, p. 321)

8 (Martin, 1988, p. 298)

9 (Syrkin M. , *Golda Meir–Israel's Leader*, 1969, pp. 175-176)

10 (Martin, 1988, p. 295)

11 (Martin, 1988, p. 296)

12 (Martin, 1988, p. 296)

13 (Mann, 1971, p. 147)

14 (Mann, 1971, p. 147)

15 (Martin, 1988, p. 321)

16 (Martin, 1988, p. 321)

17 (Martin, 1988, p. 321)

18 (Martin, 1988, p. 322)

19 (Martin, 1988, p. 300)

20 (Shenker, 1970, p. 15)

21 (Martin, 1988, p. 342)

22 (Gold, 2004, p. 68)

23 (Syrkin M. , *Golda Meir–Israel's Leader*, 1969, p. 182)

24 (Martin, 1988, p. 301)

25 (Martin, 1988, p. 301)

26 (Martin, 1988, p. 303)

27 (Martin, 1988, p. 304)

28 (Martin, 1988, p. 309)

29 (Martin, 1988, p. 307)

30 (Martin, 1988, p. 307)

31 (Martin, 1988, p. 308)

32 (Martin, 1988, p. 317)

33 (Martin, 1988, p. 311)

34 (Syrkin M. , *Golda Meir–Israel's Leader*, 1969, p. 191)

35 (Martin, 1988, p. 316)

36 (Martin, 1988, p. 316)

37 (Syrkin M. e., 1973, p. 73)

38 (Mann, 1971, p. 149)

39 (Martin, 1988, p. 331)

40 (Martin, 1988, p. 327)

41 (Martin, 1988, p. 327)

42 (Martin, 1988, p. 331)

43 (Martin, 1988, p. 331)

44 (Martin, 1988, p. 331)

45 (Martin, 1988, p. 328)

46 (Martin, 1988, p. 332)

47 (Martin, 1988, p. 332)

48 (Martin, 1988, p. 334)

49 (Martin, 1988, p. 335)

50 (Martin, 1988, p. 336)

51 (Shenker, 1970, p. 11)

52 (Shenker, 1970, p. 42)

53 (Shenker, 1970, p. 13)

54 (Mann, 1971, p. 155)

55 (Naamani, 1974, p. 82)

56 (Meir G. , 1975, p. 227)

57 (Meir G. , 1975, p. 227)

58 (Martin, 1988, p. 340)

59 (Meir G. , 1975, p. 228)

Part Four

1 (Reeves, 2010, p. 41)

2 (Reeves, 2010, p. 65)

3 (Reeves, 2010, p. 107)

4 (Reeves, 2010, p. 44)

5 (Barasch, 2005, p. 179)

Chapter 13

1 (Martin, 1988, p. 317)

2 (Martin, 1988, p. 340)

3 (Martin, 1988, p. 341)

4 (Meir G. , 1975, p. 229)

5 (Martin, 1988, p. 342)

6 (Martin, 1988, p. 342)

7 (Mann, 1971, p. 158)

8 (Hitzeroth, 1998, p. 75)

9 (Syrkin M. , *Golda Meir–Israel's Leader*, 1969, p. 210)

10 (Syrkin M. , *Golda Meir–Israel's Leader*, 1969, p. 210)

11 (Syrkin M. , *Golda Meir–Israel's Leader*, 1969, p. 211)

12 (Slater, 1981, p. 81)

13 (Naamani, 1974, p. 189)

14 (Slater, 1981, p. 85)

15 (Slater, 1981, p. 88)

16 (Slater, 1981, p. 90)

17 (Syrkin M. , *Golda Meir–Israel's Leader*, 1969, p. 230)

18 (Mann, 1971, p. 168)

19 (Mann, 1971, p. 168)

20 (Hitzeroth, 1998, p. 77)

21 (Hitzeroth, 1998, p. 77)

22 (Meir G. , 1975, p. 252)

[23] (Meir G. , 1975, p. 251)

[24] (Meir G. , 1975, p. 251)

[25] (Meir G. , 1975, p. 252)

[26] (Meir G. , 1975, p. 250)

[27] (Mann, 1971, p. 169)

[28] (Meir G. , 1975, p. 254)

Chapter 14

[1] (Syrkin M. , *Golda Meir–Israel's Leader*, 1969, p. 237)

[2] (Slater, 1981, p. 13)

[3] (Slater, 1981, p. 101)

[4] (Slater, 1981, p. 101)

[5] (Meir G. , 1975, p. 256)

[6] (Meir G. , 1975, p. 143)

[7] (Shenker, 1970, p. 58)

[8] (Syrkin M. , *Golda Meir–Israel's Leader*, 1969, p. 253)

[9] (Hitzeroth, 1998, p. 78)

[10] (Hitzeroth, 1998, p. 79)

[11] (Dobrin, 1974, p. 63)

[12] (Mann, 1971, p. 179)

[13] (Dobrin, 1974, p. 65)

[14] (Meir G. E., 1973, p. 82)

[15] (Syrkin M. , *Golda Meir–Israel's Leader*, 1969, p. 243)

[16] (Burkett, 2008, p. 176)

[17] (Martin, 1988, p. vii)

[18] (Slater, 1981, p. 92)

[19] (Syrkin M. , *Golda Meir–Israel's Leader*, 1969, p. 264)

[20] (Syrkin M. , *Golda Meir–Israel's Leader*, 1969, p. 264)

[21] (Martin, 1988, p. 212)

[22] (Martin, 1988, p. 212)

[23] (Syrkin M. e., 1973, p. 80)

[24] (Shenker, 1970, p. 64)

[25] (Syrkin M. , *Golda Meir–Israel's Leader*, 1969, p. 263)

[26] (Syrkin M. , *Golda Meir–Israel's Leader*, 1969, p. 259)

[27] (Syrkin M. , *Golda Meir–Israel's Leader*, 1969, p. 260)

[28] (Syrkin M. , *Golda Meir–Israel's Leader*, 1969, p. 263)

[29] (Martin, 1988, p. 245)

[30] (Syrkin M. , *Golda Meir–Israel's Leader*, 1969, p. 217)

[31] (Shenker, 1970, p. 68)

[32] (Slater, 1981, p. 109)

33 (Burkett, 2008, p. 248)

34 (Syrkin M. , *Golda Meir–Israel's Leader*, 1969, p. 157)

35 (Meir G. , 1975, p. 271)

36 (Meir M. , 1983, p. 153)

37 (Burkett, 2008, p. 176)

38 (Meir G. , 1975, p. 276)

39 (Meir G. , 1975, p. 278)

40 (Meir G. , 1975, p. 279)

Chapter 15

1 (Slater, 1981, p. 118)

2 (Mann, 1971, p. 182)

3 (Mann, 1971, p. 189)

4 (Robinson, 1908)

5 (Meir M. , 1983, p. 165)

6 (Mann, 1971, p. 187)

7 (Brad, 1999)

8 (Shenker, 1970, p. 27)

9 (Shenker, 1970, p. 20)

10 (Shenker, 1970, p. 20)

11 (Mann, 1971, p. 196)

12 (Meir G. E., 1973, p. 90)

13 (Meir G. E., 1973, p. 94)

14 (Meir G. E., 1973, p. 91)

15 (Syrkin M. , *Golda Meir–Israel's Leader*, 1969, p. 285)

16 (Syrkin M. e., 1973, p. 104)

17 (Meir G. , 1975, p. 293)

18 (Shenker, 1970, p. 51)

19 (Mann, 1971, p. 200)

20 (Dobrin, 1974, p. 68)

21 (Shenker, 1970, p. 46)

22 (Meir G. , 1975, p. 320)

23 (Dobrin, 1974, p. 68)

24 (Meir M. , 1983, p. 159)

25 (Slater, 1981, p. 139)

26 (Meir G. , 1975, p. 178)

27 (Meir M. , 1983, p. 170)

28 (Shenker, 1970, p. 65)

29 (Shenker, 1970, p. 43)

30 (Meir G. , 1975, p. 177)

31 (Meir G. , 1975, p. 177)

32 (Syrkin M. , *Golda Meir–Israel's Leader*, 1969, p. 245)

33 (Atkins, 2011, p. 149)

34 (Martin, 1988, p. 313)

35 (Meir M. , 1983, p. 167)

[36] (Slater, 1981, p. 131)

[37] (Mann, 1971, p. 214)

[38] (Shenker, 1970, p. 66)

Chapter 16

[1] (Shenker, 1970, p. 13)

[2] (Shenker, 1970, p. 15)

[3] (Meir G. , 1975, p. 105)

[4] (Shenker, 1970, p. 21)

[5] (Mann, 1971, p. 226)

[6] (Shenker, 1970, p. 36)

[7] (Meir M. , 1983, p. 193)

[8] (Jewish Virtual Library)

[9] (Meir G. E., 1973, p. 96)

[10] (Burkett, 2008, p. 288)

[11] (Dobrin, 1974, pp. 68-69)

[12] (Slater, 1981, p. 176)

[13] (Meir G. , 1975, p. 379)

[14] (Mann, 1971, p. 231)

[15] (Burkett, 2008, p. 239)

[16] (Shenker, 1970, p. 64)

[17] (Mann, 1971, p. 240)

[18] (Shenker, 1970, p. 46)

[19] (Shenker, 1970, p. 50)

[20] (Shenker, 1970, p. 49)

[21] (Shenker, 1970, p. 49)

[22] (Jewish Virtual Library)

[23] (Burkett, 2008, p. 264)

[24] (Burkett, 2008, p. 5)

[25] (Mann, 1971, pp. 278-280)

[26] (Syrkin M. , Golda Meir–Israel's Leader, 1969, p. 132)

[27] (Burkett, 2008, p. 310)

[28] (Mann, 1971, p. 250)

[29] (Mann, 1971, p. 246)

[30] (Burkett, 2008, p. 207)

[31] (Burkett, 2008, p. 285)

[32] (Munich Massacre)

[33] (Burkett, 2008, p. 286)

[34] (Burkett, 2008, p. 287)

[35] (Burkett, 2008, p. 287)

[36] (Burkett, 2008, p. 287)

Chapter 17

[1] (Shenker, 1970, p. 33)

[2] (Dobrin, 1974, p. 73)

[3] (Mann, 1971, p. 242)

[4] (Mann, 1971, p. 242)

[5] (Meir G. , 1975, p. 215)

[6] (Meir G. , 1975, p. 419)

[7] (Meir G. E., 1973, p. 201)

[8] (Meir G. E., 1973, p. 201)

[9] (Burkett, 2008, p. 258)

[10] (Burkett, 2008, p. 258)

11 (Burkett, 2008, p. 263)

12 (Burkett, 2008, p. 263)

13 (Mann, 1971, p. 241)

14 (Syrkin M. , *Golda Meir–Israel's Leader*, 1969, p. 11)

15 (Mann, 1971, p. 242)

16 (Burkett, 2008, p. 378)

17 (Burkett, 2008, p. 268)

18 (Burkett, 2008, p. 378)

19 (Martin, 1988, p. 170)

20 (Burkett, 2008, p. 258)

21 (Burkett, 2008, p. 259)

22 (Burkett, 2008, p. 367)

23 (Syrkin M. , *Golda Meir–Israel's Leader*, 1969, p. 339)

24 (Burkett, 2008, p. 320)

25 (Burkett, 2008, p. 319)

26 (Burkett, 2008, p. 324)

27 (Burkett, 2008, pp. 323-324)

28 (Burkett, 2008, p. 283)

29 (Burkett, 2008, p. 327)

30 (Burkett, 2008, p. 337)

31 (Burkett, 2008, p. 338)

32 (Burkett, 2008, p. 360)

33 (Burkett, 2008, p. 360)

34 (Burkett, 2008, p. 333)

35 (Burkett, 2008, p. 359)

36 (Meir M. , 1983, p. 190)

37 (Meir M. , 1983, p. 191)

38 (Letter Maurice Swan , 1975), (Official Gazette of Syria , 1974)

39 (Burkett, 2008, p. 369)

Chapter 18

1 (Burkett, 2008, p. 365)

2 (Burkett, 2008, p. 365)

3 (Burkett, 2008, p. 352)

4 (Burkett, 2008, p. 375)

5 (Burkett, 2008, p. 360)

6 (Burkett, 2008, p. 374)

7 (Burkett, 2008, p. 375)

8 (Burkett, 2008, p. 376)

9 (Slater, 1981, p. 266)

10 (Slater, 1981, p. 270)

INDEX

Golda Meir ~ True Grit

Eleanor Roosevelt's Life of Soul Searching and Self Discovery

Marie Curie ~ A Nobel Life (available 2016)

Paperback and ebook—available through
your favorite book dealer,
Amazon
or from the author at her website:
Ann@AnnAtkins.com